SEXUALITY IN MEDIEVAL EUROPE

Challenging the way the Middle Ages have been treated in general histories of sexuality, *Sexuality in Medieval Europe* shows how views at the time were conflicted and complicated; there was no single medieval attitude towards sexuality any more than there is one modern attitude. Focusing on marital sexual activity, as well as behavior that was seen as transgressive, the chapters cover such topics as chastity, the role of the church, and non-reproductive activity.

Combining an overview of research on the topic with original interpretations, Ruth Mazo Karras demonstrates that medieval culture developed sexual identities that were quite distinct from the identities we think of today, yet were still ancestral to our own. Using a wide collection of evidence from the late antique period until the fifteenth century, this fully revised third edition has been updated to include the latest scholarship throughout, including expanded coverage of Islamic and Jewish cultures and new ideas on how medieval sexual violence relates to the modern world. A new companion website supplements the text featuring an interactive timeline of key events, links to key primary sources, and references to further reading.

Sexuality in Medieval Europe is essential reading for those who study medieval history and culture.

Ruth Mazo Karras is Distinguished Teaching Professor of History at the University of Minnesota. Her books include the *Oxford Handbook of Women and Gender in Medieval Europe* edited with Judith M. Bennett (2013), *Unmarriages: Women, Men, and Sexual Unions in the Middle Ages* (2012) and *From Boys to Men: Formations of Masculinity in Late Medieval Europe* (2002).

SEXUALITY IN MEDIEVAL EUROPE

Doing Unto Others

3rd Edition

Ruth Mazo Karras

Routledge
Taylor & Francis Group

LONDON AND NEW YORK

This edition published 2017
by Routledge
2 Park Square, Milton Park, Abingdon, Oxon OX14 4RN

and by Routledge
711 Third Avenue, New York, NY 10017

Routledge is an imprint of the Taylor & Francis Group, an informa business

First edition published by Routledge 2005

Second edition published by Routledge 2012

British Library Cataloguing in Publication Data
A catalogue record for this book is available from the British Library

Library of Congress Cataloging in Publication Data
Names: Karras, Ruth Mazo, 1957– author.
Title: Sexuality in Medieval Europe : Doing Unto Others /
    Ruth Mazo Karras.
Description: 3rd edition. | London ; New York : Routledge, 2017. |
    Includes bibliographical references and index.
Identifiers: LCCN 2016035208 | ISBN 9781138860889 (hardback :
    alk. paper) | ISBN 9781138860896 (pbk. : alk. paper) | ISBN
    9781315269719 (ebook)
Subjects: LCSH: Sex customs—History—To 1500. | Europe—Social
    conditions—To 1492. | Social history—Medieval, 500–1500.
Classification: LCC HQ14 .K37 2017 | DDC 392.6—dc23
LC record available at https://lccn.loc.gov/2016035208

ISBN: 978-1-138-86088-9 (hbk)
ISBN: 978-1-138-86089-6 (pbk)
ISBN: 978-1-315-26971-9 (ebk)

Typeset in Sabon
by Apex CoVantage, LLC

Visit the companion website: www.routledge.com/cw/karras

FOR THEODORA AND FLORENCE

CONTENTS

FIGURES

ACKNOWLEDGMENTS

The idea for this book, and for the revised edition, came from Victoria Peters of Routledge, who read a chapter I wrote for a general book on the Middle Ages and suggested that I expand it. I am grateful to a number of fellow medievalists and other historians who read the entire draft of the first edition and made suggestions: Joan Cadden, Anna Clark, Matthew Kuefler, Jacqueline Murray, John Van Engen. A number of published reviews of the earlier editions were helpful in revision. I am also grateful to non-academic readers who helped give me a sense of what would be most interesting and helpful for them to know: Christopher Karras, Nicola Karras, Henry Langsam, Barbara Ziv. Research assistance on the first edition was provided by Ellen Arnold and Kathryn Kelsey Staples. Jesse Izzo helped with research for the third edition. I am also grateful to Laura Mothersole of Routledge for her work on the permissions.

I owe a huge intellectual debt to a group of scholars too large to list here, but whose names and works appear in the Further Reading section at the end of the book. Although I have used notes only when I have quoted directly, a broad synthesis like this inevitably relies on the scholarship of others, and I have indicated which parts of the book have drawn on the ideas of which scholars.

PUBLISHERS' ACKNOWLEDGMENTS

The publishers are grateful to the following for their permission to reproduce copyright material: Albertina, Vienna; Bibliothèque du Chateau de Chantilly; Bibliothèque municipal, Agen; Bibliothèque Nationale de France; The British Library Board; Heidelberg University Library; Houghton Library, Harvard; Médiathèque François-Mitterrand, Poitiers; The Metropolitan Museum of Art, New York; Musée de la Tapisserie de Bayeux; Musée Rolin; Museu de Mallorca; Osterreichische Nationalbibliothek; Painton Cowen; Reading Museum; Staats-und-Universitätsbibliothek, Hamburg; Walters Art Museum.

1

SEX AND THE MIDDLE AGES

The combination of "medieval Europe" and "sexuality" conjures up one of several images in most people's minds. One is a vision of total repression. A church controlled by celibate men defines all sexual acts and thoughts as impure. Any sexual behavior or thought is a sin calling for severe acts of penance. Even marital sex for the purpose of reproduction is barely tolerable; it becomes a sin if the participants enjoy it. Sexuality threatens human salvation: it is a nearly irresistible force, but a force for evil. The devil is always at the ready to use sexual temptation to drag humankind to destruction and damnation.

Plenty of medieval texts support this vision of negative and repressive medieval attitudes toward sexuality. We can look, for example, at the Desert Fathers tradition. In the late antique period (fourth to fifth centuries) there were several collections of the sayings and deeds of the monks who lived in individual cells (eremitic monasticism) or in groups (cenobitic monasticism) in the Egyptian desert. These texts were translated into Latin and then into the various European vernaculars, and became quite popular. The tales include stories of heroic penance for sexual thoughts. In one story, the devil sends a woman to tempt a monk. She claims to be lost and asks to stay in his cell because she is afraid of wild beasts. As a thirteenth-century French poetic version tells it:

> The monk soon had great desire of her . . . and he knew well that it was the devil who caused him so much anguish. . . . And when he burned with the most passion he said, "Those who do such things go into torment. This will test whether you can suffer the eternal fire where you must go." And he extended his finger and put it in the flame. . . . But the finger did not feel the heat, because he was so filled with fleshly fire. Thus one after the other he held his fingers in the fire, so that they were all burned by daybreak.[1]

When we reflect on the pervasiveness and popularity of stories like this, we cannot help thinking of medieval Europe as a culture with a very negative

1

attitude to sex. Sexual desire had to be combated even at the cost of great personal hardship; it was a pollutant and a threat to the soul. This book treats the whole period of the Middle Ages in western Europe – roughly 500–1500 CE – and attitudes of course changed over this time period, but, as the thousand-year popularity of this particular story indicates, some understandings of the role of sex in human affairs were very persistent.

Opposite this strict and sin-wracked image stands an earthier one. Lusty priests seduce the women who confess to them; noblemen keep mistresses; monks and nuns engage in secret liaisons; peasants couple behind hedgerows. This view dismisses the church and its repressive teachings as full of hypocrisy and generally ignored by medieval people, who went about their daily business with a zest that disappeared later in a more puritan age.

Medieval texts support this earthy, lustful, playful version as well. The stories of Chaucer, Boccaccio, or the French fabliaux (humorous rhymed stories) are good examples. In one story of a wife deceiving her husband with a young lover:

> She, acting as guide,
> ushered her paramour inside
> and got him underneath the quilt,
> and right away he went to tilt
> in the tourney prescribed by Love.
> Less than a nut's all he thought of
> playing at any other game,
> and, as for her, she felt the same.[2]

In stories like this, both men and women find joy in sexual intercourse. They do what comes naturally. Sin is not an issue, nor is reproduction. This story is not subversive, underground literature, nor is it the medieval equivalent of the porn video. Scholars argue about whether the audience for fabliaux like this one, and similar literature, was aristocratic or bourgeois, but these stories were read and enjoyed openly by both men and women, no doubt including many members of the church hierarchy.

A third image of medieval sexual attitudes and practices is much darker, born out of a twenty-first-century awareness of sexual violence against women, gay men, transgender adults, children, anyone who is vulnerable. This image appears most prominently in neomedieval cultural artifacts like the *Game of Thrones* television series, in which not only rape but also sadism appears to be endemic. It is true that in the Middle Ages women who traveled without men's protection, like Margery Kempe, could fear sexual assault; that Christians could envision sexualized torments inflicted by pagans, who could cut off women's breasts to get them to renounce Christianity; that for girls to be married as soon as they hit menarche was, if not routine, at least not surprising; and that for clerics to molest boys under their educational regime was also not uncommon. And yet the pagans in medieval texts torture Christians because they want them to stop being Christian, not because they get pleasure from it; men who rape in medieval texts generally do so because they want to have sex, not because they want to dominate, unlike in modern depictions of the medieval period (although as we will see, these two things were in some ways not entirely separable in a world that thought of sex and penetration as being largely the same thing). It is the difference between a world in which the pilgrim Dante can observe sinners tortured by demons, and one in which a crusader Dante, as reimagined in a video game, can participate in inflicting a torment more sexualized than that suffered, at least by women, in the poet Dante's work.

All of these views of medieval sexuality have some truth to them, but all are based on modern readings. Yet it is not just that attitudes changed over time, although they did; it is also the case that many different attitudes coexisted within a single culture. Medieval Europe, of course, was not a "single culture"; Latin Christendom can be seen as one, in many ways, with some regional variation, but there were also Muslim polities in Iberia and in Sicily, as well as Jews under Christian and Muslim rule throughout. Sexuality in the medieval Islamic world is also subject to the same sorts of cultural stereotypes as in Christian Europe, and perhaps even more so: the harem as a place for elite men to indulge themselves entirely, the sexual exploitation of male and female slaves, the seventy-two houris who are the heavenly reward of the martyr are part of Western cultural vocabulary. Here too there is some support in the medieval texts: the frame tale that begins the *One Thousand and One Nights* in its oldest existing version involves the infidelity of a queen and her slave girls with African slaves in the palace:

> The private gate of his brother's palace opened, and there emerged, strutting like a dark-eyed deer, the lady, his brother's wife, with twenty slave girls, ten white and ten black. . . . they sat down, took off their clothes, and suddenly there were ten slave girls and ten black slaves dressed in the same clothes as the girls. Then the ten black slaves mounted the ten girls, while the lady called "Mas'ud, Mas'ud!" and a black slave jumped from the tree to the ground, rushed to her, and, raising her legs, went between her thighs and made love to her. Mas'ud topped the lady, while the ten slaves topped the ten girls, and they carried on till noon.[3]

The wife and the ten slaves, who the text makes clear are the king's concubines, are put to death (the story does not say what happened to the male slaves), and the monarch's conclusion that there is no such thing as a chaste woman leads to his regime of sleeping with a different woman each night and putting her to death in the morning, a regime broken only by Shahrazad's successful storytelling. Even in the Middle Ages this story was set in the remote past and in a distant country (India), so it hardly describes actual practice. But the paramount importance of chastity for women, together with relative freedom for (at least elite) men, emerges from texts across the Islamicate world so that here too a frankness about sex is combined with a stringency reinforced by religion.

Yes, these images are contradictory, even within Christian culture. So are many of the views on sexuality found in contemporary culture. If you think about the sexual attitudes of people you know, you will find not only that different people have different views but even that a single individual may hold many different views, depending on circumstances. People learn and understand culture at many different levels. Sex is a particularly complicated issue because it involves questions of religious morality, public order, gender relations, and representational cultures, as well as the individual psyche. It should not be a surprise that a complicated issue generates a complex web of attitudes. This book, then, will not search for the medieval view of sexuality, but rather for the multiplicity of views that describes the medieval experience.

The stereotypical images of medieval sexuality are heavily gendered. It is fair to say that the first, repressive attitude, associated with the medieval church, carried over into the secular culture more commonly with regard to women's sexuality, seen as active but sinful; the second, earthy attitude, associated with lay culture, carried over into the ecclesiastical realm more commonly with regard to men's, seen as active but celebrated; and the third involves women mainly as passive victims. Women's behavior was sinful, polluting, or simply irrelevant; men's was obeying the dictates of nature. Again, the concept of a double standard is familiar to any modern reader. My argument throughout this book goes beyond saying that the same act was seen differently for men and for women. In many cases, medieval people did not see what the two partners did in sexual intercourse as the same act at all.

Medieval people, for the most part, understood sex acts as something that someone did to someone else. The subtitle of this book, *Doing Unto Others*, reflects this idea. The most common verbs used for sexual intercourse today – "to have sex," "to make love" – are intransitive. They are actions that two people do together, not actions that one person does to another. Even "to fuck," which began as a term implying penetration, has come to be used intransitively, or interchangeably of men and women: "they fucked" or "she fucked him" are perfectly comprehensible.

Medieval terminology was different. The subject of the French verb *foutre*, for example, in modern French can be a man, a woman, or a couple, but the older meaning was "to penetrate" and the subject was always a man. The same was usually true of the English *swiven*. The *Middle English Dictionary* recognizes two meanings of *swive*, "to have sexual intercourse" and "to have sexual intercourse with (a woman)." There are many more examples of the second, transitive meaning, and in all the man is the subject and the woman the object.[4] The Latin *concubere* has an original meaning of "to lie with," and might seem gender neutral but in fact is most often used with a masculine subject. For example, in the 1395 interrogation of a male transvestite prostitute in London, the summary of his testimony reported that a certain priest "lay with him [*concubuit*] as with a woman," but that he himself "lay [*concubuit*] as a man with many nuns."[5] A medieval English text about the sinfulness of lust carefully explained that the sin was on both parties, "the man that doth and the woman that suffreth."[6]

These linguistic forms reflected a general way of thinking about sex in the Middle Ages. Indeed, the relation between the active and passive in grammar and the active and passive in sexual intercourse was not lost on medieval people. In the twelfth century Alain of Lille wrote a poem entitled "The Plaint of Nature," in which he drew an analogy between grammar and men who pervert nature by playing a passive role in intercourse. "The active sex shudders in disgrace as it sees itself degenerate into the passive sex. A man turned woman blackens the fair name of his sex. . . . He is subject and predicate; one and the same term is given a double application." Personified Nature herself says that "the human race, fallen from its high estate, adopts a highly irregular (grammatical) change [metaplasmus] when it inverts the rules of Venus by introducing barbarisms in its arrangement of genders."[7] The role of nature and the natural in medieval understandings of sexuality will be discussed later in this chapter; for now, the important point is that medieval people in general understood the active and the passive role in sex to be two very different things.

The roles of "active" and "passive" partner did not necessarily have anything to do with who was pursued and who was pursuer, or who enjoyed sex more. Many medieval writers thought women were more lustful than men. Their supposed passivity didn't mean that they did not initiate the sexual relationship, nor did it mean that they were expected to lie still on their backs. It meant that they were the receptive partners; they were penetrated. Similarly the distinction between "active" and "passive" in male–male intercourse referred to the penetrator and penetrated. (This distinction sometimes breaks down in discussions of fellatio, but as noted in Chapter 5 such discussions were rare in the Middle Ages.)

Sexual intercourse was understood as something that one person did to another. One consequence of this was that the two partners were not understood to be doing the same thing or having the same experience. Mutuality was not important in the medieval conceptualization of sex. Since it was most often the case that the two partners were of different sexes, it follows that medieval people understood men's and women's experiences of sex acts as quite different. Where the partners were of the same sex, this created further conceptual problems. Medieval texts reveal, for example, a good deal of confusion about the moral status of erotic acts between women, which often were not considered sex unless one of the women penetrated the other with a dildo.

The fact that men and women were seen as experiencing sex differently dictates in part the organization of this book. Although modern scholars have recognized that the experience of rape in the Middle Ages was different for the perpetrator and the victim, they have seen other sex acts (fornication, adultery, prostitution, homosexual behavior) as a single type of act, roughly the same in social and moral terms for both partners. Because the acts were not really the same for both partners, this book is organized not by the type of sex act but by the status of the individuals who committed the act (or who did not commit it, in the case of the chapter on chastity).

Organizing the book with separate chapters on men and women may not seem particularly controversial, but it is worth making explicit the underlying assumptions. Some scholars have argued that medieval understandings of sex and gender were not binary. Some say that for medieval scientists who followed Aristotle, for example, there was only one sex, the male, and females were defective males. Others argue that because sexual reproduction was so common an expectation for men and women in medieval society, those who chose celibacy and renounced reproduction became not men or women, but a third gender. Still others argue that medieval gender was fluid, that people could occupy a variety of gender positions depending on the situation.

On the contrary, the binary opposition between men and women was extraordinarily strong in medieval society. Although theorists might write that females were defective males, their defects were significant enough that no one seriously considered them the same as males; they were in a quite different category. The category was lower in the hierarchy – it was definitely not "separate but equal" – and the category difference was very real both to scientists and to other medieval people. Similarly, those who did not reproduce might be considered in some ways "not real men" or "not real women," but no medieval person would have any problem identifying nuns as women and monks as men. Women who transgressed the expectations for their gender did not thereby become not-women, even temporarily; they became deviant women, and the same was true for men. Indeed, sometimes such deviants would even be considered hyper-feminine or hyper-masculine, deviating from expectations by taking to an extreme the qualities that others of their gender kept under control. A woman who played a masculine role in sex, or a man who played a feminine role, did transgress, but they did not thereby become a member of the opposite, or a third, gender. The dichotomy remained.

The way people understood particular sex acts is not the same thing as the way they understood sexuality as a field of human experience. Before turning to medieval sexuality specifically, I need to digress and discuss the concept of "sexuality." Like most other general concepts, it can be used to mean a number of different things, and it is important to specify what it means in a given context. Many scholars would argue that it is anachronistic even to talk about sexuality with regard to medieval Europe, but this is not the case. It may not be a concept medieval people had – there is no word in any of the medieval languages that translates precisely as "sexuality" – but nor is there any word that translates precisely as "political culture" or "affective piety" or "patriarchal family" or a host of other terms we have no problem using to describe the Middle Ages.

The study of sexuality

The term "sexuality," as scholars use it, refers to the whole realm of human erotic experience. As Anna Clark puts it, sexuality is "the desires, relationships, acts, and identities concerned with sexual behavior. Desires, relationships, acts, and identities do not automatically flow from one to another; they must be considered separately, and they are often constructed separately."[8]

Sexuality is the universe of meanings that people place on sex acts, rather than the acts themselves. As a field of study the history of sexuality is different from the history of sex, which has to do with who did what with (or to) whom. Some authors prefer to use "history of sexualities" in the plural to emphasize difference: sexuality is not just one thing, dissident sexualities must be included in any history. But "history of sexuality" is not the same thing as "history of sexualities." "A sexuality" is a way of being or a form of desire that is more fundamental to the individual than a preference: "sexual identity" and "sexual orientation" are related (modern) terms used to express this. In the contemporary world, heterosexuality and homosexuality would be the most prominent sexualities. A "history of sexualities" would be one that traced the antecedents of those and other categories. But a "history of sexuality" is a more comprehensive term. Just as one may speak of different chemistries but "chemistry" can still be used to describe the field as a whole, the study of sexuality comprises the study of different sexualities and also the meanings of sex for people who did not identify themselves with particular sexualities as we now understand them.

The terms "sex," "gender," and "sexuality" (as both scholarly discourse and casual conversation today use them, and as they are used here) have distinct meanings. "Sex" refers to the physical facts of male and female bodies: genes, hormones, genitalia, and so forth. "Gender" refers to masculinity and femininity, patterns of behavior and identity. "Sexuality" refers to orientation or desire. Thus a person today born with a male sex might have a female gender identity and a bisexual orientation. The three terms overlap in common usage even today. It is important for our purposes to recognize that in the Middle Ages the distinction among the three was not just blurred, it did not exist. If someone deviated from the expected models of sexual behavior, people did not assume that the variation was a matter

7

of biology *or* gender identity *or* sexual desire; the three worked together. Whereas we might say that an individual has a female body, a feminine identity or behavior, and a sexual desire for women, medieval people would have assumed that the desire for women came from a masculine body and, in itself, constituted masculine behavior. For them, sexuality was not separate from sex and gender; therefore this book will have much to say about what we moderns call sex and gender in the Middle Ages as well as about sexuality.

The media and popular discourse today frame the discussion about different sexualities around the question of whether they are inborn ("hardwired") or a matter of choice or lifestyle. Scholarly discussion has focused on a somewhat different question: are sexualities essential (that is, do they have a reality on their own and exist across cultures?) or are they socially constructed (are they created by the meanings given by different cultures to sex acts?)? The general consensus today is that sexuality is socially constructed. It is not written in the body but created by society. A person might perform the same acts in a variety of cultures, but they would not express the same sexuality in all those cultures because the acts would have different meanings and are understood differently. As the classicist David Halperin puts it: "Sex has no history. It is a natural fact, grounded in the functioning of the body, and, as such, it lies outside of history and culture. Sexuality, by contrast, does not properly refer to some aspect or attribute of bodies. Unlike sex, sexuality is a cultural production: it represents the *appropriation* of the human body and of its physiological capacities by an ideological discourse. Sexuality is not a somatic fact; it is a cultural effect."[9]

One of the worst things someone can do in contemporary Western society is to abuse children sexually – with "children" generally defined as those under eighteen years old. Medieval people would find that idea absurd. Girls could be married at twelve, boys at fourteen, but someone who had sex with them when they were below this age did not come in for more opprobrium than for non-marital sex with an adult. There was a concept of "age of consent" but it applied only to permanent vows, such as marriage or entrance into a religious order. In fact, for a man to have sex with a boy could be considered more normal than to have sex with an adult man. The act might be the same in the two time periods, but it had very different implications for the identity of the actor. An essentialist would argue that a pederast is a pederast wherever and whenever you find him; the social constructionist position, that the sexual and social identity of a man who has sex with underage boys (or girls) depends on the culture in which he lives, is much more useful in understanding sexuality within the context of the wider society.

This idea that sexuality is a function of culture and society is especially important in tracing the history of same-sex relations. Even to refer to the "history of homosexuality" can be problematic. "Homosexuality" is not a *thing* that one can find in all cultures. Scholars of the ancient Greek and Roman world argue that people at that time classified sexual behaviors or identities not by the gender of the participants but by the sexual role each plays; thus a man who penetrates others is simply playing the appropriate male role, he does not become a "homosexual" merely because those he penetrates are also male. Some scholars deny that there was any concept of the "homosexual" at all before the second half of the nineteenth century, when the term was coined and when sexuality became part of the study of abnormal psychology. Others find that particular sexual identities in other cultures resemble that of the modern "homosexual." But most would agree that to label anyone in the past who had sex with someone of the same sex as "a homosexual" would be to impose a modern category. The same argument also applies to other categories of sexual behavior: heterosexuality, bisexuality, prostitution, or any other. The acts may be the same, but each society will determine what the meaning of those acts is and whether they create identities.

Heterosexuality may seem somewhat simpler. It may seem at first glance that, whether or not a certain minority of people in the Middle Ages should be called "homosexual," the majority certainly were "heterosexual." In thinking about heterosexuality, however, it is especially important to keep in mind the question of whether behaviors and attitudes add up to an identity. Heterosexuality both in the Middle Ages and today tends to be an unmarked category: most people assume it is normal and thus often do not notice that it is socially constructed in the same way homosexuality is.

If medieval people did not think of "homosexuals" as a category, they did not think of "heterosexuals" as one either. It may be the case that most medieval men had sex only with women and most medieval women had sex only with men, but it would be wrong to attribute to them a consciousness of a heterosexual orientation unless we find evidence for it. In fact, for the most part we do not. Medieval people did not draw the line between gay and straight, but between reproductive and non-reproductive sex. Same-sex activity was not reproductive, but much opposite-sex activity was not reproductive either, and was not excused by the fact that it was "heterosexual."

Perhaps it would be wrong to call marriage the norm for medieval people, since many ecclesiastical writers saw marital sex as a necessary evil, but it was certainly the expectation for most. That does not mean that heterosexual desire was a good thing, or even the default condition against which other desires were set; it was "concupiscence," the result of Eve's and Adam's disobedience. As Karma Lochrie writes:

> Procreation and chastity more than heterosexuality are the reigning norms of medieval theological culture, and this makes a tremendous difference. Sodomy as a subcategory of lechery, although it is set apart as an abomination, is more or less on a continuum with

9

other "heterosexual" vices in which desire waxes inordinate and gender roles morph.[10]

The opposite of the social constructionist point of view, which the social constructionists call "essentialism," would argue that there are fundamentally different kinds of people in the world, that in every culture there are those with homosexual, heterosexual, and various other orientations. The popular lists of "famous gays in history" are essentialist in conception. Essentialism is implicit in the contemporary search for genetic markers or biological corollaries of a predisposition to homosexuality. It is also congenial to activists who believe that society will be more tolerant if it understands homosexuality as something inborn, not chosen. But the social construction of sexuality does not imply that individuals choose their own identities – it is the way the broader culture gives meaning to sex through medical, legal, or religious systems that creates sexual identities for them, and these identities are very real.

This book works from the assumption that we must look at how medieval people thought about sexuality, rather than impose our own categories on them. Some people, however, would go much farther and say that not only the particular categories familiar to us but also the very notion of a sexual orientation or a sexuality are creations of bourgeois capitalism. This point of view has its roots in the insights of the French philosopher Michel Foucault in his important work *The History of Sexuality*. According to this argument, only in nineteenth-century Europe and North America did people come to view their sexual preferences as part of what constituted them as individuals. People in other societies may have had preferences for a particular type of partner, role, or act, but these preferences did not define them as a type of person. As Foucault wrote:

> As defined by the ancient civil or canonical codes, sodomy was a category of forbidden acts; their perpetrator was nothing more than the juridical subject of them. The nineteenth-century homosexual became a personage, a past, a case history, and a childhood, in addition to being a type of life, a life form, and a morphology, with an indiscreet anatomy and possibly a mysterious physiology. . . . Homosexuality appeared as one of the forms of sexuality when it was transposed from the practice of sodomy onto a kind of interior androgyny, a hermaphrodism of the soul. The sodomite had been a temporary aberration; the homosexual was now a species.[11]

A classification of persons based on sexual behavior was a categorization of convenience in earlier eras, but not psychically deep. (Some influential interpreters argue that saying there was no sexuality before capitalism is a distorted reading of Foucault's views. When Foucault drew his famous

10

acts/identities dichotomy, he was not really saying "earlier there were only acts, in the modern era identities developed," he was speaking of types of discourses or ways of talking about sex. Earlier we have legal enactments that mention only acts; later we have medical and psychological analyses that discuss identities.)

This book rejects the *a priori* argument that sexuality is not a relevant concept for the Middle Ages. As we shall see in Chapter 2, the identities of medieval people were fundamentally shaped by their sexual status – not whether they were homosexual or heterosexual, as today, but whether they were chaste or sexually active. This distinction created a dividing line between two very different kinds of people in medieval society. When it comes to other sexual categories, we have to look at the medieval evidence and decide what kind of sexual categories medieval people used to think with, if they did at all. To dismiss out of hand the possibility that they could have had a concept of sexuality is just as reductive as automatically assuming that their concept of sexuality was the same as ours.

Recently scholars have used the concept of "queer" to describe a variety of sexual and gender transgressions. This is not the place for a detailed discussion of "queer theory" in the various humanistic disciplines, especially literature, but it is worth saying a few things about the way it is applied to the Middle Ages. In one sense to be "queer" is simply to challenge norms; thus the term can be associated with homosexuality in the contemporary era, but it can also be used by people who want to claim for themselves an identity that does not map onto the homosexual–heterosexual binary. Anyone who is outside of cultural expectations can be labeled as "queer": thus Tison Pugh suggests that Harry Bailly, the host in Chaucer's *Canterbury Tales*, is "queer" because his domestic masculinity is impugned by his wife's dominance and shrewishness. But "queer" can also signify a new way of looking at medieval texts, rejecting contemporary heteronormativity; approaching a medieval text without assuming that the people and actions depicted in it are heterosexual (unless otherwise noted) can open up a new set of interpretive possibilities. This work seeks to "unsettle the heterosexual paradigms of scholarship."[12] It can also include attention to transgression of gender identity since, as many scholars argue and as this book will further discuss, medieval sexual identity is very much about gender identity. To read in this way has become the verb "to queer." Queering the Middle Ages does not mean arguing that particular historical figures or literary characters were homosexual, but rather displacing the entire homo/hetero binary. William Burgwinkle suggests that the fact that any non-reproductive sexual behavior could be labeled "sodomy" means that all readers can identify with "sodomites." There is no homosexual and heterosexual; all are together in a sort of "queer utopia" in which "all readers get to play at being marginal and subversive."[13] Of course, being marginal and subversive may not have been as exciting in the Middle Ages as it may seem today, and the fact that all

11

kinds of behavior were deemed sodomy may have harmed the practitioners of that behavior more than it universalized sodomy.

Queering a text can also involve a reinterpretation on a very basic and concrete level: when the object of love in a poem is masculine, scholars long assumed that the speaker is a woman, or vice versa, but this assumption may not have been the same that medieval readers would have brought to it. The Anglo-Saxon poem commonly known as "The Wife's Lament" is one example. Scholars disagree on the basis of grammar, word choice, and historical plausibility as to whether the speaker who mourns an absent male lover is in fact a woman or a man. Queering a text also involves examining the way the text constructs sexuality, rather than how it describes or depicts a sexuality that exists outside the text; in this sense it is essentially a literary technique, but historians need to understand the nature of literary and other texts in order to use them as historical sources. Queer theory reminds us once again that texts are not faithful representations of concepts that have a prior independent existence outside the texts.

"Queer" has come now to refer not just to sexuality but to gender identity as well. "Genderqueer" is an alternative to "transgender" used to refer to people of non-binary gender (who do not identify as either men or women). Gender identity is somewhat separable from sexual orientation (that is, a woman can be attracted to women, men, or both), but genderqueer also implies queer in terms of sexuality, since a genderqueer person cannot be "straight" (or "gay" either). Medieval people did not draw the distinction between gender and sexual identity that modern people do, although they did sometimes query the correspondence between biological sex and gender identity. This book focuses on sexuality but it is impossible to discuss it without questions of gender entering the mix.

Sources for medieval sexuality

To look at the medieval evidence, of course, is to open up several additional cans of worms. Medieval attitudes about sex have to be pieced together from a variety of sources. Medieval people did not keep diaries. When they did write first-person accounts or memoirs they were rarely explicit about sexual experiences; literature is sometimes more explicit, but brings with it its own problems of interpretation. The bulk of the extant documents that survive from Christian Europe was written by monks and clergymen, who had taken vows of chastity. Texts written by women, while not as rare as scholars once thought, are still not common. Much of what we know about sexuality in the Middle Ages, then, is what theologians and canon lawyers thought about it, not what the sexually active common people thought.

Some general issues apply to all medieval sources. First of all, we need to take into account the author. A medieval text does not represent "the medieval attitude" toward a given subject, it presents the attitude of one particular writer, shaped by her or (usually) his social status, education, religion, and occupation. Second, we need to take into account the audience. We do not always know for whom a particular text was written, although sometimes we can tell from evidence in the text itself, or from what we know about ownership of manuscripts (until the very end of the fifteenth century all medieval texts circulated exclusively in hand-copied form). Only a small segment of society could afford to own the texts or were sufficiently literate to be able to read them. What a text seems to mean to a modern reader is often not the same thing it would have meant to its medieval audience. Third, we need to take into account the purpose of the document. This question includes many of the issues involved in a consideration of genre. No medieval text was written for the purpose of providing information to historians of sexuality hundreds of years later. Some were to entertain, some to persuade, some to inform, some to demonstrate the author's erudition, some to record information for posterity. Most medieval writings, too, were written for public distribution or at least public reading. There were undoubtedly a great many personal letters and perhaps journals, but few have survived. Letters that we have from the Middle Ages mostly exist because they were copied into collections for public consumption (although a few were preserved as part of histories or because they were evidence in court cases). It is difficult to find medieval texts that are truly "private" in the way modern people have private papers.

The main types of sources fall into the categories of literary, historical, religious, legal, and medical texts. These categories overlap (biographies of saints, for example, are both religious and historical, while Muslim *fatwas* are both religious and legal). A brief discussion will indicate both the richness and the variety of material from which conclusions about medieval sexuality can be drawn, and the tentativeness of what we know. Beyond a few illustrative examples here, most of the discussion of individual sources and how they might be interpreted will come in subsequent chapters.

Literary sources can be among the most useful sources for the history of sexuality because (in the absence of private letters) imaginative literature gives us the most vivid examples of actual medieval life – or so it seems. They may be no more accurate representations of how medieval people actually lived than pulp fiction is of the way people live today. Literary representations of human behavior do not reflect lived experience in any simple way – or even, necessarily, in any complex way. In fact, they may have influenced experience – by affecting how people understood and interpreted it – more than they reflect it, and they certainly influence how we reconstruct medieval experience. The behavior of literary characters cannot be taken as typical (although we may perhaps say that it can be taken as plausible). Authors are often not attempting to describe the culture in which they live but to imagine what a past, or a mythical, culture would have been like. Medieval literature often relies on complex systems of metaphor and allegory, so that what seems to be about sex may be about something else (love poetry being about poetry itself, or the impossibility of representation) and what seems to be about something else (the quest to pluck a rose, the pursuit of a gazelle) may be about sex. It may be difficult or impossible, at our chronological distance, to determine which aspects of a literary work are supposed to be straightforward and which are supposed to be humorous, or how obvious what we see as double-entendres would have been to medieval readers or hearers. And medieval literary works often drew very heavily on models – other medieval texts, or preferably ancient ones – so that in order to discern a particular author's original contribution we have to figure out what was taken from other sources.

Many of the same considerations apply to visual representations too; they may contain ambiguous allusions that may or may not be seen as sexual or erotic, depending on the viewer's preconceptions. Here again, it is important to understand not just what associations images bring to contemporary minds but what they would have meant to medieval people, and as with literature this is a topic of lively debate. As art historian Diane Wolfthal writes, "Although some art historians accuse those who 'see sex' in medieval and early modern art as anachronistic in their approach, in fact the reverse is true."[14]

The considerations that affect the use of literary texts as sources also affect other kinds of texts, including historical works that purport to recount actual events. Of course, many literary texts purport to do this too, and the line is not always easy to draw. Many historians writing in the Middle Ages wrote to entertain as much as to record. They also wrote to edify, and their selection of what to include was shaped by this goal. Writers of historical texts, like those of more fictional works, sometimes relied on classical models so their work cannot be taken as accurate descriptions of medieval cultural practices. However, using these sorts of texts to understand the history of sexuality is a bit less problematic in one way at least than using them to sort out an accurate narrative of events. While they may be notoriously inaccurate about who did what, for a variety of reasons, the history of sexuality is concerned not so much with who did what as with how it was understood. The texts present a set of attitudes and assumptions that, if they do not reflect those of the society around them, at least reflect what the author thought the audience would find plausible. If the author treats a particular liaison in a matter-of-fact way, this does not prove that the liaison took place, but it may indicate that liaisons of this type would not be especially surprising.

The term "religious texts" covers a huge variety of medieval writings. Some were very similar to what I've called historical texts – within Christianity, edifying narratives about saints (hagiography) or sacred history. Traditions about the practice, or *sunna*, of the Prophet Muhammad could also be considered historical. Some texts were didactic, explaining the complexities of religious teaching to the people (some for lay reading directly, and some for the use of preachers in composing their sermons). Some works were written for educated audiences, like theologians in universities, madrasas, or yeshivas; others were sermons delivered to the general public. Many were commentaries on scripture. Many of the same kinds of texts were found in Islam and Judaism as in Christianity. The important thing to remember about religious texts is that in none of the three religions was there a single authority that controlled all of religious doctrine. Christianity, with the Pope, came closest, but even within medieval Christianity there was still substantial room for differing views. If extreme, these might be considered heresy, but there were many issues on which people who were all considered perfectly orthodox could disagree. In particular, attitudes in medieval texts may appear quite different depending on whether the audience was intended to be monks (vowed to celibacy) or lay people.

Each of the three religions also produced a substantial body of legal texts. In Christianity these constituted canon law, which was a compilation of decretals by the Popes and the writings of patristic and other authorities. Judaism had commentaries on the Torah and Talmud, as well as a body of *responsa* or replies by well-known rabbis to cases put to them. Islam had a huge body of jurisprudential writing. In all three religions proper sexual behavior constituted one of the topics of legal regulation. Sexuality does not appear as prominently in secular legislation in western Europe as one might expect, in part because it was considered within the church's jurisdiction. Nevertheless, various towns and states did regulate prostitution, sodomy, and other sexual practices. The problem with such prescriptive and theoretical writings is that their relation to attitudes and practices is not straightforward. If something was prohibited, that does not mean that it did not happen; in fact, many would take as a general principle that if something is prohibited, that means the authorities were concerned about it, meaning that it probably did happen. However, the laws do not tell us the underlying reasons for the authorities' concern, nor do they tell us the seriousness and depth of that concern – often laws are repeated over generations and do not necessarily reflect issues that were of concern at the time of writing. Nor do they tell us whether the laws were generally followed or generally ignored.

We also possess numerous documents of legal practice, from court records reflecting actual testimony and decisions, to inquisition records, to contracts and wills. These documents may get us as close to actual medieval life as it is possible to get, but even so they must be consulted with care. Church court records are in Latin even if the actual words spoken were in the vernacular, and thus reflect the scribe's views and understandings of the issues at hand. They are often highly formulaic, with people sticking to stylized legal language rather than speaking spontaneously from their own experience. And we cannot know how typical are the events recorded in a court case or legal opinion. Are they anomalies? Are these the few people who got caught, out of the many who practiced the same behavior? Were the accused, in fact, guilty as charged? In the case of prescriptive law, contracts, and wills, were these meant to be performed precisely as written or were they guidelines? What kind of negotiations that do not show up in the written texts went on in the process of creating them?

Medical texts constitute a specialized subject of study. They include learned works written by and for scholars, practical works for practitioners, and popularizations for the reading public (which was not at all the same thing as the general populace). To a modern eye, medieval understandings of the body may seem rather ludicrous. It is important to understand that they were not simply a bizarre agglomeration of erroneous beliefs, but constituted a coherent system. The system owed much to ancient authorities who held that the human body was made up of four humors that corresponded to four elements. The balance of these humors determined a person's health, personality, and even gender conformity. Some of the medications and herbal remedies used in the Middle Ages were quite efficacious, but the explanations for their working were phrased in terms of the balance among the humors rather than in terms of chemical properties we might cite today. Medieval medicine had no concept of genes or of germs. Of course, medieval medical thought, like any of the other bodies of work discussed here, changed over time, with Arabic writers in the vanguard and Latin writers gradually drawing on their work. A great many of the medical writers of the Christian Middle Ages were also members of religious orders, and for them medicine was never entirely separate from theology; the understanding of bodies was not just in order to keep them healthy, but in order better to understand God's creation.

Let one medieval literary text stand here as an example of the problems of interpretation that can arise when working with medieval sources. This story comes from one of the French fabliaux of the late twelfth century. A fisherman has married a young wife, whom he satisfies sexually, in the words of the poem:

> for a young wife who gets her food
> will frequently want to be screwed.

She claims that she loves him because he supports her and buys her things; he says it's only for the sake of sex.

> I push myself to do my stuff
> for your sake. Clothes are not enough
> to keep a wife's love; satisfaction
> depends much more on fucking action.

16

(Note how different this is from a contemporary scenario, in which a wife would be much more likely to protest that she loves her husband for the great sex, while he would accuse her of wanting him only as a meal ticket.)

The fisherman finds a dead body in the water one day – a priest who had drowned while escaping from a jealous husband – and decides to test his wife. He cuts off the penis and takes it to his wife, claiming that it is his, cut off when he was attacked by three knights. She immediately says to him:

> I pray to God you soon will die!
> Your body is the thing that I
> now most hold in abomination.

She makes ready to leave the house, but he calls her back and tells her God has miraculously restored him. She says:

> My darling husband, dearest friend,
> today you gave me such a fright!
> Never since I first saw the light
> of day has my heart known such pain!

while embracing him, and holding his penis, just to be sure.[15]

What are we to make of this story? It describes the behavior of the common people, but it was written for an audience of higher social status, aristocratic or bourgeois. Were they laughing at working people for being so driven by their lust? Is the story poking fun at the woman for being so lustful? Would the audience have considered a woman who was so interested in sex with her husband a positive or a negative thing? Does the story really tell us anything about women's attitudes to sex or only about what men thought those attitudes were, or wished they were? Did medieval women really believe that their sexual satisfaction required a penis, or was it men who thought so? It becomes clear that we can't use a story like this to tell us "the" medieval attitude about sex. And yet it is from small building blocks like this that any broad conclusions about medieval sexuality must be built.

We must consider another possibility here too. In a culture with effective methods of birth control, we are able to separate sexual intercourse from reproduction. For medieval people the two were much more connected. When medieval texts talk about women wanting to have sex with their husbands, they may be attributing to these women not sexual desire as we would think of it, but rather the desire for offspring. And this leads us to yet another level of uncertainty: if medieval texts attribute to women the desire for motherhood, is this a reflection of their actual desires or a male writer attributing to them the desires he thought appropriate?

Images, like texts, can be interpreted in various ways, and unless we know something about the artist, context, and audience, we do not have a basis for knowing what the work meant to medieval people. As one example, the famous Bayeux Tapestry, embroidered to commemorate the conquest of England by the Normans in 1066, has naked men and women among the fabulous beasts in its marginal spaces, whose meaning scholars have much debated. Churches across Europe have stone carvings of both men and women, generally quite grotesque, exhibiting their genitalia. These were once interpreted as survivals of pagan fertility cults, incorporated into churches in a syncretistic manner, or as celebrations of fertility within a more Christian context. More recently they have been seen as misogynistic, equating woman with sex organ and emphasizing the threat of feminine lust and temptation. Perhaps marginal figures in a manuscript or even embroidery represent little more than the artist having his joke, but stone carvings on churches are usually part of a planned program. Some carvings we recognize as part of biblical narratives or traditional iconography. What do we make of these sexualized figures? How would medieval people have "read" them, and would different people have read them differently? Does the man with an erection chasing the naked woman in the Bayeux embroidery, just below the main image of Harold being escorted to Duke William, indicate fertility, or is it a symbol of the loose sexual mores of the English? (See Figure 1.1.) Is the man threatening the woman or are they engaged in foreplay? If the work was indeed embroidered by nuns, was it their idea, and what would it have meant to them to embroider it? In the late nineteenth century a copy of the famous embroidery was made, stitched by thirty-five ladies of the Leek Embroidery Society and first exhibited in 1886, then moved to the Reading Museum in 1895. The Victorian ladies of the society worked from photographic reproductions that had been slightly edited: the visible genitalia were omitted in several scenes. (See Figure 1.2.) The difference in the degree of graphicness of the images tells us something about what was considered acceptable in polite company in the eleventh century.

No entirely convincing explanation for this image and similar ones in the margin of the embroidery has been put forward, although Madeline Caviness stresses that the marginal scenes must be read in the context of the main scene in the panel, and that this is likely to be some kind of comment on Harold.[16] It may represent the rape that is attendant on war. It may be analogizing a victorious leader to a virile man and the captive loser to a woman. It may, like the more abstract pictures of birds and animals, be simply decorative, perhaps a joke inserted by the designer. It is unlikely to have been considered obscene, or it would not have been included in this context. And it is unlikely that it was actually pornographic, that is, included for the purpose of titillation. Scholars disagree on where the embroidery was displayed, some thinking that the marginal figures make it unsuitable for a church, but without knowing how the figures would have been interpreted

Figure 1.1 Detail from the Bayeux Tapestry – eleventh century, Musée de la Tapisserie, Bayeux. With special permission of the town of Bayeux

Figure 1.2 Detail from a replica of the Bayeux Tapestry, Reading Museum, Reading

we cannot say for sure that a church would not have permitted it; parallel though not identical images can also be found on churches.

The questions about the interpretation of this image from the Bayeux Tapestry are largely unanswerable, and even if we could answer them, it would be in regard only to this one artifact, a creation of late eleventh-century Anglo-Norman culture and not of a general "medieval" ethos. Medieval texts and artistic works may be interpreted in a variety of ways. On many topics this book will not make a definitive statement, merely suggest some of the possibilities to which the evidence points. Some readers may find this frustrating. Historians find it frustrating too, and yet it is the way that historians have to work. The past is like a puzzle, but it is a puzzle with many of the pieces missing. Sometimes there are enough pieces available for us to be able to determine where they fit and easily see the shape of the missing pieces, but sometimes we can only conjecture what the missing pieces might look like.

The puzzle-piece analogy does not go far enough to describe the problems of working with these sources, however. Medieval people often did not write frankly about sex. But even when they did write erotically, or in terms that seem to us erotic, that does not mean the texts unproblematically reflect their desires. We are reading the texts in a different world, a world that has learned from Freud and from various literary schools of interpretation to see sex lurking everywhere as an underlying motive or theme. Medieval people may not have seen things this way. Does that mean that sexual meanings are still there although the medieval writers did not know it, or does it mean that their world is totally incommensurable with ours and therefore inaccessible to us?

Take, for example, a piece of erotic poetry that was very widely read and commented on during the Middle Ages:

> How fair and pleasant you are,
> O loved one, delectable maiden!
> You are stately as a palm tree,
> And your breasts are as its clusters.
> I say I will climb the palm tree and lay hold of its branches.
> Oh, may your breasts be like clusters of the vine,
> And the scent of your breath like apples,
> And your kisses like the best wine that goes down smoothly,
> Gliding over lips and teeth.

You may have guessed that this comes from the Bible: the Song of Songs or Song of Solomon (Song of Sol. 7:6–9). Medieval theologians explained this erotic poem as an allegory: it was really about the soul's love for God, or Christ's love for the church. If people habitually heard language like this in a religious context, and had it explained to them as spiritual rather than

20

carnal, the way that they wrote and read love poetry could well have been affected. Where we see eroticism, they may have seen biblical allusion. If someone today wrote:

> Oh! Good and desirable love, well-formed body, slender and smooth, fresh and fair-complexioned face, which God formed with his hands! I have always desired you, for no other lady pleases me in any way. No other love do I want at all![17]

we would assume that the speaker (if not the poet) was experiencing sexual desire for the woman in question. It is not quite so clear that we can assume that in the case of a medieval poem.

Medieval people often wrote with an emotionality that would seem out of place today except between lovers. Thus, when Aelred of Rievaulx, a twelfth-century English Cistercian abbot, wrote about spiritual friendship, he described it in a way that would be rather unusual for a man today:

> a friend is a man who will weep with you in troubles, rejoice with you in good fortune, seek an answer with you in times of doubt; who with the chains of love you will bring into the secret place of your mind, so that even when absent in body he will be present in spirit, where you alone will converse sweetly and secretly with him alone, you alone will confer with him alone, and as the bustle of the world is silenced, in the sleep of peace, in the embrace of love, in the kiss of unity, with the sweetness of the Holy Spirit flowing between you, you alone will rest with him alone; thus you will join and unite yourself to him, and mix your soul with his, so that one being is created from several.[18]

Whatever deep and passionate feelings Aelred may have had for his friends, it is clear from his writings that he was not physically involved with them. Do we then say that this language is not erotic? If so, do we discount the eroticism of similar language between a man and a woman? Or do we say that such language must always be erotic on some level, even if not consciously? If so, we are going to find eroticism in a lot of places in medieval Europe.

The most important conclusion that we can draw from texts like this is that medieval people understood the bonds of love and friendship differently from the way we do today. We expect the most intense emotional relationships in our lives to be with our sexual partners, especially spouses. They did not. As David Clark suggests for Old English literature, we must "leave open the questions of where platonic and erotic love part company (if indeed they can be truly said to do so), and how far sexual and emotional relations coincide."[19] Many people today would not be able to answer those

21

questions about relationships in their own lives; we certainly cannot answer them definitively for people who lived a thousand years ago. Whatever desires may lurk beneath the language of friendship and love, it is not useful historically to label medieval people who did not recognize them as victims of false consciousness who were unable to come to terms with their own sexuality. Rather, it is more helpful to use such texts to understand how they approached friendship, love, and sex.

Just as medieval people's views of what was and was not erotic differed from each other's and from our own, so did their views of what was and was not natural. This was an issue to a larger extent within Christianity, but Muslim and Jewish natural philosophers also took from Aristotle and other ancient philosophers the idea of "nature" as a single entity that things could be either in accordance with or against. Medieval Christian texts frequently make reference to "the sin against nature," which is sometimes used interchangeably with "sodomy." The personification of Nature in Alain of Lille's *Plaint of Nature* objects to the practice of this sin. "Many other youths, too, clothed by my favour in grace and beauty, intoxicated with thirst for money, converted Venus' hammers to the function of anvils."[20] But if we look more closely at what Christian writers meant by nature or the natural, we find a good deal of conflict. Natural is what animals do – sex for the purpose of reproduction, according to medieval authors – and yet for humans to have sex in a rear-entry position, the way animals do, was considered unnatural. William Peraldus, a moral writer much quoted and translated throughout the Middle Ages, distinguished between two kinds of sins against nature: that which is "against nature in terms of the manner," when the woman is on top or some other unusual position is used for heterosexual vaginal intercourse, or "against nature in terms of the substance, when someone obtains or consents that semen be spilled elsewhere than in the place deputed by nature."[21] Nature, in Alain of Lille, objects to non-reproductive sex of any sort: it is sterility, not the choice of love object, that offends her.

People today, too, use the concept of nature as a means of criticizing whatever they disagree with. Whatever I feel in my gut is wrong is "unnatural," and this has little to do with whether it occurs "in nature," that is, in the non-human world, or not. What could be more "natural" than incest? Animals are not concerned with how closely related they are to their sexual partners. Of course, when we label behaviors like incest "unnatural," we are talking about human nature, not the natural world. But we will never agree on what human nature is. For those who follow the great thirteenth-century scholastic Thomas Aquinas, everything has a purpose for which God created it, and its nature is to fulfill that purpose; the study of the nature of each thing is "natural philosophy," the category under which Aristotle (and his medieval heirs across religious traditions) placed the areas of investigation that we might call "science." For Aquinas, human nature, divinely implanted, is to be rational, and any sexual act that defies rationality (which tends to mean any act that is not procreative) is unnatural. For other modern people, "doing what comes naturally" means following the dictates of one's body, as opposed to the artificial conventions of society. Nothing could be farther from a medieval view in which there existed a natural law, far stricter than social convention. "Nature," then, is also a socially constructed concept, and the nature that medieval people recognized is not the same as what we recognize. As Karma Lochrie points out, " 'Natural' and 'unnatural' . . . were not medieval code words for 'heterosexual' and 'perverse.' "[22]

Many people tend to assume that sex was not much spoken of in the medieval period. Because the popular perception today is that religious people think sex is an inappropriate topic of discussion, in the Middle Ages, when religion so dominated the culture, people assume a discreet silence must have been observed. This, however, is not the case. It is not always easy to know exactly how to interpret what medieval people said when they talked about sex, but talk about it they did. Michel Foucault famously repudiated what he called the "repressive hypothesis" that in Victorian and other nineteenth-century societies sex was something that could not be talked about. In fact, Foucault argued, nineteenth-century bourgeois culture talked about sex all the time, even if these discussions focused on why particular sexual behavior was wrong. Legal, medical, literary, and political discourses all discussed sex. The same was true in medieval Europe.

Medieval discussions about sex are not only discussions by religious or secular authorities about how to repress it, although those were certainly present. It was discussed in everyday conversation perhaps more than is acceptable in many circles in North American society today. Most people in the Middle Ages lived off the land, and the breeding of animals would have been no secret. Many lived in small houses where there were no private bedrooms, so children might be aware of parental behavior that takes place today behind closed doors. The terms in which sex was discussed, though, indicate not only a familiarity with the behavior – not a surprise – but also a frankness in its discussion.

Two instances from two different medieval literatures, where discussions of sex cause problems, can give us some indication of what was permissible to say and what was not. In one of the French fabliaux, "La damoiselle qui ne pooit oïr parler de foutre" ("The Young Woman Who Couldn't Bear to Hear about Fucking"), a farmer's daughter cannot bear to hear the word "foutre" ("fuck" seems the closest equivalent, since although the audience was aristocratic and/or bourgeois, "foutre" was definitely on the vulgar side) – indeed, she is so delicate that the word makes her physically ill. She and her father's farm hand name the parts of the body in euphemisms – his penis is a horse, her vagina is a spring, and so on. She eventually tells him to "Go water him there in my spring."[23] The humor of the story derives from the fact that although she is too prudish to hear or speak the words, she has no problem with the actions. It implies, however, that a young woman who was bothered by this particular word would be rare. Normally, the story implies, anyone who was willing to engage in the act would be willing to call it by its colloquial name.

In medieval Scandinavia, according to laws from Norway and Iceland, there were certain insults that were punishable by full outlawry (a punishment under which, if the perpetrator did not leave Iceland, anyone could kill him with impunity). These insults included calling any man by the name of a female animal. This type of insult was connected with accusations of passive homosexual behavior. The Icelandic sagas, written in the thirteenth century but depicting events of the ninth to eleventh centuries, give several examples of this type of insult (see Chapter 5). The words are unspeakable, or must be avenged with violence, not because they are offensive or polluting in themselves, but because they shame the man who is insulted by casting doubt on his masculinity. It is not that the speaker has been too blunt or graphic; it is not a failure of euphemism. Particular words are against the law not because they are obscene in themselves, but because of the power of the ideas behind them, ideas that would not be any more acceptable if euphemized.

These examples – and many others could be cited – indicate that people could and did speak about sex, and when people objected to it, it was not because the talk about sex was in itself polluting or improper. Sex was very problematic for medieval European Christians, but they did not for the most part deal with the problem by attempting to silence any mention of it. By the later Middle Ages in western Europe, some scholars have identified a tendency toward euphemism, exemplified by Chaucer's Reeve, who complains when someone uses "churls' terms" about him.[24] Chaucer may here be satirizing the objection to vulgar language more than the use of vulgarity itself, although he has warned his audience that both the Reeve and the Miller are churls and tell tales accordingly; whoever wants edification should choose another story. But this seems a bit tongue in cheek, and in any case the objection is to the language rather than to the topic of discussion. Sex in the Middle Ages could be talked about. Chaucer and the fabliau authors, or the authors of the *One Thousand and One Nights*, which includes much sexual activity, may have intended their stories largely for entertainment rather than edification, but once again it is clear that things that today would be considered dirty jokes were in the Middle Ages appropriate for middle- to highbrow entertainment.

That something was talked about does not mean that it was tolerated. To speak of toleration or acceptance raises the question of "tolerated by whom? Accepted by whom?" Some forms of sexual behavior may have led to labeling with a stigmatized identity. Labeling meant recognition, albeit of a negative sort; it could mean official tolerance accompanied by policing, as with prostitutes. Other sorts of behavior were against religious teaching, but perhaps not against social expectations, and not acknowledged by regulation. Anna Clark has called these "twilight moments": "these acts and desires were hidden because they were regarded as shameful and embarrassing," including those "sexual acts and relationships which take place without ever being acknowledged or named."[25] Sexual relations between women might be an example: discussed in sources very allusively rather than directly, so that many scholars have hesitated to see them, they were neither accepted nor stigmatized.

Sodomy sometimes formed an exception. Some writers called it "the unmentionable sin," and certain discussions of sexual sin, as we will see in Chapter 5, deliberately avoided talking about it, some on the grounds that it would give people ideas. But preachers like Bernardino of Siena were not afraid to talk about it, in the most scathing terms. The act may have been taboo for Bernardino, but talking about it was not. Medieval people certainly talked about sex in a great variety of ways, but the only ones that we know about are those that appear in the surviving sources, and in trying to draw conclusions about medieval sexuality we have to take into account that much of our information comes from hostile sources like Bernardino or criminal records.

The Middle Ages and the modern world

This chapter so far has devoted a lot of attention to the concept of "sexuality," but we need to think also about the concept of "medieval Europe." The time period of the Middle Ages covers roughly the millennium between 500 and 1500. This period is particularly important in the history of sexuality because it is the period during which the basic parameters of Christian teaching and attitudes, which underlie much of the thinking about sexuality even in today's secularized Western world, were set. Contemporary European attitudes as well as those of cultures around the world in which European cultural influence predominates (or did during and after the colonial era) were shaped in significant ways by the ideas about sexuality formulated in the Middle Ages.

The Middle Ages were not, of course, a unified period. If we consider the kinds of sources discussed above by time period rather than by type, we find great variation. From the early medieval West, for example, we have chronicles that tell us about the behavior of the highest aristocracy, and here we learn about plural marriage or perhaps concubinage (since the church did not recognize more than one marriage, even though the aristocracy persisted in plural marriage or at best serial monogamy). We also have handbooks for confessors that prescribe penances for particular sexual offenses, which can give us some indication of how seriously various transgressions were taken. But even if we could assume a direct correspondence between the magnitude of the penance and the magnitude of the offense – which is difficult to do when the penalty for intercourse between two men is one year while that for a priest's going hunting is three – this does not tell us much about how the offenses were perceived by the laity at large. The handbooks were written by and for priests, many of them monks, as a guide to hearing confession; many penances are for the clergy, or for monks and nuns. The laity are of course included, but they are not the core audience, and the handbooks do not necessarily reflect their concerns. Nevertheless, what we see is a church trying to impose its rules of morality on a laity, from the aristocracy on down, who want to be good Christians but chafe at the restrictions on their behavior.

And although the church did try to impose rules, it by no means banned the discussion of sex within its own walls. The *Exeter Book*, a tenth-century manuscript compiled and copied by monks and containing both Christian and secular poetry, includes a collection of nearly a hundred riddles, some of them with sexual double-entendres:

> A small miracle hangs near a man's thigh,
> Full under folds. It is stiff, strong,
> Bold, brassy, and pierced in front.
> When a young lord lifts his tunic
> Over his knees, he wants to greet
> With the hard head of this hanging creature
> The hole it has long come to fill.[26]

The *Exeter Book* gives no solutions to the riddles. Most scholars have taken this one to be a key, although a dagger has also been suggested. But whatever the "clean" meaning, it is obviously also meant to call to mind a penis. The riddles with double-entendres do not use unambiguously sexual language; they are capable of tame interpretations, thus allowing the monks deniability, and in any case they do not constitute the bulk of the riddles. Yet they show us something of the universality of sexual humor even among the devout celibate.

In the tenth and eleventh centuries in Muslim Spain, among Jews as well as Muslims, and the twelfth century in Christian Europe, we get a different type of source, literary texts, which provide the affective background to what appears in earlier sources simply as behavior. The twelfth century seems to be an era when love came into its own in Europe, both spiritual and profane love, and where sexuality was connected with deep, passionate emotion. This does not mean that people before this time did not have these feelings, but that they did not leave behind the kinds of evidence that would reflect them. Despite efforts by the church to enforce clerical celibacy, the twelfth century seems to have been a rather unrepressive time. When Abelard had his affair with Heloise (see Chapter 4), it was her uncle, not the secular or religious authorities, who had him castrated for it, and while church councils condemned some of his writings as contrary to true doctrine, it was not his sexual behavior that they condemned. A relatively more repressive era seems to have begun in the middle of the thirteenth century. This may be due in part to the codification of knowledge in compendia like those of Thomas Aquinas, who systematized theology and the Christian position on various sexual issues. Towns began to regulate prostitution and other aspects of the sexual behavior of their citizens. Church courts punished adulterers, fornicators, and other sinners. Again, it is not clear whether the repression was new or whether the institutions through which it worked merely became more effective. Did a church bureaucracy come into existence because of a need to regulate sexual behavior, or did it begin regulating sexual behavior simply because it existed and needed a purpose?

Attitudes about sexuality varied and changed over the course of the Middle Ages, but there are certainly common themes that look familiar at the beginning of the twenty-first century. In the Christian world a normative religious discourse taught that sexuality was something sinful and evil, and yet large segments of the society chose to ignore that teaching. The diversity of viewpoints about sexuality in contemporary culture is paralleled by the diversity of viewpoints in the Middle Ages. That is not to say the contemporary ideas are still the same; many factors have altered them over the last five hundred years, including the Protestant devaluation of celibacy, increased encounter with non-European peoples, the development of science as an alternative source of authority, and massive social and economic changes including especially the results of the women's movement and the development of reliable methods of birth control. The reader of this book will find moments of "plus ça change, plus c'est la même chose," and other points at which the medieval substratum appears beneath the superstructure of modern ideas. Nevertheless what makes medieval Europe particularly interesting to the study of sexuality is that it is a set of cultures at once like our own, because it is ancestral to it, and yet profoundly different, shaped by different assumptions.

Fundamental differences do separate contemporary and medieval outlooks. One major difference concerns the place of the normative religious discourse. While many parts of contemporary Euro-American culture are still dominated by a Judeo-Christian view of monogamous heterosexual marriage as the only appropriate place for sexual expression, these societies also espouse pluralism, as witnessed by the legalization of same-sex marriage in Canada, the United States, and many European countries. Religious people may condemn the behavior of others, but in a secular society the views of religious leaders or institutions are not binding on anyone except their own followers. Their views sometimes find their way into legislation, but this legislation has to be justified by some reason other than "God wants it this way," for example by concerns about social order.

In the Middle Ages the situation was quite different. On the Christian side, there was only one church, and although there was a diversity of views within the church, there were some points on which there was little disagreement, such as the sinfulness of extramarital sex, especially for women. The fact that the Bible or the church said that it was wrong was sufficient. Toleration of other viewpoints was not a positive value, although in fact none of the schools of jurisprudence within Islam, nor Jews nor many Christian heretics, would have disagreed about the sinfulness of extramarital sex for women. Sermons frequently taught that the worst of sins could be wiped away by sincere confession, but people still would have been aware of a unified, normative teaching. Not all Christians in the Middle Ages took the church's teaching on sex very seriously, but very few took no account of it whatsoever.

The greater importance of religious teaching in the Middle Ages than today is not just the result of secularization but also a function of modern concepts of individual freedom and of privacy. Many people today would say that what other people do in their own bedrooms is their own business and should not be regulated by the state. In medieval Europe it was not their own business. One's choice of sex partner affected one's family and the inheritance of property. One's choice of sex act affected the social order and therefore was of concern to the entire community. The US Supreme Court's statement that homosexuals are "entitled to respect for their private lives. The State cannot demean their existence or control their destiny by making their private sexual conduct a crime"[27] would be incomprehensible to medieval people.

Another difference between sex in the Middle Ages and today is the extent to which it can be separated from reproduction. The impact of the availability of reliable forms of birth control on all heterosexual relations, including marital, can hardly be overestimated. The effects of the link between sex and reproduction would have been greater on women than on men, since they were the ones whose lives were changed by pregnancy, but for men too heterosexual intercourse was the act of generation as well as an act of pleasure.

Attitudes toward sodomy, at least in Christian Europe, were also quite different from contemporary ones. Sodomy was reviled precisely because it was non-reproductive, sterile, an argument not much used today in a world in which most heterosexual acts are also non-reproductive because of contraception. It was also blasphemy; it went against the God's creation, an argument that appears today in a slightly different form: "God created Adam and Eve, not Adam and Steve." It could subvert the gender order by making men into women. What was not a major part of the medieval polemic against sodomy was the defense of marriage, the idea that same-sex relations would undercut the social order by discouraging people from marrying. This idea appeared in fifteenth-century Florence, but was not common elsewhere. For the most part the emphasis was on the way sodomy disrupted the natural order because it undermined fertility, rather than on how it disrupted the social order because it undermined male dominance via the household. Indeed, in the Middle Ages a man's interest in sex with other men was not thought to be exclusive or to prevent him from marrying and having children. A wife was not considered to be the focus of a husband's emotional life or even his sexual life. Marriage was a sacrament, but because it was so often arranged, and even if arranged by the parties themselves was often undertaken for economic reasons, the conjugal unit did not have the same emotional importance it has for many people today, and thus was not so threatened by sodomy.

The biggest difference between medieval attitudes and those of today, however, is in the idea of sex as a transitive act, something done by someone to someone else. While mutuality may not be the reality in many sexual relationships today, it is taken by many as the ideal, and sex is commonly thought of as something done by a couple, not as something done by one person to another (although indeed this is not the case in all contemporary subcultures). The line between active and passive partner in the Middle Ages was very sharp, and closely related to gender roles. To be active was to be masculine, regardless of the gender of one's partner, and to be passive was to be feminine. One can find examples of such strict dichotomization between active and passive in the modern period – the butch/femme organization of lesbian communities in the United States in the 1940s and 1950s is one example – but for the most part both same-sex and opposite-sex couples have abandoned these strict roles today.

These differences between medieval outlooks on sexuality and contemporary ones do not mean that there are no points of connection. The idea that sexual pleasure is in itself evil, that sex even in marriage is somehow polluting, comes to us from early Christianity via the Middle Ages, even if it was not a view universally held either then or today. Many of the legal categories we use to talk about sex – fornication, adultery, rape, prostitution, sodomy – come from medieval western Europe, though ultimately from ancient Rome. The double standard, in which men have substantially more sexual freedom than do women, was hardly a creation of medieval European culture, but it comes down to us directly from there.

If we identify contrasts between contemporary views on sexuality and medieval ones, it is logical to ask when the break occurred. Is the change an effect of modernity? Was the medieval the last period to conceptualize sex as something one does to another, where what was important was gender role rather than object choice? Clearly this was not the case. Recent scholarship has shown that sexual economies far into the modern period shared these patterns. The work of George Chauncey on the gay male world in New York in the first half of the twentieth century, for example, reveals a system in working-class communities in which men had sex with either women or "fairies," effeminate men who played the passive role. The men who took the active role were not considered "gay" or indeed, for the most part, to have a particular kind of sexual identity. If their preference was exclusively for fairies they might be termed "wolves," but mostly they were just considered "normal" men. In essence, then, the binary division in sexuality was not between those identified as gay and straight, but between those identified as masculine (mostly men, a few "bull daggers" or butch women) and those identified as feminine (mostly women, some fairies). Sexual and gender identities were much less separable just a century ago than they are today.

That we can find persistent patterns in the construction of sexuality from the ancient Greeks to twentieth-century New York does not mean that the modes of sexual categorization were the same, nor that the patterns were continuous across the millennia. It does mean, however, that we cannot identify a sharp break that comes with modernity. The same is true of the persistent pattern of age-differentiated partner choice. The contemporary importance of reminding people that homosexuality does not in itself imply pedophilia may seem contradictory with a long history of discourses about men loving boys. These must, however, be seen in the context of an equally long history of men loving girls, or loving women whom they juvenilize by calling them girls. In a culture in which sex is hierarchical, a dominant partner doing something to a subordinate partner, it makes sense that the subordinate partner would typically be younger, or thought of as younger. In addition, the equation of youth with beauty, both masculine and feminine, is pervasive in western culture, and the young are seen as more desirable. The change that has taken place in sexual and love relationships in the past century or even half century, which is still not as complete as we would like to think, has been a shift toward more equality between the two partners, whether they are of the same sex or the opposite sex. That this was not the case until fairly recently tells us something not about homosexuality but about the relation between sexuality and dominance.

Of course homosexuality and heterosexuality are not the only modern sexual categories whose application to the Middle Ages are open to discussion. Cross-dressing is not much discussed in this book; although it may be considered a sexual paraphilia today, in the Middle Ages it had much more to do with gender performance and much less with sexual preference. Masochism is a bit trickier. Certainly many medieval people took pleasure in pain and suffering: saints desired and took pleasure in union with God, and they desired and took pleasure in pain because it led them to God. It is not always possible to draw a line between the erotic and the divine, and this is true of pain as well as of pleasure; people who suffer pain to achieve salvation are not the same as those who suffer it to achieve orgasm, but there may be parallels. We need to remember that the beating of children or subordinates was common in the Middle Ages. Peter Abelard beat his student Heloise: "To avert suspicion there were some beatings, yes, but the hand that struck the blows belonged to love, not anger, to pleasure, not rage – and they surpassed the sweetness of any perfume."[28] The twelfth-century monk Guibert of Nogent similarly was beaten by his tutor: "I had such a liking for him – striped as my poor little skin might have been by his many whiplashes – that I obeyed him, not out of fear (as would generally be the case in relationships like these) but out of some curious feeling of love, which overwhelmed my whole being and made me forget all his harshness."[29] The connection of love with suffering pain, then, appeared often in medieval society, but was not specifically configured as a sexual preference or identity.

The connection of sexual desire with causing pain to another, so prominent in contemporary pornography, is also hard to identify in the Middle Ages. Certainly rape as an instrument of power was not uncommon; but depictions of the rape of peasant women by aristocratic men are prettified in the *pastourelle* genre, and there are few detailed descriptions of the rape that often accompanied military campaigns. There is little suggestion in the texts that violence increased men's enjoyment. In the few instances where literary sources depict rape in some detail, as with the giant of Mont St. Michel in some versions of the Arthurian legends, they elicit horror rather than pleasure. Sexual violence in a religious context – stories and pictures of Christian virgins threatened with rape or mutilation by pagans – underscored the severity of the threat or torture in order to emphasize the saints' remarkable steadfastness. Of course, these stories may at the same time have appealed to hearers' or viewers' prurient interests, but while this may have been an effect – we cannot tell, since we cannot get into individual beholders' eyes or minds – it was not the purpose of the texts.

The examples in this book are mainly restricted to western Europe, in part because this is the region that left its legacy to modern western culture, and in part because local and national differences, while important, are less striking than overall broad cultural similarities across the region. However, within western Europe, the book looks at Muslim and Jewish culture as well as the Christian majority. These comparisons help us to see how much of the period's understanding of sexuality was shaped by religious texts and thinkers, and how much was influenced by particular historical circumstances. Occasional comparisons with eastern Europe, which shared some of the same religious assumptions, help illuminate the road not taken and the historical specificity of western European developments.

In building up a general picture of a culture, it is always difficult to preserve the picture of differences within that culture. I have tried to make general statements about the European Middle Ages as a whole, while still stressing variation. The variations are significant. Medieval society changed over time, and at any given time social relations varied across Europe. Few of the sources used in this book tell us something about how "medieval people" felt or behaved, although they may tell us something about how some medieval people – for example, fourteenth-century English aristocrats – felt or behaved. The variation was great even across western Christendom, but was even greater if we take into account other religious/legal traditions.

31

Jewish society took a somewhat different attitude from the majority Christian culture: the mainstream Jewish view did not treat sexual pleasure within marriage as suspect for either women or men, although there were certainly writers who did. On the other hand, extramarital sexual behavior by men came in for more opprobrium than it did among Christians. In Muslim society, where slave women were also available, men had more extramarital opportunities, but free women fewer.

One thing that all three religio-cultural groups agreed upon was that sexual relations between members of different groups were to be discouraged at all costs. Or, rather, none of the groups minded so much if its men had sex with women of one of the other groups, but they all minded a great deal if men of another group took "their" women. Christian exempla are full of stories of men marrying and converting Jewish women, and chansons de geste and romance are full of "Saracen" women who marry Christians and convert. Yet the Fourth Lateran Council of 1215 ordered Jews to wear a distinguishing badge on their clothing explicitly for the purpose of avoiding miscegenation: the fear was of Jewish men having sex with Christian women. Everywhere Jews were forbidden to frequent Christian prostitutes, and in Spain, where this sort of activity was most likely, it was forbidden most severely. Local town laws provided, for example, that if a Jewish or Muslim man had sex with a Christian woman, the man should be drawn and quartered and the woman burned at the stake.

The reasons behind these provisions are similar to those behind miscegenation laws in the United States and the lynchings that followed rumored violations of the norm by black men with white women (but not white men with black women). Penetration symbolizes power. For men of one group to have sex with women of another is an assertion of power over the entire group. Jews and Muslims policed the inter-religious sexual behavior of their women far more stringently than that of their men. Muslim women who had sex with Christian men were often enslaved by Christians if not punished by their own communities.

Attitudes about sexuality varied not only across religious lines but also across class lines. As with religion, men of various status groups did not mind if they had sex with women of other groups, but objected strongly if men of subordinate groups took "their" women. (We do not really know what women of the various groups thought about the matter, since the evidence for these attitudes comes from the writings of men.) When it comes to the level of toleration of sexual activity overall, and within social groups, however, as far as we can tell attitudes differed more by degree of piety than by social class. Adultery may have been more condoned among the aristocracy than elsewhere, at least when it did not lead to illegitimate children, but it seems to have been condoned mainly when a king or someone very powerful had sex with someone's wife and there was not much to be done about it. The literature that glorified adultery – like the story of Tristan and

Iseult – showed what some of the consequences of an older man's arranged marriage with a younger woman might be, but while the audience is meant to sympathize with the lovers, they do not end up triumphing; it is a tragedy for all involved. Literature showed adultery as a great passion but did not indicate that it was accepted; even the complaisant Arthur is forced to take notice and thereby lose his queen and his best knight.

We don't know much about the sexual behavior that was expected at the lower end of society, but from the later Middle Ages there are enough fornication cases in church courts to indicate that marriage was no more sacrosanct there than it was at the upper echelons. The constant thundering from the pulpit against sexual temptation and extramarital sexual behavior seems to have been responding to a not uncommon phenomenon among the public generally. And the fact that chastity is so remarkable in saints' lives would seem to indicate that it was not expected in normal people's behavior.

Across Europe in the later Middle Ages church courts regulated Christians' sexual behavior, both inside and outside of marriage. They enforced the same basic rules, but they enforced them differently depending on local synodal legislation and on local customs. But although the church claimed jurisdiction over these kinds of offenses, secular authorities also claimed it, as for example in the territory of the count of Savoy in northern Italy, where local chatellanies held courts that regulated fornication, adultery, incest (understood as marrying someone to whom one was too closely related by birth or marriage), and other offenses.

This book is intended as a broad survey of medieval sexuality, but it is an interpretive survey. It begins from the position that we must pay attention to medieval categories rather than impose our own categories on the Middle Ages. It also assumes that the question of whether or not there were sexual identities in the Middle Ages is a question to be answered by reference to the medieval evidence, rather than saying "yes" because we think sexuality is universal or "no" because we think sexuality is a creation of the nineteenth century.

From those points of departure, this book will make several arguments. The first is found throughout: that medieval attitudes toward sexuality were conflicted and complicated; there was not one universal and hegemonic point of view imposed by a totalitarian church upon everyone. The second is that there were sexual identities in the Middle Ages, but that those identities were different ones from today's, and not determined by object choice. The third is that the dichotomy between active and passive partner played a major role in the way medieval people thought about sexuality.

As a corollary to this argument, the fourth and perhaps most important point to be made is that gender played a fundamental organizing role in medieval sexuality. The experience of any heterosexual act was different for the man and the woman, both because they were conceived of as doing different things and because the social consequences for them of their sexual involvement (whether marital or not) were quite different. Gender also played an important role in the meanings placed on homosexual behavior: a man who took a passive role or a woman who played an active role was not transgressing the boundaries of sexual identities as much as the boundaries of gender.

Because this book is intended for non-specialists, I have kept the footnotes to a minimum, giving sources for direct quotations only. Where a translation is available I have cited it rather than the original; if no translation is cited, the translation is my own. A book as broad as this one cannot rely on the research of one individual, and I have huge intellectual debts, which are acknowledged in brief bibliographical essays for each chapter that indicate the works from which I have drawn and to which readers may wish to turn for further information.

Notes

1 *Henri d'Arci's Vitas Patrum: A Thirteenth-Century Anglo-Norman Rimed Translation of the Verba Seniorum*, ed. Basilides Andreas O'Connor (Washington, DC: Catholic University of America Press, 1949), 40.

2 "The Good Woman of Orléans," in *The Fabliaux: A New Verse Translation*, trans. Nathaniel E. Dubin (New York: Liveright, 2013), 629.

3 *The Arabian Nights*, ed. Daniel Heller-Roazen, trans. Husain Haddawy (New York: W.W. Norton, 2010), 7.

4 *Middle English Dictionary*, ed. Robert E. Lewis (Ann Arbor: University of Michigan Press, 1988), s.v. swiven.

5 David Lorenzo Boyd and Ruth Mazo Karras, "The Interrogation of a Male Transvestite Prostitute in Fourteenth-Century London," *GLQ: A Journal of Lesbian and Gay Studies* 1 (1995), 463.

6 *Memoriale Credencium: A Late Middle English Manual of Theology for Lay People, Edited from Bodley MS Tanner 201*, ed. J.H.L. Kengen (Nijmegen: n.p., 1971), 141. "Suffer" here does not imply pain, but rather passivity.

7 Alain of Lille, *The Plaint of Nature*, trans. James J. Sheridan (Toronto: Pontifical Institute for Medieval Studies, 1980), 67–8, 133–5.

8 Anna Clark, *Desire: A History of European Sexuality* (New York and London: Routledge, 2008), 3.

9 David M. Halperin, "Is There a History of Sexuality?" *History and Theory* 28 (1989), 257–74, quote at 257.

10 Karma Lochrie, "Presidential Improprieties and Medieval Categories: The Absurdity of Heterosexuality," in *Queering the Middle Ages*, eds. Glenn Burger and Steven F. Kruger (Minneapolis: University of Minnesota Press, 2001), 87–96, here 90–1.

11 Michel Foucault, *The History of Sexuality, vol. 1, an Introduction*, trans. Robert Hurley (New York: Vintage, 1990), 43.

12 Karma Lochrie, "Mystical Acts, Queer Tendencies," in *Constructing Medieval Sexuality*, eds. Karma Lochrie, Peggy McCracken and James A. Schultz (Minneapolis: University of Minnesota Press, 1997), 180.

13 William Burgwinkle, "Queer Theory and the Middle Ages," *French Studies* 60 (2006), 79–88, here 79.

14 Diane Wolfthal, *In and Out of the Marital Bed: Seeing Sex in Renaissance Europe* (New Haven: Yale University Press, 2010).

15 "The Fisherman of Pont-sur-Seine," in Dubin, 443–51.

16 Madeline H. Caviness, "Anglo-Saxon Women, Norman Knights, and a 'Third Sex' in the Bayeux Embroidery," in *The Bayeux Tapestry: New Interpretations*, eds. Martin K. Voys, Karen Eileen Overbey and Dan Terkla (Woodbridge, Suffolk: Boydell Press, 2009), 85–118.

17 Bernart de Ventadorn, "Lo tems vai e ven e vive," in *Troubadour Lyrics: A Bilingual Anthology*, ed. and trans. Frede Jensen (New York: Peter Lang, 1998), 159.

18 Aelred of Rievaulx, *Speculum Caritatis*, 3:109, in *Opera Omnia, vol. 1*, ed. Anselm Hoste, Corpus Christianorum Continuatio Medievalis 1 (Turnhout: Brepols, 1971), 159.

19 David Clark, *Between Medieval Men: Male Friendship and Desire in Early Medieval English Literature* (Oxford: Oxford University Press, 2009), 18.

20 Alain of Lille, 136.

21 Gulielmus Peraldus, *Summa de Vitiis*, 3:2.2. I am grateful to Siegfried Wenzel for the use of his draft normalized edition of the *Summa de Vitiis*.

22 Karma Lochrie, *Heterosyncrasies: Female Sexuality When Normal Wasn't* (Minneapolis: University of Minnesota Press, 2005), xxii.

23 Dubin, 883. Dubin translates another version of the title "La damoiselle qui n'oit oïr parler de foutre qui n'aüst mal au cuer," as "The Maiden Who Couldn't Abide Lewd Language," 873. The title as I have given it is in *Nouveau recueil complet des fabliaux*, vol. 4, 82.

24 "The Reeve's Prologue," l:3917, in Geoffrey Chaucer, *The Riverside Chaucer*, ed. Larry D. Benson, 3rd edition (Boston: Houghton Mifflin, 1987), 78.

25 Clark, *Desire*, 7.

26 *The Exeter Book Riddles*, trans. Kevin Crossley-Holland (London: Penguin, revised edition 1993), 44, 48.

27 Lawrence v. Georgia, 123 S.Ct. 2472 (2003), 2484.

28 Peter Abelard, "The Calamities," in *Abelard & Heloise: The Letters and Other Writings*, trans. William Levitan (Indianapolis: Hackett, 2007), 12.

29 Guibert of Nogent, *A Monk's Confession: The Memoirs of Guibert of Nogent*, trans. Paul J. Archambault (University Park, PA: Pennsylvania State University Press, 1996), 19.

2

THE SEXUALITY OF CHASTITY

Medieval European Christian society inherited Christianity's vexed relationship with the flesh. While teaching that all creation – including the human body – was good, church authors also taught that the flesh must be controlled and subdued for the sake of the salvation of the soul. Sex was not the only bodily drive that had to be subdued. The desires for necessities like food, drink, and sleep, as well as luxuries like comfortable clothing, also had to be combated. Sex, however, as perhaps the most tempting of the human desires, got more than its share of attention from medieval writers. Indeed, whether one was sexually active or chaste came to be a fundamental definition of what kind of person one was.

Why was the medieval church so concerned with avoidance of sexual activity? Why was this activity polluting even if involuntary (as with nocturnal emissions)? Why did it disqualify individuals from the highest spiritual status? In part the answers have to do with the idea of ritual separation. Most religions have something that sets their priestly caste apart from common believers, usually the observance of particular taboos. For Christianity the important taboo was sexual. The idea of ritual separation and ritual purity owed much to Jewish sources, but in Jewish practice ritual impurity (as opposed to moral impurity) could be cleansed by ritual ablution. Christianity was, rather, characterized by a dualist strain – the spirit is good but the flesh is bad. This dualism received more emphasis at some times than at others, and it has never so dominant as to exclude all positive valuations of the flesh (after all, Christians believe that God chose to be incarnated in a material body and born of a woman), but it still characterizes the teachings of some Christian churches and the views of many Christians.

The idea that sex was polluting also had a great deal to do with gender. For men, it was not just the sex act that was polluting, but also the women with whom they committed it. Of course, to commit it with other men could be even worse, and effeminate men were considered a temptation just as women were. The general expectation was, however, that women were the temptresses who led men astray. To be too involved with women – to have sex at all, if a cleric, or to have sex other than with one's wife for

36

reproductive purposes, if a lay man – was to turn away from higher things and to become, like a woman, bound to the body.

Lust (and the disobedience that went along with it) was for Christians the original sin, and Eve the original sinner (here shown depicted by the twelfth-century sculptor Gislebertus on the lintel of the cathedral church of Autun, serpent-like and seductive; see Figure 2.1). According to medieval theologians Adam and Eve did not feel concupiscence in the Garden of Eden. They did have sexual intercourse but it, like eating, was for the creation and sustenance of life, not for pleasure. The original sin was disobedience to God, but concupiscence was its clear result. Eve came in for most of the blame, since she persuaded Adam to sin, although some theologians thought that since a woman could not help being weaker, Adam actually bore more responsibility.

The terms "chastity," "celibacy," "abstention," and "virginity" loom large in this chapter. While they overlap, none are synonymous. Chastity in the Middle Ages generally meant the absence of sexual activity, but could also be used to mean the absence of illicit sexual activity; thus married people who had sex only with their spouses for reproductive purposes might be called chaste, although this was not the usual usage. Abstinence, too, in medieval as well as modern usage, means the absence of sexual activity, but the connotation is slightly different, for abstinence refers only to refraining from the act, whereas chastity has moral overtones. Someone who refrained from sexual activity for medical reasons would be abstinent, but would probably not be called chaste unless moral reasons were involved as well.

Figure 2.1 Eve. North portal lintel, Cathedral of St. Lazare, Autun, attributed to Gislebertus, now in Musée Rolin, Autun.

© Ville d'Autun, Musée Rolin, cliché S. Prost

In contemporary usage celibacy is more or less equivalent to abstinence, but that was not the medieval meaning. Celibacy meant the unmarried state. It was not oxymoronic, although it might be sinful, to be celibate and engage in sexual activity; a cleric who did so violated his chastity, not his celibacy. Indeed, although the main point of clerical celibacy was to maintain the chastity and purity of the clergy, it also served to minimize the pull of worldly ties on them. If a priest did engage in heterosexual activity, it was better for the church if he did it with a woman he was not obligated to support, and if he had children, it was better if they had no legal claim to a share of his (or the church's) property.

Of course, in a normative sense, celibacy implied chastity, because medieval people were not supposed to have sex unless they were married. The term "celibate" was generally reserved for those for whom the unmarried state was permanent. Someone who had simply not yet gotten married was more likely to be called simply a youth, or (if female) a virgin, since it was assumed that women's sexual activity began with marriage. The term "virgin" was rarely used of men. For women the meaning could vary; the physical state of having an intact hymen was not always the defining feature of virginity.

For most medieval people of whatever religion, virginity, marriage, and widowhood were life-cycle phenomena rather than choices of particular forms of life; marriage was the normal expectation. Chastity as a life phase loomed rather larger for women than it did for men, because it was considered much more important for them than it was for men to abstain from sexual activity during the time that they were not married. In discussing virginity and chaste widowhood here, I am following medieval theologians in focusing on women who chose those statuses, rather than on those who happened to be unmarried because they had not found a spouse.

It may seem strange for a book on sexuality to start off with a chapter on people who abstained from sex. This abstention, however, did not mean that sexuality was not an issue for them. The choice to abstain often came as a result of what medieval people would have described as a vocation or call from God, and what modern people might consider an inner compulsion or an orientation. Often it required strong effort to overcome sexual temptation; the person who abstained from sex was nevertheless continually conscious of his or her sexual desires and the struggle to overcome them. The absence of sexual activity does not mean the absence of eroticism, involving both people of opposite and of the same sex.

The discussion here is largely drawn from Christian literature: prescriptions from church authorities about virginity, as well as accounts from individuals who chose it, or their biographers. But the ideal of virginity also found its way into secular literature. In particular, romances about the Grail quest suggest that only a knight of particular purity can achieve the grail. Even though Lancelot is perhaps the knight of greatest prowess ever, his unchastity disqualifies him, and it is the chaste Galahad who can discover the grail. In this body of literature, as in the religious texts that will be discussed, temptation and its overcoming loom large.

This chapter focuses on Christianity, unlike the other chapters which also include material on medieval Muslim and Jewish cultures. Chastity as a goal, and virginity as a lifelong state rather than as a temporary situation, were not central to Islam and Judaism, although the latter especially was also concerned with sexual temptation. Jews and Muslims expected women and (usually) men to be chaste in the sense of being faithful to their spouses, but not in the sense of abstinence. Both religions expected or required people to marry. Some movements within these religions diverged – the Sufis in Islam encouraged celibacy, and the German Jewish Pietists (Hasidei Ashkenaz) of the thirteenth century and some Jewish philosophical schools and branches of Kabbalah expressed some qualms about sexual activity – but in these two religions the divine command to multiply took precedence over the demands of bodily purity. The German Pietists, for example, urged marital intercourse to combat sexual temptation, whereas Christians would urge prayer and fasting, allowing marital intercourse to avoid greater sin only if absolutely necessary.

Not all church thinkers taught that sexual intercourse was always sinful. Indeed, the church condemned some teachers as heretical for saying that it was. Rather, mainstream western Christian doctrine taught that sex for purposes other than pleasure – to have children, to prevent one's spouse from falling into sin – was acceptable. However, chastity was always preferable. Some medieval writers believed that any sexual act, no matter how conjugal and procreative, could not be accomplished without concupiscence and "itching of the flesh," and even those canonists and theologians who argued against this position were deeply suspicious of intercourse. To understand why, we must go back before the Middle Ages, to the early centuries of Christianity, and see how Christian teaching on chastity developed.

Early Christianity

Jesus himself had much to say about love but little to say about sex. His moral teaching was more concerned with the avoidance of hypocrisy and with love than with sexual abstinence. His approbation of those who "have castrated themselves for the sake of the Kingdom of Heaven" (Matt. 19:12), whether meant literally or figuratively, however, clearly indicates that the avoidance of sexual activity was pleasing to God.

Some Christians took this passage literally: for example, Origen of Alexandria (185–253), an important theologian, castrated himself. The church historian Eusebius reported that the act was "proof enough of his young and immature mind, but also of his faith and self-control."[1] The Council of Nicaea in 325 (the first church council after Christianity became a tolerated religion of the Roman Empire) required that clerics who castrated themselves be removed from office. The bishops assembled there found castration repulsive and reminiscent of pagan worship. Nevertheless, as Eusebius recognized, Jesus's words implied that even if men should not castrate themselves, at least it was possible to do so with good intentions. A good Christian should behave as though he had been castrated, replicating in spirit what pagans might have done in body.

More important for the development of Christian thinking about sexuality than Jesus's few explicit teachings about it was the example of Jesus's life. None of the canonical gospels describe Jesus as having any erotic relationships. The idea that Jesus was celibate and chaste, and that all Christians should therefore strive to be so, was powerful in the Middle Ages. Even today, when sexual abstinence is not urged on all believers, the idea of the imitation of Christ is used to justify the requirement of a celibate clergy in the Roman Catholic Church (as well as to exclude women on the grounds that only a man can truly imitate the male Jesus).

While Jesus himself said little about sexual behavior, Paul of Tarsus, whose letters to various Christian congregations around the Mediterranean became part of the Bible, was much more concerned with it. He did not state explicitly that sexual intercourse made one impure, and his dictum that "unto the pure all things are pure" (Titus 1:15) has sometimes been taken to permit varieties of behavior that he surely never intended. He suggested that those who were virgins should remain so until the second coming of Christ, but also that those who were married should remain so (1 Cor. 7:27). In his famous admonition that "it is better to marry than to burn" (1 Cor. 7:9), he ranked marriage low in the moral hierarchy, as a crutch for those who were too weak to abstain. For Paul, reproduction was not an important goal of marriage, because the imminent second coming obviated the need to reproduce the Christian community.

The intellectual and cultural traditions out of which Christianity grew – those of the Near East, notably Judaism, and those of the Hellenistic world – had not traditionally been hostile to sexual activity. They may have tried to restrict it to permanent unions (for women especially), but, although the issue was contested, mainstream thought in neither the Jewish nor Hellenistic tradition taught that remaining a virgin or minimizing the frequency of intercourse within marriage was a positive good. Jewish tradition did in fact minimize the frequency of marital intercourse by decreeing that women had to be purified after their menstrual periods before marital relations could resume. However, whatever the reason for this prohibition, it was not based on an idea that sex itself was sinful. The biblical accounts of Mary stress her virginity in order to guarantee the miraculous nature of her son's birth. The absolute good of virginity was a later development.

At the time when Christianity appeared on the scene, however, both Jewish and Hellenistic cultures were witnessing ascetic movements that urged sexual abstinence, at least for men (women did not have a choice, as they were still supposed to bear children). The Jewish community of Qumran, which created the Dead Sea Scrolls, included men vowed to celibacy. While few pagans urged total abstinence from sex, either at the time of Christ or in the first few Christian centuries, there were those like the Stoics who believed that sex could be a disruptive force and urged that men control their passions. This view influenced many early Christians, even those who did not reject sex altogether.

Although these cultural undercurrents meant that Christianity did not emerge out of nowhere to contradict a pro-sex culture, Christianity's innovation was in making the belief in abstinence part of the mainstream. Not everyone could take it up, but everyone recognized the holiness of those who did. And the reasons that Christianity gave for sexual abstinence were different from those of the Hellenistic philosophers, who believed that sexual activity could distract one from the things of the mind. With Christianity sin and purity entered the picture.

The emphasis on sexual renunciation in early Christianity was especially strong for women. This does not mean, however, that Christianity was a patriarchal movement aimed at controlling women's bodies. It may have been women themselves who chose virginity and initiated the movement toward a special status within the church for female virgins. Rather than cutting back on women's choices, virginity offered them new options. Virginity was the opposite of sexual activity, but because the only sexual activity that was at all acceptable for women came within marriage, virginity was also the opposite of marriage. Rejection of sex meant the rejection of the control of a husband. Celibate women could avoid male domination, at least to some degree (the spiritual authority they amassed could help them gain their independence from fathers and brothers as well). Yet, as the third-century writer Tertullian warned, renouncing sex did not free a woman from her basic sexual nature; a virgin was still a woman and therefore should still wear a veil to signify her shame.[2]

Some Christians believed that Christian women were able to transcend their femininity and become masculine. They understood this in a positive sense: femininity meant being tied to the body and things of the world in a way in which masculinity did not. One of the texts found at Nag Hammadi in Egypt, among a cache of documents written by Gnostics (a group condemned as heretical, who believed that they had some secret knowledge given them by God), promises that "every woman who makes herself male shall enter the Kingdom of Heaven."[3] Since this text was suppressed as heretical, we do not have a tradition of how ancient and medieval writers understood it. It is not clear whether this transcendence of femininity placed renunciation of marriage and motherhood at the center, or indeed whether all Gnostics, let alone other Christians, would have agreed.

The story of saints Perpetua and Felicity, who were put to death at Carthage in 203, is an orthodox text that also supports the idea of transcending femininity as a goal for women. Perpetua was a young married woman with a child. Despite repeated importuning by her father and husband, she refused to make the pagan sacrifices that would have allowed her to escape death. Her father couched his request explicitly in terms of gender roles: daughter, sister, mother. "Do not make me disgraced before men. Behold your brothers, behold your mother and your aunt; look at your son, who cannot live without you." She, however, refused the family ties and chose martyrdom. Before her death she had a vision in which, in the arena, her clothes were removed from her and she became male.

> Then there came forth against me a certain Egyptian, horrible in appearance, along with his assistants, ready to fight with me. There came also to me comely young men as my assistants and helpers. I was smoothed down and changed my sex. And they began to rub me down with oil as is customary for a contest.[4]

Perpetua clearly had not renounced marriage and sexual activity as part of her acceptance of Christianity; yet when she took her Christian beliefs to their extreme, they did require such renunciation. Her companion Felicity, meanwhile, had cause to regret not having been sexually abstinent, because she was pregnant, and the Romans would not put to death a pregnant woman. Felicity therefore feared she would miss out on the opportunity of martyrdom. Miraculously, however, she delivered her child in time to die with her companions.

Perpetua and Felicity were not virgins, but they nevertheless symbolized the idea that a truly good Christian woman rejected marriage and motherhood, the social roles dictated by her possession of a female body. Perpetua became independent of men's social domination in rejecting her husband's and father's requests to give in and save her life. One might argue that this did not make her independent, because she traded submission to the will of a father and husband for submission to the will of God. But submitting to God was her choice, and in terms of human society she declared her independence by rejecting these gender roles. Perpetua demonstrates the difficulty in distinguishing between women's sexual activity and the social roles they were required to play.

Although an ascetic ethos had been present in some streams of Judaism in the pre-Christian era, it did not become the dominant theme in rabbinic (post–Second Temple) Judaism. Chastity was certainly valued in women, and language similar to that found in Christian texts was sometimes used about women as temptation or gateway to evil, but virginity was not valued for either men or women. A woman's highest calling was to marry and bear children. A man's was to study, but in contrast to Christianity this was by no means incompatible with marital sexual activity. Indeed, stories in early rabbinic literature depict the sages boasting of their sexual prowess in a way that in a Christian context would have been mockery. And a Jewish or Muslim Perpetua would have been unthinkable.

The most important early Christian writing about female virginity to be handed down to the Middle Ages was not written in the cause of female independence. St. Jerome had close friendships with a number of chaste women, widows, and virgins, with whom he corresponded frequently and to whom he gave spiritual advice. However, when it came to treating women as a group, rather than the individual women whom he respected, his point of view was much more negative. Jerome's most famous writing about women, in his *Against Jovinian* (written about 393), was cited in misogynistic treatises throughout the Middle Ages.

The purpose of Jerome's work was not a critique of women, but rather a critique of the work of the priest Jovinian, who had taught that virginity was not superior to the married state. Jerome, in rather intemperate style, critiqued marriage by stressing the advantages of virginity for women and the disadvantages of marriage for men. He implied, however, that all sexual intercourse even in marriage partakes of sin. "For the time past is sufficient for us when we walked in lasciviousness, lusts, and other vices."[5] He criticized sexually active men as well as women, including priests who had previously been married.

Jerome presented virginity for women as a positive choice. His arguments were practical as well as based on ideas of purity. Virginity would free them from the tyranny of a husband and the agony of childbirth. He also argued against marriage for men, using misogynistic arguments to paint freedom from a wife as a desirable state. Jerome did not place much emphasis, however, on sexual desire. He was concerned with detaching oneself from ties and obligations in this world more than with overcoming the lusts of the body. "Just as the man who has a wife is anxious for the things of this world, how he may please his wife, so the married woman thinks of the things of the world, how she may please her husband."[6]

Ambrose of Milan, bishop from 374 to 397, also wrote about the positive value of virginity. He suggested that women who remained virgins transcended the defects of womanhood: "chastity makes angels; [she] who preserves it is an angel, who loses it, a devil."[7] He too stressed freedom from the cares of the world, but he also placed a strong emphasis on purity or bodily integrity: "what is virginal chastity, but integrity without contagion?"[8] Both authors clearly believed that a woman becomes a totally different kind of human being if she is a virgin. Note here the assumption that virginity is an unusual state. We today think of virginity as the default, the state of all people until they become sexually active; but in late antiquity the default state was marriage (a girl might be temporarily a virgin only because she had not yet entered marriage), and virginity was a deviation from the norm. Women in late antique culture may have had more freedom than in early classical times, but they still operated within a system that valued them mainly as household managers, bearers of children, and tokens in political alliances. Virginity was not just a sexual choice, it also took women out of their gender-defined roles and made them honorary men. This state of virginity was different from virginity in the pagan Roman world in that it was permanent. Pagans and Jews valued virginity in not-yet-married daughters, but that was a temporary state dictated by circumstance, not a fundamental identity.

Unlike some later writers, these church fathers did not substitute a passionate relationship with God for the human passions. The choice not to reproduce, implicit in the decision to remain a virgin, meant a denial of the traditional feminine identity, not a transfer of women's dependence and emotional bonds to God. A woman's whole being, then, was defined by her sexual activity or lack thereof. This choice was made on the basis of faith rather than sexual inclination; it could be based on intense desire, but desire for salvation rather than human love.

Virgins were not the only ones who could be chaste; Jerome also praised chaste widowhood. Some theologians considered widowhood an "order" akin to virginity. Not all widows were classified as chaste, however, and the "order" consisted only of those who either took vows or made a less formal commitment to chastity. They could not become virgins again, but they could do penance for their earlier involvement in the flesh, which some authors considered a pollution even though they also taught that marriage was a good. Even a former prostitute could repent and become holy, and the stories of Mary Magdalene, Mary of Egypt, and Thaïs, told in late antiquity, provided examples. Virginity was not necessary to salvation. But nevertheless it was something very special that, once lost, could never be regained.

The sense of purity and bodily integrity connected with female virginity would be found, throughout the Middle Ages, in images of the Virgin Mary: for example, as a glass through which light (impregnation by the Holy Spirit) passes without breaking it, or as an enclosed garden, an image from the Song of Songs. Peter Damian in the mid-eleventh century argued that Mary remained a virgin even after the birth of Jesus, implying her hymen was not broken even then.[9] To be truly pure was to be unpenetrated, impenetrable. The difference between virginity for men and virginity for women, then, had to do with the transitive nature of sexual relations, as something a man does, something a woman has done to her. For a man to have sex might be a sin, but for women it was a violation. To be pure and virginal, however, meant renouncing not only sex but also its purpose and result: reproduction. This is why the Virgin Mary was so specially venerated in medieval culture. She alone was able to have the reproductive result without losing virginal purity; for her alone among not only women but also men, the twin desiderata of purity and fertility were compatible.

The arguments made by these church fathers were cited repeatedly throughout the Middle Ages. Originality was not considered a great virtue among medieval writers; rather, they placed a great deal of emphasis on textual authorities. Ambrose and Jerome were foundational to the tradition of medieval writing on virginity and chastity, but the most important patristic writer on sex and marriage (as well as on other aspects of Christian society) was Augustine of Hippo (354–430).

Augustine, writing a few years after Jerome, faced a very different problem and opponent than Jerome did in Jovinian. Jerome was defending virginity against someone who claimed that marriage was just as beneficial spiritually; Augustine was defending marriage and indeed human sexuality against those who claimed that all flesh was the creation of an evil divinity, designed to entrap the soul and keep it from salvation. Augustine had himself formerly been a Manichean and wrote against his former co-religionists with the zeal of a convert. The next chapter will have more to say about his treatises in defense of marriage; it is important here simply to note that he was very careful to defend the moral worth of sexual intercourse in the context of a marriage, even if performed out of motives other than reproduction.

Virginity, in Augustine's view, was a good thing, better than marriage, but this did not mean that the loss of virginity through marriage was a sin or an obstacle to salvation. His critique of non-marital sex was not based on impurity, but on lack of control and disobedience to God's will. In the proper context and frame of mind, however, sex was not in itself evil. "Marriage and fornication," he wrote, "are not two evils, the second of which is worse; but marriage and continence are two goods, the second of which is better." He drew an analogy between marriage and health: health is not as good as immortality, but that does not mean it is not a good thing.[10] He warned virgins that "they must not, on account of the superiority of the more perfect gift which they have received from on high, despise, by comparison with themselves, the fathers and mothers of the people of God."[11] Yet virgins too could be mothers of the people of God. Like their model, the Virgin Mary, they could be fertile, although in their case the motherhood was spiritual: "with Mary, they are mothers of Christ, if they do the will of his Father."[12]

These authors all concentrated particularly on the importance of sexual abstinence for women, but they did not ignore men. The idea of chastity after a period of sexual activity was considered normal and acceptable for men (Augustine's recounting of his prayer, "Give me chastity and continence, but not yet," was meant to illustrate his wrong-headedness, but it was probably not all that atypical).[13] For men, virginity held no special magic. Having had sex once did not make a man permanently impure, because men in heterosexual intercourse were not penetrated. This was a crucial distinction for Roman culture and an integral part of the double standard in sexuality that had developed. Christianity did not do away with the double standard, but Augustine and others did suggest that men had the same responsibility to chastity that women did. In the later Roman period a number of writers suggested that sexual moderation was good for men both for health reasons and because it allowed them to focus on the life of the mind. The fourth-century historian Ammianus Marcellinus, himself a pagan, described the pagan emperor Julian's sexual abstinence in his widowhood: "he was so conspicuous for inviolate chastity that after the loss of his wife it is well known that he never gave a thought to love."[14] Pagan authors did not often go as far as Christians in suggesting total abstinence, but in their promotion of moderation they helped create a new ideal of masculinity based on self-control rather than on aggressive penetration of as many other people as possible.

Christianity fit well with this set of ideas. Whereas it provided women with a way of transcending femininity by renouncing the social bonds that sexual activity created for them, it provided men with a way of not transcending but redefining masculinity. Being manly did not have to mean being aggressive, sexually and militarily; it could mean being strong in the sense of controlling oneself and one's body as well as controlling others. This self-control was not only sexual but also applied in many other areas of life. A new type of Christian, the monk, practiced it most completely.

Monasticism

Although Augustine had a profound effect on the teachings of the church throughout the medieval period, as did Ambrose and Jerome to a lesser degree, none of these three authors were monks. A discussion of chastity and sexuality in medieval Christian culture will inevitably devote a great deal of attention to monasticism, both male and female, so we must digress just a bit further and look at the traditions about sex in early monasticism.

Chastity, closely related to sexual purity, played a major role in the medieval church, and monasticism was its main vehicle. Monks were not the only men expected to be sexually abstinent; so were secular priests (although their celibacy was not enforced until the twelfth century). Monks, however, participated in a wider project of renunciation – of food, clothing, daily comforts, and social relations – that secular priests did not. In the case of women, nuns were the main sexually abstinent group; although in the central and later Middle Ages anchoresses, beguines, tertiaries, and vowed widows might commit publicly or privately to celibacy, this was not as widespread as the monastic phenomenon. In the eastern church, married men could be ordained priests, so monks were the sole bearers of sexual abstinence. Bishops had to be celibate, so in practice it was mainly monks who were promoted to that rank.

Monasticism had its origins in the Egyptian desert. As Christianity became legalized and firmly established within the Roman Empire, there were fewer opportunities for the display of one's faith through martyrdom, which had been a sure road to salvation. Some people turned to monasticism as a substitute, a sort of martyrdom in this life, in which an individual becomes dead to the world, withdraws and concentrates on prayer and the state of his or her soul. This withdrawal is also coupled with ascetic practices meant to tame the flesh and purify the heart: specifically, abstinence from sex, from food and drink beyond what is necessary to sustain life, and from luxury and comfort. Ascetic forms of life were not unique to Christianity, but known in other religions as well; it is the Christian form, however, that most influenced the European Middle Ages. The first monks were hermits, following in the footsteps of St. Anthony, whose biography circulated widely in the late fourth and fifth centuries.

Of the various varieties of monasticism, the cenobitic type, where the monks lived in communities, had the greatest impact on medieval culture. In order to regularize monastic life, several authors in the early fifth century wrote rules for the monks to follow. John Cassian's *Institutes*, written in Gaul, introduced into the west an account of eastern monastic practice, while the rule of Benedict of Nursia (380–457), written for his monastery of Monte Cassino in Italy, became the basis for most medieval western monasticism. The first rule for nuns was that of Caesarius of Arles (d. 542), possibly written in collaboration with his sister. Benedict does not give much attention to issues of sexuality, demanding chastity but saying little more about it. Cassian devotes more space to threats to chastity, including "nocturnal pollution" and the development of inappropriate relationships between monks. Early works on religious women focused on protecting virginity and chastity through enclosure and obedience. In some ways the rejection of sexuality for a nun was a given, and in early Christianity the theme of continual sexual temptation of women was not as prominent as it was for men.

While cenobitic rather than eremitic monasticism became the model for medieval developments, the eremitic tradition (from the Greek word *eremos*, "desert," and the origin of the English word "hermit") had a profound effect on perceptions of sanctity in medieval culture, both within and without monasticism. Stories of the heroic asceticism of the desert mothers and (mainly) fathers were collected and circulated widely. These collections abound with stories of men and women who ate practically nothing, and who combated the devil's assaults on their chastity with self-mutilation, or at a minimum drastic asceticism:

Since the time that I became a monk I have never given myself my fill of bread, nor of water, nor of sleep, and tormenting myself with appetite for these things whereby we are fed, I was not suffered to feel the stings of lust.[15]

The paradigmatic desert saint, Anthony,

> defended his whole body by faith, by praying at night and by fasting. At night the devil would turn himself into the attractive form of a beautiful woman, omitting no detail that might provoke lascivious thoughts, but Antony called to mind the fiery punishment of hell and the torment inflicted by worms.[16]

It could be, too, that early monks' strict fasting may have limited their sexual activity (including nocturnal emissions), although not necessarily their sexual thoughts.

Heroic asceticism was not a universal demand or standard; there were also stories that counseled moderation and noted that those who tried too hard could be guilty of pride in their ascetic achievements, just as great a sin as indulgence. When a brother asked aloud for a little salt to eat since he ate no cooked food, Father Theodore told him: "It had profited thee more, my brother, to eat flesh in thy cell, than to hear this spoken in the presence of the brethren."[17] However, the stories of asceticism were more gripping than those of moderation. They painted a picture of the holy life as a constant struggle against temptation, either from other humans at the devil's prompting or from demons themselves.

A holy woman might not fight against her own temptation at all, but against the temptation of another, thereby taking upon herself the responsibility for men's sexual behavior. The fifth-century writer Palladius tells the story of one of the desert saints, Alexandra, who walled herself up in a tomb, seeing no other human being for ten years. She explained her motivation: "A man was distracted in mind because of me, and rather than scandalize a soul made in the image of God, I betook myself alive to a tomb, lest I seem to cause him suffering or reject him."[18] This story stands at the head of a long medieval tradition of stories of women mutilating themselves in order not to tempt men; there was a strong strand in medieval thought that wanted women to internalize the blame for men's desires.

The stories of the desert mothers and fathers became important in medieval traditions because they painted the chaste individual not as someone without sexual desires, but as someone who had managed to overcome those desires through an act of will. The goal was not to feel the desires any more, but there was little glory in never having felt them in the first place. This aspect of attitudes to chastity would interact in complex ways with medieval medical theory. Those who were more tempted – who had stronger desires – were more virtuous for overcoming them. Yet some medical writers thought that women's pleasure in intercourse was greater than men's. Women's lust was also seen as harder to control because of women's innate weakness. It was more difficult for women to remain chaste than for men, and therefore they had to be more strictly controlled; on the other hand, when they did remain chaste, it was more praiseworthy than for men, because they had overcome greater obstacles. As Peter Abelard wrote, "As women are the weaker sex, their power is more perfect and finds greater favor with God."[19]

The idea that virtue lay not only in abstinence but also in fighting against temptation was especially pronounced in attitudes toward eunuchs. The western church argued against taking Jesus's words about "those who have made themselves eunuchs for the sake of the kingdom of heaven" literally. To castrate oneself physically took a one-time great act of will, but, once it was done, there was no further struggle against temptation, whereas castrating oneself metaphorically was a constant battle. (In fact castration after puberty may eradicate neither desire nor the ability to have an erection, but medieval people believed that it did.)

In the eastern church, eunuchs did serve as priests, monks, even bishops (though some monasteries refused to admit them because they might become temptations to other monks). But churchmen writing about them did not give them credit for great ascetic virtue because chastity no longer required of them an effort of will. In the early Middle Ages eastern Christian writers tended to regard eunuchs as dangerous (because they were sexually tempting to men) and not especially virtuous. They could not struggle against temptation or achieve the triumph of *apatheia* (sexual disinterest) since it was already physically determined. On the other hand, some writers thought self-castration a virtuous act because it allowed eunuchs to serve God without worrying about accusations of sexual misconduct. In the central Middle Ages eunuchs in the Byzantine Empire were understood as able to achieve sanctity through other means: most were castrated young and given to court or church service, allowing them to become powerful patrons of religious institutions.

In the west, castration to maintain chastity was frowned upon, unless it was purely metaphorical. Caesarius of Heisterbach in the thirteenth century tells the story of a monk who could not control his lustful feelings. He dreamt that a man with a long knife

> rushed upon him with terrible swiftness and cruelly mutilated him. Then awakening from the horror of this nightmare he thought that he had been made a eunuch, which indeed was true, though not as the vision showed, with a material knife, but by spiritual grace.

After this dream, he was no longer troubled by lust, although his testicles physically remained.[20]

When a man was spiritually castrated in this way, or when a man or woman achieved *apatheia* or sexual anesthesia, it represented a fundamental change in his or her life. To a few absence of desire came naturally, for others it was achieved, but for all it meant an identity of chastity that went beyond mere acts (or absence of acts). Those who had transcended sexual desire became a different type of person, and this transformation became a goal for many throughout the Middle Ages. Alongside those who sought this transformation were those who did not need it because their orientation was already to chastity.

By the early Middle Ages, the church did not emphasize chastity as purity and the means to salvation for lay Christians as much as in the early Christian period (or as much as in the later Middle Ages). People had clearly adopted the underlying assumption, however, that chastity was better than sexual activity. Most early medieval saints were monks or nuns, so they had already taken a vow of chastity. Some, most often women, had been married and came to monasticism only in their widowhood; their holiness did not rely on virginity. Virginity, however, was still considered the best, if not the only acceptable, state. As Caesarius of Arles preached around 500, using a topos borrowed by many other writers: "Indeed there are three professions in the holy catholic Church: virgins, widows, and the married. Virgins produce a hundredfold reward, widows sixtyfold, the married indeed thirtyfold."[21]

The life of Radegund, a saint of the sixth century, is a good example of Merovingian-era attitudes toward chastity. Because of her family position, remaining a virgin was not an option for Radegund. After her uncle's defeat in war she became a prisoner of the Frankish king Clothar, who later married her. She did, however, succeed in making clear to her husband that she preferred to avoid sex and other fleshly indulgences if at all possible, so that "people said the King had yoked himself to a *monacha* (monk-ess) rather than a queen."[22] According to her biographer, she used to get up from her husband's bed during the night, put on a hair cloak and pray on the cold ground near the privy. An illustration from an eleventh-century manuscript (see Figure 2.2) of her biography illustrates her praying while her husband sleeps, although here she appears on the floor next to his bed, with no privy in sight, and wearing her crown: her dignity remains more intact in the image than the text.

Eventually Radegund fled from Clothar and became a nun. But both of her biographers, Venantius Fortunatus and the nun Baudonivia, put more emphasis on Radegund's rejection of ties to the world and the trappings of royalty than on sexual pollution.

The stories of other saints contain similar motifs, in part perhaps because the life of Radegund was well known and later biographers used it as a source. In the seventh century an Anglo-Saxon slave named Balthild was serving at the palace of Neustria, one of the Frankish kingdoms, and a high royal official named Erchinoald wished to marry her. She hid in a corner under some "vile rags" to escape the marriage: "She hoped that she might avoid a human marriage bed and thus merit a heavenly and spiritual spouse."[23] Later, however, her commitment to heroic chastity dissolved as

Figure 2.2 Radegund prays next to her husband's bed. Life of St. Radegund by Venantius Fortunatus. Poitiers, Médiathèque François-Mitterrand, Ms 250 (136), fol. 24r, detail. Image by Olivier Neuillé.

she married the Merovingian king Clovis II; she remained active in political and financial support of the church, and eventually retired (voluntarily or involuntarily) to a monastery for the last fifteen years of her life.

The stories of these holy women belong to a genre known as hagiography, or writings about saints. Like many other genres of medieval writing, hagiography is stylized; there are certain conventions to which the life of a holy man or woman must adhere. The purpose of the account is to make a case for the canonization of this individual or to edify readers and provide them with an example to follow. It does not aim to provide an objective account of the individual's life. What the stories tell us, then, is not how a woman like Radegund felt, or even how she acted, but rather how the author envisions that a holy woman would have behaved. In other words, we learn a set of ideals about female sanctity, among which chastity has a role to play, even if not always a central one.

Nor did it play a central role in the lives of early medieval male saints. Saints like Benedict, Amandus, Benedict of Aniane, Remigius, and Boniface were known for their humility, their miraculous power, their unwavering faith, and their championing of the rights of the church, but their chastity was a given rather than an important achievement. Benedict, indeed, as his story was retold in the central Middle Ages, had an experience of temptation in his youth, but its resolution spared him having to deal with the issue later:

> And another time the devil set before his eyes the image of a woman whom he had seen in the past, and kindled in him such a fire of passion that little was wanting to make him yield to desire and to abandon his solitary life. But of a sudden he recovered the mastery of himself, stripped off his clothing, and rolled in the thorns and brambles which lay thick about his cell, until his whole body was lacerated. Thus he forced out the sickness of his soul through the wounds of his body, and conquered sin. And thenceforth he never again felt the sting of the flesh.[24]

Early medieval texts discussed chastity mainly as a means to attract (or frighten) people into the monastic life. Handbooks of penance, compiled largely for use within monasteries, prescribed very high penances for violations of monastic chastity, but did not penalize marital intercourse – chastity was not required for all. Monks considered themselves spiritually superior to married lay people because of their chastity, especially if they were virgins. Monastic chastity, along with individual poverty (as opposed to poverty of the monastic institution), came by the high Middle Ages to be a part of the justification for the wealth and privileges of monasteries. Monks retained a greater purity than lay people, and they also were at least in theory free of the family ties that kept the concerns of the nobility on worldly things.

The importance of chastity to monks has led some scholars to suggest that they were in effect a third gender, no longer men. The implication of this view is, of course, that sexual activity was an important part of manliness in medieval culture. In some circles, indeed, it was; fathering children, or simply having a large number of sexual partners, could be an important measure of masculinity. However, it was not the only one. Struggling against and overcoming a foe – even when that foe was one's own desires – was a manly activity. (It could be a manly activity for women too; celibate women who had overcome their sexual desires could be called viragos, manly women, in a positive sense; they had transcended the weakness of femininity.) Those whose struggle had been so complete and successful that they no longer felt temptation, it is true, might be considered as no longer men. Indeed, they might be considered no longer quite human: they ceased in a sense to be embodied at all, because the flesh mattered not at all to them. They, however, were very few and far between.

The admonitions repeated throughout the Middle Ages to monks against any behavior that might lead to increased sexual desire, or to placing oneself in circumstances of temptation, indicate that most monks were expected to have sexual desires. Threats to monastic chastity came not only from the opposite sex (monks, especially, might have very little contact with women, though nuns would need to have male confessors), nor even from the same sex, but from the monks' minds and imaginative processes. For example, the Byzantine abbot Theodore of Stoudios (c. 759–826) wrote to his monks:

> Don't grasp or handle your member at all, and don't stare deeply at your nudity, lest you bring the curse of Cain upon you. . . . For it is *porneia* [fornication] even when one does not come close to another's body. . . . And when mother nature calls, let yourself down decently, and make water, without looking at what comes out, without manipulating your member with a finger.[25]

Both those desires and the successful struggle to overcome them were signs of masculinity. Monks did not father families, or participate in military activity, but their rejection of these traditional attributes of masculinity did not mean that they were not considered men; they represented a different way of being men. Compared to third-gender groups in various societies around the world – the so-called *berdache* in some Native North American societies and the *hijra* in India are two of the best-known examples – monks were much less distinctive, and no medieval writer seriously questioned that they were indeed men. Similarly, although some scholars argue that virgin women could be considered not-women because they did not exhibit the misogynistic attributes women were thought to have, medieval people would still have identified them as women in all but a metaphorical sense.

Clerical celibacy

Attitudes toward monastic and clerical chastity began to change with the emergence of the reform movement of the eleventh century. Up until that time, although monks were celibate, little effort had been made to impose celibacy on the secular clergy (those, like parish priests, who served in the world). In the eleventh century, however, as part of a wider move toward separating the church from the world (but at the same time giving it dominance over the world, particularly over temporal rulers), the popes attempted to set higher standards of moral behavior for priests, including the proviso that they should not marry. A whole new literature developed about the harms of marriage and the importance of chastity to salvation. While it was intended largely for priests, it had widespread repercussions for the laity as well.

While literature supporting virginity and chastity had long existed, directed at monks and nuns, the new body of literature directed at the secular clergy placed a new emphasis on ritual purity. Much of the monastic writing had stressed the symbolic significance of chastity as a way to reach God. The chastity of the soul was more important than the chastity of the body. The chastity of the body was by no means unimportant, it was a *sine qua non*; but it was taken for granted, not really in question. In the seventh century the Anglo-Saxon Aldhelm had written:

> For every privilege of pure virginity is preserved only in the fortress of the free mind rather than being contained in the restricted confines of the flesh; and it is beneficially safeguarded by the inflexible judgment of the free will, rather than being diminished out of existence by the forced servitude of the body.[26]

These ideas continued to be expressed in the central Middle Ages. The monk Guibert de Nogent in the twelfth century wrote a treatise on virginity in which he treated it as a spiritual process rather than a state of physical purity. It is not just a question of purity of the flesh, but of moving the focal point away from the flesh to the soul. This did not mean the chastity of the body was unimportant. Saints' biographies describe them as sitting in freezing water, fasting, or flinging themselves into a briar patch to quell their lust. Medieval writers repeated the story of St. Benedict rolling in a briar patch, and other monks copied him. Of course, self-control through prayer was superior to physical means, but physical means were also appropriate to maintain chastity.

An emphasis on ritual purity and on physical virginity became more important from the eleventh century on in writings directed to the secular clergy. The latter lived among people who were sexually active, and even if they remained unmarried as the church demanded, they were exposed to constant temptation. Their image among the laity, as presented in various satirical genres, included a great deal of womanizing. They required constant exhortation to maintain their state of chastity, and a variety of treatises appeared to fill this need. The idea of pollution, of sexual activity as ritual impurity, appears frequently in these treatises. In a 1064 letter to Bishop Cunibertus of Turin, Peter Damian called priests' wives, specifically:

> Charmers of clerics, appetizers of the devil, expulsion from paradise, venom of minds, sword of souls, poison of drinkers, toxin of banqueters, matter of sin, occasion of ruin . . . harem of the ancient enemy, hoopoes, screech-owls, owls, wolves, leeches . . . whores, prostitutes, lovers, wallows of greasy pigs, dens of unclean spirits, nymphs, sirens, witches, Dianas . . . through you the devil is fed on such delicate banquets, he is fattened on the exuberance of your lust . . . vessels of the anger and furor of the Lord, stored for the day of vengeance . . . impious tigers, whose bloodstained mouths

cannot refrain from human blood . . . harpies, who fly around and seize the lord's sacrifices and cruelly devour those who are offered to the Lord . . . lionesses who like monsters make careless men perish in the bloody embraces of the harpies . . . sirens and Charybdis, who while you bring forth the sweet song of deception, contrive of the ravenous sea an inescapable shipwreck . . . mad vipers, who because of the impatience of the burning lust of your lovers mutilate Christ, who is the head of the clergy.[27]

It is such a commonplace in Western society, which has inherited some of these ideas, that impurity stems from sexual activity that it may not strike us as all that surprising that the church condemned such activity by the clergy. It was not, however, a foregone conclusion. The early church identified other things that put the clergy in a state of ritual impurity: shedding blood or touching a corpse, for example. Yet no one fulminated like this about clerics who shed blood or touched corpses. Exchanging ecclesiastical offices for cash (simony) was the only thing that excited nearly as much rancor. Of course, there were other reasons for the demand for clerical celibacy besides ritual purity and the separation from the laity; keeping church property from falling into familial hands was the most important one. But its fundamental effect, and the rhetoric used to promote it, had to do with sexuality.

The eleventh century represented a watershed in ideas about clerical purity. This period witnessed a reform movement within the western church that insisted on upholding standards of clerical behavior in a variety of areas (for example, prohibiting simony or the purchase of church office). Part of this reform movement was the Investiture Controversy, in which the popes (most notably Gregory VII, 1073–1085) and secular rulers (especially the German emperors) disputed who had the right to choose clerics and invest them with their symbols of office. The church insisted on its independence from and primacy over the secular state. In order to maintain this independence and primacy, it had to be able to assert that members of the clergy were different, purer, and better than the laity. Particularly since the church's teaching on this topic was heavily influenced by monastic writers, celibacy became an important element of this difference.

The insistence on clerical celibacy in the west in the wake of the church reform movement of the later eleventh century served to draw a sharp line between clergy and laity, a line that was defined in terms of sexual activity. The clergy were not the only ones who were unmarried and therefore presumed not to be sexually active, but they were the ones for whom the unmarried state was considered permanent. Much as the church encouraged chastity for the unmarried laity (and even for the married laity, as we shall see in the discussion of chaste marriage), it was a calling only for a few, mainly the regular and secular clergy. The chastity of those few was necessary to maintain their special, sacred status, underscored by a new focus on the Eucharist and the miracle of transubstantiation, which only a priest could perform. By presenting sexual activity as polluting, the church could maintain its own representatives on a higher moral plane. Bishops, in particular, were bridegrooms of the church. This allowed it to justify clerical privileges such as freedom from taxation and from royal justice. The line between clergy and laity thus had immense practical as well as symbolic importance.

Condemnations of clerical marriage had their effect. The first Lateran Council in 1123 forbade it and required that the spouses separate. The second Lateran council in 1139 went further and declared such marriages invalid: henceforth there was technically no such thing as a priest's (or any clergyman above a subdeacon's) wife, because any such woman was a concubine. Although reformers fulminated against clerical incontinence throughout the entire Middle Ages, the distinction between clergy and laity eroded from the thirteenth century on. The clergy were not really expected to be a different type of man, and although it was accepted that they could not marry, their sexual activity came in the later Middle Ages to be seen as typical. Both neighbors and church authorities often turned a blind eye to it. For example, a priest named Richard Lucas in late fifteenth-century Paris had lived with his concubine Antoinette for eighteen years. They had not been reported to the local court. What finally brought Lucas to the attention of the local promoter (prosecutor) was that some of his parishioners discovered him in his stable with the wife of a local tailor. Antoinette became very upset and railed at him in front of the witnesses, "Am I not good enough for you?" Apparently the years of concubinage did not offend his neighbors nearly as much as adultery, and his concubine considered herself entitled to fidelity.[28] Yet Lucas was prosecuted for the concubinage (the result of this case does not survive), as were hundreds or thousands of other clergymen across Europe who were living in domestic partnerships. On a day-to-day basis their behavior might be tolerated, but church doctrine remained in place that considered priests separate and opened their partners to prosecution and economic ruin. Records of the papal penitentiary, who issued dispensations from illegitimate birth for young men who wished to become priests, show thousands of priests' children requesting such dispensations. Their existence bespeaks a certain level of toleration, but the fact that they could not take up their choice of career without paying for a dispensation indicates that they still remained marked as the fruits of sin.

By the fifteenth century some church leaders were speaking out against clerical celibacy on the grounds of its impracticality and the hypocrisy it engendered, and some indeed on the basis of human nature. Reformation leaders like Martin Luther who held that very few people were actually called to chastity and that the celibacy requirement made the rest into hypocrites and fornicators were following in an established late medieval tradition. Yet the idea of separation of the clergy from the laity on the basis of their celibacy continued in the writings of churchmen before and after the Protestant Reformation, in preaching, and in prosecution of concubinary clergy by church courts.

By contrast, sexuality, and in particular the denigration of women as polluting and of any sexual contact as filthy, was not as important a part of the discourse in the Byzantine Empire. Clerics in the eastern (Orthodox) church were allowed to marry (though monks and bishops could not); indeed, it became customary for them to marry prior to ordination, and if they preferred celibacy, they became monks. Sexual activity, or the abstinence from it, did not constitute such an integral part of a person's identity, or of the dividing line between lay and cleric. The clergy did not obsess over it to the same extent. This had repercussions for attitudes toward women and gender relations in the society in general.

In the Orthodox world, however, ritual purity was to some extent projected onto clerics' wives. A man could not be ordained if his wife had not been a virgin at the time of their marriage; if she were a widow, or the two of them had sex before the marriage, or even if she had previously been betrothed but never consummated the marriage, she was not chaste enough to be a priest's wife. This restriction may go back in part to Old Testament laws prohibiting priests from marrying widows or divorced women.

A look at medieval Christian ways of classifying people indicates how, in the west, the fundamental distinction between clergy and laity was understood in terms of sexuality. The medieval mode of classification with which people are most familiar is probably the division into those who pray, those who fight, and those who work. This division became popular in the eleventh century, and scholars have noted who is omitted from it, notably women, but also merchants. There were other classification schemes, however, that structured the way people thought about society. One was a simple division between clergy and laity. Other writers, especially in the twelfth century, however, phrased this distinction as one between "the married," "widows," and "virgins," the last often equated with monks and nuns, or between the prelates, the continent, and the married. Sexual status was central to the distinction between clergy and laity, so that we may say indeed that chastity was a sexual identity that was constitutive of how individuals would have understood themselves and their role in life.

Choosing chastity

Both the secular and the regular clergy (both men and women, in the case of the regulars) took sexual abstinence as an important part of their identity. Some Christian lay people did too. Stories of saints who were lay people (the minority of saints during the Middle Ages) often told of their struggles to maintain their chastity. Christina of Markyate, a twelfth-century Englishwoman, had vowed her virginity to Christ. Her aristocratic parents, who wanted her to marry for political reasons, went so far as to encourage her fiancé to rape her. She managed to convert him on their wedding night to a chaste marriage.

Christina eventually ended up living as a holy recluse, maintaining her virginity for her entire life, although the monk who wrote her biography seems to have downplayed the spiritual significance of the state. In the process she entered into passionate friendship with several men, including a hermit named Roger and the abbot of St. Albans monastery. She lived for some time with an unnamed cleric, and they were inflamed with desire for each other; only her prayers brought relief. Christina had not made a monastic profession at that point, although she later did so. In the twelfth century the options were such that lay people – women at least – could choose a chaste and eremitic life without joining a religious order. Their choices were respected by many people, if not by all (like Christina's parents). Other spiritual friendships, such as that between Goscelin of St. Bertin and Eve of Wilton, followed the same pattern as Christina's with Roger and with Abbot Geoffrey: deep and fervent spiritual intimacy.

Choosing chastity could be dangerous, however. In the twelfth century, particularly, several heretical sects argued that all flesh and all sexual experience were evil. This could lead in several different directions. One was antinomian (rejection of established laws): if sex was a creation of the devil, marriage could not sanctify it. You might as well commit fornication, adultery, sodomy, incest, whatever you wished, because it was no worse than marital sex. Orthodox writers often accused heretics of adopting the antinomian point of view, but the only evidence suggesting that they were actually doing so comes from hostile sources.

The other direction in which this sort of dualist heresy (soul created by God, flesh created by the devil) could go is toward a rejection of the works of the flesh, including sex. Gérard of Cambrai wrote in the early eleventh century that heretics taught that "married people could in no way be counted among the faithful." Obviously Gérard did not wish to label as heretical anyone who rejected sexual activity, since clerics, monks, and nuns were required to remain chaste. Gérard argued that "since there is a distinction of orders between men of the world and men of the church, a distinction should be maintained between their behavior."[29] The condemnation of lay sexual activity, not sexual activity in general, was characteristic of heretics.

The attribution to heretics of a requirement of chastity meant that any rejection of sex (except by those under monastic vows) could be suspect. Ralph of Coggeshall tells a story that in the 1170s Gervase of Tilbury accused a young woman in Rheims of heresy. His evidence was that when he had propositioned her, she had refused to have sex with him, "because if I lose my virginity and my flesh once becomes corrupt, without a doubt I should be subject to eternal damnation with no remedy." Obviously, in such a case the cleric was using the threat of a heresy accusation to coerce sex, but the important point here is that he was believed and the woman burned along with others whom she implicated.[30] Wishing to cling to virginity and insisting that any sexual activity would prevent one's salvation, especially without the backing of a religious order, was a dubious course. From the twelfth century to the end of the Middle Ages and beyond, accusations of sexual deviance, including sodomy and group sex, were also leveled against various groups that authors wished to depict as heretical.

The twelfth century in the west saw chastity take a leading role both in the discourse about the clergy and their difference from the laity, and also in the discourses that surrounded various heretical movements. But the discussion of chastity was by no means restricted to theological writers or ecclesiastical contexts. Chastity also began to play a role in Arthurian literature, the flourishing of which dates from this time. In the pursuit of the Holy Grail, only the knights Perceval and Galahad are pure enough to achieve the quest because they have maintained their chastity. Yet their resolve, while admirable, is also a bit out of place in this Arthurian world where so much of a knight's value is measured in the currency of attaining the love of women. Love makes the chivalric world go round (as discussed in Chapter 5), and the Grail quest seems at times like an uncomfortable graft attached to that world. Scholars have often attributed the Grail stories, with their emphasis on chastity, to ecclesiastical influence on a folk tradition. Whether or not this is the case, the development of this literary theme shows that ideas about sexual purity reached an audience well beyond the ecclesiastical elite.

The church hierarchy was determined, however, that lay people who chose sexual abstinence should do so with the sanction of the church. From the thirteenth century on, the church attempted to regulate the religious life more thoroughly, requiring formal vows and entry into a religious order if someone made a permanent decision not to marry. This option became so popular among women in late medieval Italy that so-called third orders of the Franciscan and Dominican friars were established for women. The tertiaries did not become full members of the order, they did not have the preaching mission as the men did, nor did they live communally as did the nuns of St. Clare of Assisi, who were affiliated with the order of St. Francis.

The story of Catherine of Siena (1347–1380), one of the most famous Dominican tertiaries and one of only four women to have been named a Doctor of the Church, illuminates the role chastity could play in the life of such a woman. Catherine knew from early childhood that she would never marry, and she had a revulsion from the idea of sexual intercourse. She had difficulty persuading her parents that she should not marry, but eventually managed to do so. Other women seem to have followed her pattern (or perhaps their biographers followed the pattern of biography set by Catherine's confessor/biographer Raymond of Capua). Her story is reminiscent of the recollections of those gay men and lesbians today who say that they knew from a very young age where their sexual inclinations lay. For some people chastity was an adult "lifestyle choice," but for some it felt as though they were born with a calling to it.

Not everyone born with a calling to chastity was able to maintain it, because many were forced into marriage. Angela of Foligno, another late medieval Italian holy woman, for example, prayed successfully for the death of her husband, mother, and children, in order to strip herself of worldly ties. "Because I had already entered the aforesaid way, and had prayed to God for their death, I felt a great consolation when it happened." In Angela's case it was not so much the escape from the obligation of sexual intercourse but the escape from the responsibilities of caring for a family that she sought; she wanted no distractions from a concentration on the sacred. Nevertheless, she had also prayed that God allow her to keep her promise "to observe chastity with all the members of my body and all my senses."[31] Angela illustrates how social norms might force people with a vocation or, as we today might say, an orientation to celibacy into marriage.

Both men and women came under pressure from their families. The noble family of Thomas Aquinas (1225 or 1227–1274), for example, is said by his biographers to have gone to great lengths, including imprisoning him and bringing a young woman to seduce him, in order to shake him in his vocation (although they were only trying to shake his commitment to the Dominican order so that he could become an abbot, not to make him marry). When they brought the woman, "whorishly dressed," to his room, "and he felt the pricking of the flesh rise up in him, which he always kept under the subjection of reason," he chased her from the room with a burning stick and prayed for a "belt of chastity." When he fell asleep, two angels appeared and girded him with such a belt. From then on, "his virginity, which had been preserved undefeated in such a serious struggle, remained inviolate up till his death."[32] Thomas's resistance to his family's pressures was considered especially virtuous, and other less saintly figures no doubt succumbed.

Some women and men managed to answer the call to chastity even within the context of marriage. According to the teachings of the church, neither spouse was allowed to deny the other sexual intercourse. If someone did deny it, he or she, and not the erring spouse, was responsible for any sin of extramarital sex or masturbation that the spouse committed. To agree to intercourse only in order to render the debt to one's spouse and for no other reason did not, in the view of many medieval writers, pollute one's chastity. Although stricter canon lawyers like Huguccio (active c. 1188) thought that some sin was always present, others, like Rolandus (active c. 1150), thought there was positive merit in having intercourse at the request of one's spouse in order to render the debt. But to avoid sex not by simply denying one's spouse's needs, but rather by persuading the spouse to the ideal of chastity, was a higher good. In some stories the marriage was chaste throughout; in others the couple opted for chastity after they had enough children to ensure the succession.

Perhaps surprisingly, the western church did not really encourage chaste (abstinent) marriage. This may have been in part because it threatened to erode the boundaries between clergy and laity, and the clergy's claim to special holiness through chastity. It may have been, also, that chaste marriage was most often something sought by the female rather than the male partner, and churchmen did not want to be accused of encouraging wives to rebel against their husbands in any way. Chastity in marriage was a good thing, but only if freely chosen by both parties. Some stories, like that of St. Alexis, told of men who sought chaste marriages, in some cases by converting their wives, or, as in the case of Alexis, by fleeing on the wedding night.

It is difficult to discern the exact tangle of motives behind the choice of chaste marriage. A call to, or orientation toward, sexual abstinence could certainly be part of it, as could the belief that sexual activity constituted an obstacle to the pursuit of holiness. But social factors must often have played a role too. When spouses did not choose their own partners, sex must sometimes have been an obligation rather than a mutually enjoyable activity.

It is possible that women also saw abstinence as a way to avoid childbearing with its attendant medical risks and its consequent long years of childrearing. However, the sources that tell us about chaste marriage are mainly the biographies of those considered saints. They come largely from the elite in society, and they are written by churchmen who want to make them seem as holy as possible, so they do not describe chaste marriage as empowering to women in a secular sense. That is a modern interpretation of the sources, although a very likely one.

In the central Middle Ages, many treatises on virginity were written for women and even perhaps requested by them. But women did not have to maintain the ideal of physical virginity manifested by the saints in order to benefit from their example. Not only nuns and recluses could measure themselves by the standard of saints, but also what Jocelyn Wogan-Browne has called "honorary virgins," married women or widows who tried to lead a holy life in their own particular circumstances. Through prayer and penance they could attempt to reconstruct their virginity. The distinction between marriage and virginity, Wogan-Browne argues, "is not always constituted by sexual activity"; married women who had sex with their husbands for procreation could claim some of the value of virginity for themselves.[33]

If the element of bodily integrity did not always remain central for women, it did not for men either. The line between virginity and chastity for them was much less sharply drawn. John Arnold has argued that for men chastity meant a constant fight against temptation, but virginity meant having overcome lust, usually by divine intervention – the state of *apatheia* as the Greeks called it. Whereas female chastity was seen as rare because of the nature of women, male chastity was achievable through hard work and could show masculine strength.

Different groups of people in the Middle Ages understood chastity differently and had different reasons for it, even though many of the writings we have about it come from men who themselves had taken vows of chastity and celibacy. Another set of writings, however, treated sexual abstinence quite differently – medical writings. Many of the important medical writers of the Middle Ages, like Albert the Great, were also theologians, and even those whose education was primarily medical were often ordained clerics. Nevertheless, in their scientific approach to issues of sex they sometimes disagreed with, or at least looked at the topic from a different angle than, those who considered it from the point of view of morality. This was not always, however, separated from medicine. Monica Green recounts the story of a couple in early fourteenth-century Marseilles, Elzéar of Sabran and his wife Delphine de Puimichel, who had been married for several years without children. The well-known physician Arnau of Villanova was asked by their families to determine the cause of the infertility so that it could be treated. The couple confided to Arnau that they had secretly made a vow of chastity. Arnau, spiritually edified (according to the biographer who wished to claim that Elzéar and Delphine were saints), reported back that both partners had incurable medical conditions which prevented conception. Since both were afflicted, their marriage could not be annulled under canon law.[34] Whether or not this story is true, it is certainly the case that Arnau became one of the most important medical writers on infertility. It is telling, however, that according to the story the couple had to hide the fact that they had made the vow. Although the church valued chastity more highly than reproduction, families who wished to pass on their lineage did not necessarily have the same set of priorities.

From a medical point of view sexual abstinence might be harmful. Of course, medieval medicine owed a great deal to Greek and Arabic medical texts, which came from cultures that did not put a spiritual value on chastity. Regular ejaculation in men might be necessary to maintain the balance of humors within the body. Medieval medical theory held that there were four humors, blood, phlegm, yellow bile, and black bile, and that their balance within the human body determined both personality and health. Semen was thought to be a product of blood (as was breastmilk in women), and to allow it to build up created an imbalance of the humors, although nocturnal emission might help alleviate the problem. Of course, overindulgence might lead to equal if not worse problems.

The issues were very similar for women, because medieval theories about the human body held that in certain respects male and female bodies were homologous. There was significant disagreement about some questions, however, including whether or not women ejaculated as men did, but there were many authorities who held that they did, and that this ejaculation in moderation was beneficial to their health. Indeed, virginity was considered to be especially unhealthy for women. Women, who were thought to be cooler than men, had more pollutants in their bodies (which is why they menstruated). Men's superfluities were more fully refined and expelled in nocturnal emissions, which women did not have. Some handbooks for midwives suggest that the pain caused by retention of seed in widows and virgins could be relieved by the midwife's manipulation of the woman's genitals, a possible oblique reference to orgasm via manual stimulation. Medical texts are notably silent, on the other hand, about any possible health benefits from virginity.

Medical writers also recognized that the level of sex drive varied from individual to individual. This might be, but rarely was, extrapolated to argue that some people were more suited than others to chastity. More often, it was couched as a problem for the married, if one spouse's sex drive was much weaker than the other's, or if the lack of desire resulted in their being unable to conceive. Medical texts took infertility, not impotence or frigidity, as the problem to be solved; it might be caused by anatomical problems that prevented one spouse from having intercourse. In general, however, despite disclaimers by medieval writers, the blame for infertility was usually placed on the woman, though it was not necessary for her as passive participant to have a sex drive.

As we have seen, moral and theological writers stressed that it was possible but not conducive to salvation to have chastity of body without chastity of soul. Chastity of body was a sine qua non for salvation, although a married person could be considered chaste if he or she engaged in sex only for the purpose of begetting children or rendering the marriage debt to his or her spouse. Medical writers, however, provided additional theories to help answer the question whether it was possible to have chastity of soul without chastity of body.

The question arises in cases of rape: is a woman who is forced into sexual intercourse against her will still chaste? Some medieval writers suggested that she was not. One common medieval exemplum (a story meant to be used by preachers in composing their sermons) told of a woman who came into court and accused a man of rape. The judge commanded the man to pay her a sum of money in compensation for the loss of her virginity. After he paid her and she left the court, the judge told the man to follow her and forcibly take the silver from her. He was unable to do so, so hard did she defend herself, and he returned to the court. The judge called the woman back in, took back the silver, and said she had lied: "if she had preserved the treasure of her virginity as she did the money, it would never have been taken from her."[35] This anecdote reflects the common medieval view that raped women are complicit. The woman is not treated as impure because of what has been done to her, but rather because she has allowed it to be done. Other stories of attempted rape, particularly of saints in the early

Christian era, show them either protected by God (who addles the brains of the rapist, makes the woman invisible, or performs some other trick), or choosing death or dismemberment over rape. There are a few medieval texts that state that a raped woman can still be considered chaste if she did not consent, but these did not receive anything like the same kind of elaboration in genres intended for a popular audience.

Medical theory had another twist to contribute, however. The "two-seed" theory of sex and reproduction held that both a male and a female seed were necessary for conception. Conception, then, could not take place unless both the man and the woman ejaculated, thus requiring them both to feel pleasure. This doctrine would have benefited married women, whose husbands would need to make sure their wives felt pleasure and ejaculated (probably what they meant by this was what we could call orgasm) in order to conceive. However, it had a negative effect in terms of rape law. Any woman who conceived was deemed to have consented to intercourse, since she must have received pleasure from it.[36] The implication was that she could not remain a virgin in spirit.

Some medical writers, however, argued that a woman could emit seed without consenting to it. The rational will need not play a role; the pleasure is located purely in the body, not in the mind. Nocturnal emissions provide a parallel. The latter were sinful if the sleeper had had concupiscent thoughts during the daytime or when going to sleep, or overindulged in food and drink; the sleeper might not be culpable if he (or indeed she) had done nothing to provoke the emission, which resulted merely from natural superfluity. But while medical writers might hold that the nocturnal emission was healthy, the body's way of ridding itself of excess humors, theologians held that the higher virtue was so to mortify one's flesh and subject it to the will that such an involuntary orgasm would not be possible. Although a steadfast will was virtuous even if the body was weak, a man of the highest virtue would not have wet dreams and a woman of the highest virtue would not become pregnant as the result of rape.

Virginity and temptation

I've been referring to "theologians" as though they all held one point of view, but in fact there were differences both among trained theologians and among medieval people generally as to where the real virtue of chastity lay. Is the truly chaste person one who feels no sexual temptation, or one who feels it but fights and overcomes it? Abbot Cyrus of Alexandria, one of the Desert Fathers, is reported to have said: "If thou hast not these imaginings [of lust], thou art without hope, for if thou hast not the imagination thereof, thou hast the deed itself."[37] The stories of the Desert Fathers make the point that no one is ever totally safe from temptation. When a "certain old man" told a young brother that he was vile and unworthy for admitting the harassment of the demon of lust into his mind, Abbot Apollo prayed that the old man would feel the same temptation: "Lord, who does send temptation when it is needed, turn the battle wherein that brother has suffered against this old man." He told the man that he had not felt temptation before because the devil had either forgotten him or found him unworthy of battle, but "no man can endure the assaults of the adversary, neither can any extinguish or restrain the fire that leaps in our nature, unless God's grace shall give its strength to human weakness."[38]

The twelfth-century English Cistercian Aelred of Rievaulx wrote in his *Rule for a Recluse*, directed to his sister, that temptation was constant:

> in food and drink, in sleep, in speech, let her always be on guard against a threat to her chastity . . . if she has to speak to someone let her always be afraid of hearing something which might cast even the least cloud over the clear skies of her chastity; let her not doubt that she will be abandoned by grace if she utters a single word against purity.[39]

The danger was constant and vigilance had to be constant too. The *Ancrene Wisse*, written for anchoresses in England in the thirteenth century, suggests that any exposure to a man could be dangerous to a woman. If a woman asks why it is so dangerous for her to be around a man: "But do you think that I will leap on him just because I look at him?" the author answers,

> God knows, dear sister, stranger things have happened. Eve your mother leapt after her eyes, from the eye to the apple, from the apple in paradise down to the earth, from the earth to hell, where she lay in prison four thousand years and more, she and her husband both, and condemned all her offspring to leap after her to death without end – the beginning and the root of all this sorrow was one light look.[40]

Yet other stories, like that of Christina of Markyate, told of God's answering the prayers of the virtuous by delivering them from temptation. Still other writings caution that virginity in body is not enough: virgins should not be proud but humble, and the state of the soul can be as important as the state of the body.[41]

In terms of the argument here – that chastity was a sexual identity, that whether or not individuals were sexually active was an important part of the way they defined themselves as persons and how others defined them – the question of temptation is crucial. Is the person with an orientation to chastity one who rarely if ever feels tempted to sexual activity, or is it someone whose desire for chastity is so strong that s/he is able to overcome the desire for sex? The answer is probably both/and. A lack of sexual desire might be seen as a gift from God; most people had to achieve that lack of desire through struggle. As the *Ancrene Wisse* puts it: "St. Benedict, St. Anthony, and the others – you know well how they were tempted, and through the temptations were proved as true champions, and so justly deserved a champion's crown."[42] To be chaste was to identify oneself as someone devoted enough to spiritual matters that one could transcend the flesh. This is an even more profound aspect of personal identity than simply a question of whether someone was ritually pure or not.

By the late Middle Ages, there was less emphasis on the physical integrity of virginity than there had been earlier (although it never completely went away). Even those who had once been married, as well as virgins, could attain chastity. Clarissa Atkinson, among other scholars, has identified a shift from the thirteenth century onward toward the conception of virginity as a psychological and spiritual state, a constructed identity rather than a physiological fact. While the physical nature of virginity, especially for women, was never forgotten, it became secondary to moral qualities, which meant that those who had once engaged in sexual intercourse could still acquire the same virtue. This idea remained problematic for medieval people, so that visionaries like St. Birgitta of Sweden and Margery Kempe required constant assurance that they could indeed be saved. When Margery lamented "because I am no maiden, lack of maidenhood is to me now great sorrow," Christ reassured her: "Forasmuch as you are a maiden in your soul, I shall take you by the one hand in heaven and my mother by the other hand, and so shall you dance in heaven with other holy maidens and virgins."[43] Being a "maiden in your soul" is a way of expressing a profound personal identity, comparable to what modern people would term sexual orientation.

Of course, it may have been easier for some people to transcend their desires than others simply because their desires were less easy to fulfill than others', or because medieval society did not define those desires as sexual. Women who chose to live in a household with other women rather than marrying, and who did not engage in sexual activity involving penetration, would still have been considered chaste or virgins, and may not have recognized their desire for another woman as sexual. This could be in part true of men in same-sex relationships as well, but such men's activities were perhaps more likely to include some form of penetration and thus to be classified as sexual than were women's.

Here we encounter a profound difference in perception between medieval society and our own as to what actually constitutes sexual activity. The Bill Clinton impeachment hearings in 1999 sparked a national discussion and revealed that there is little unanimity in the United States about what exactly we consider "having sex." Medieval people would not have been in entire agreement with each other either. Penetration was an important element, hence the lack of concern over women living together, but medieval authors recognized lascivious touching as an activity that could threaten chastity even if it did not in itself violate it.

Erotic chastity

Medieval and contemporary views part ways, too, when it comes to the role of love and the language of love in relationships that are not considered sexual. Contemporary westerners are, perhaps, prepared to accept that a heterosexual man and woman can be good friends without the relationship becoming sexual and without either party wanting it to – although the story of such a relationship that eventually does become sexual is a staple plot for film and popular novel. But where that relationship is couched in love language, we are less prepared to accept its chaste nature. Because many believe that homosexuality is a minority characteristic rather than a tendency present to a greater or lesser extent in all of us, we are perhaps more likely to believe that close same-sex friendships are chaste and non-erotic, but even here the presence of love language would suggest to a modern reader an erotic level to the friendship.

Who today would write:

> The sweetness of your love abundantly refreshes and soothes the ardor of my breast every hour, every minute; and the beauty of your face, which I constantly dwell upon in loving thoughts, fills all the channels of my memory with desire and an immense joy,

and expect it to be taken as chaste?[44] These words were written by the priest Alcuin to the Frankish emperor Charlemagne at the end of the eighth century. I have removed the adjective "sacred," which Alcuin used to describe their love; other than this word, nothing but a pomposity in tone betrays that this is not a passage from a recent love letter. Now, Alcuin and Charlemagne were clearly not involved in a sexual relationship, nor did either of them desire such a relationship. This was simply the kind of language that people at that time used to express friendship, admiration, respect; it was compatible with chastity. In the Byzantine east, too, as well as the Latin west, language that to a modern sensibility represents sexual desire was taken over for religious purposes so that it was used primarily for the desire for God. Sally Vaughn and Christina Christoforatou talk about "expressions of sexuality by clerical men and pious women," including "imagined sexual relationships, friendships, and theoretical meditations," as "sex without sex."[45]

Some scholars would suggest that this kind of language does eroticize the relationship between humans, or between humans and God, even if the parties involved would not have recognized this. This may indeed be so. But it is worthwhile asking whether the parties involved, or the people around them, would have seen things that way, would have seen a threat to chastity in the language of love, either for another person or for God. We can certainly identify cases where medieval texts suspect lust. Medieval readers would have agreed with modern ones that Christina of Markyate's feelings for an unnamed cleric with whom she was staying were erotic:

> in his absence she used to be so inwardly inflamed that she thought the clothes which clung to her body might be set on fire. Had this occurred whilst she was in his presence, the maiden might well have been unable to control herself.[46]

Part of the justification given for women not being able to hold official roles in the church (outside the convent) was their vulnerability to such temptation.

Yet is the vision of Christ, which cured this lust, any less erotic?

> For in the guise of a small child He came to the arms of his sorely tried spouse and remained with her a whole day, not only being felt but also seen. So the maiden took Him in her hands, gave thanks, and pressed Him to her bosom. And with immeasurable delight she held Him at one moment to her virgin breast, at another she felt His presence within her even through the barrier of her flesh. Who shall describe the abounding sweetness with which the servant was filled by this condescension of her creator? From that moment the fire of lust was so completely extinguished that never afterwards could it be revived.[47]

Christina's contemporary Aelred of Rievaulx wrote to his sister, also an anchoress (hermitess), in terms very reminiscent of Christina's experience:

> how often he infused himself into your innermost being when you were on fire with love . . . how often he carried you away with a certain unspeakable longing for himself when you were at prayer.[48]

Similar language can be found in late medieval literature for nuns and recluses: "kindle me with the blaze of your radiant love. Let me be your lover [leofmon]; teach me to love thee, living Lord."[49] The nuns in question were quite likely very aware of the erotic nature of their language. Certainly the story of St. Agnes, as retold by the late fifteenth-century Englishman Osbern Bokenham, explicitly juxtaposes the love of Christ and profane love. A Christian virgin, Agnes fends off the unwelcome attentions of the son of the Roman prefect by saying that she already has a lover:

And taken of his mouth many a kiss have I,
Sweeter than either milk or honey;
And often in his arms he has embraced me
Without blemishing of my virginity
His body to mine is now conjoined.[50]

Women like Christina (and men who had similar experiences) were not lusting after God. To suggest that they were victims of false consciousness, that their love was not really as spiritual as they thought it was, would be intellectually arrogant. And yet their spirituality was unlike that of believers today who separate the erotic from the divine. Even here, as in relationships between humans, the partners stand in a hierarchical relation to each other. The virgin is the passive partner to whom God does something; the same is true of male mystics. For them, this passionate relation to God was not unchaste.

Medieval people, both male and female, did look at and meditate on images of the nearly naked body of Christ. They might, as did Rupert of Deutz, envision Christ kissing them with open mouth. Rupert's mystical vision might be called a homoerotic one, but he would certainly not have seen it that way; the kiss was for him a call to understand the mystery of Christ. In the early fifteenth century Margery Kempe, too, had a vision of Christ in which he told her:

Therefore must I needs be homely with you and lie in your bed with you. Daughter, you desire greatly to see me, and you may boldly, when you are in your bed, take me to you as your wedded husband, as your most worthy darling, and as your sweet son, for I will be loved as a son should be loved by the mother and I will that you love me, daughter, as a good wife ought to love her husband. And therefore you may boldly take me in the arms of your soul and kiss my mouth, my head, and my feet as sweetly as you will.[51]

The reference to "the arms of her soul" indicates this was understood spiritually and metaphorically. She also had a vision of caring for the infant Christ, just as Christina of Markyate had a vision of him nursing at her breast. These are images of closeness, intimacy, merging. They are at once *both* erotic *and* spiritual.

Medieval chastity, for some people, can be called a sexual identity or orientation precisely because it was an erotic chastity. That is, it did not represent a lack of desire, or a lack of opportunity to satisfy desire, but a more or less deliberate orientation of desire toward matters of the spirit. I do not mean to suggest that this was sublimation, as Freudians call the redirection of erotic energy into other channels. Rather, these chaste medieval people continued to feel intense desire, but it became a desire for the divine rather than for a sexual relationship. Sometimes, indeed, the desire was for chastity as an end in itself. The chastity these people sought to achieve was not asexual; it was achieved not by repressing their sexuality but by redirecting it. Indeed, where we look in discussions of divine love for the underlying sexual meaning, they might look in accounts of sexual love for the underlying divine meaning. As one scholar puts it, not only is a cigar sometimes just a cigar, but "it is also important to contemplate the possibility that at other times even a penis can signify a cigar."[52]

A dream of Gilbert of Sempringham (d. 1189), the founder of the twelfth-century monastic order of the Gilbertines, provides an example. He was living in a house where an attractive young woman lived, and one night he "dreamt that he put his hand into this girl's bosom and was made to draw it out. The most chaste of men was terrified that, human frailty being what it is, his dream foretold a sin of fornication."[53] Alarmed, he quickly found somewhere else to live, removing himself from the temptation. Later in his life, this same woman became one of the first nuns in his order, and he realized that his dream had really been a divine message, that her bosom signified divine peace. We might read his dream differently. But it stands as an example of the way medieval people realized that the erotic and the spiritual could be very closely related indeed. Rather than non-sexual symbols in dreams symbolizing sexual activity, medieval people could understand sexual activity in dreams as symbolizing religious meanings.

It is not only symbols in dreams but symbols depicted in extant medieval artworks that we must beware of interpreting by solely modern standards. The wound in Christ's side created by the penetration of a lance at the Crucifixion was often depicted in later medieval art in a way that looks like a vulva, or at least that looks like a vulva to a modern observer. The image could even be abstracted from Christ's side and used on its own as a devotional object, particularly by nuns or pious laywomen (see Figure 2.3). This version was made in the first half of the fourteenth century, an illustration in a Book of Hours or prayer book made for Bonne of Luxemburg, queen of France.

Was Bonne's veneration of this image (which may have been created by a woman, Bourgot le Noir), or other women's veneration of similar images, homoerotic? First of all, it is not clear that medieval people would have immediately thought "vulva" when they saw an image like this. To medieval people a vulva might have looked like a wound, rather than a wound looking like a vulva. Indeed, Caroline Bynum has argued that the wound in Christ's side (when in the context of his body, not abstracted as in this example) is an iconographic parallel not to a vulva but to a breast: Christ

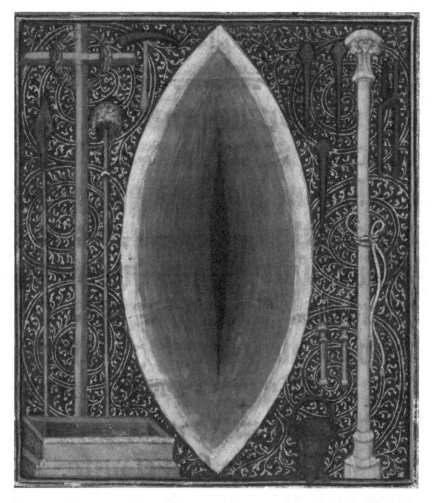

Figure 2.3 Wound in Christ's side. Jean or Bourgot Le Noir, Psalter and hours of
Bonne of Luxemburg, fol. 331r, The Cloisters Collection, New York,
Metropolitan Museum of Art.

© The Metropolitan Museum of Art. Image Source: Art Resource, NY

is depicted directing blood from the wound into a Eucharistic chalice in the
same way as the Virgin Mary directs milk from her breast to St. Bernard in a
widely illustrated miracle, or displaying the wound in the same way that his
mother displays her breast. Even if medieval people did see the resemblance
to a vulva, Jeffrey Hamburger argues that "nuns regarded [the opening in
Christ's side] as an invitation to introspection, a literal looking inward,"
a way of approaching Christ's womblike heart.[54] This is not to say that it

did not also have erotic meanings, and in a culture that treated women's genitals as sexual and shameful, suggesting that the entrance into Christ's body was like the entrance to a womb was a powerful image of inversion. It is important to note the complexities of images, to recognize that medieval people brought different meanings to them, and not to think we know what it meant because we read it a certain way.

Only someone living in the modern age could have written these last few paragraphs about how the erotic and the spiritual overlap. A medieval writer would not have put it the same way. While for us the erotic equates with the carnal, for many medieval thinkers the erotic, to the extent it over-lapped with the spiritual, was opposed to the carnal. Bernard of Clairvaux, for example, who wrote a series of sermons on the Song of Songs in which he imagined kissing Christ on the mouth and something even more holy, "that most intimate kiss of all, a mystery of supreme generosity and inef-fable sweetness," would have wanted to make a sharp distinction between his spiritual understanding of this action and a carnal understanding that would equate it with erotic activity between men, or between men and women. One was sublime, the other polluted. But he would, at least, have recognized the similarities in language and the possibility that it could be taken the wrong way; he suggested that novice monks cannot understand the true spiritual meaning until they are prepared for "nuptial union with the divine partner."[55]

Conflicts not just between "the medieval" and "the contemporary" under-standings of "the erotic," but also between different understandings in the same time period, arise when we look at images of the torture of virgin mar-tyrs (Figure 2.4). If St. Barbara or St. Agatha has her breasts removed, if other saints are threatened with rape and torture, are visual representations of these scenes about pain as a road to transcendence and salvation, or about misogyny? Are they "icons of invincibility," or are they pornography?

As Robert Mills argues, "what we now label as pornography is a pre-dominantly post-medieval invention, tied to the creation of bourgeois stand-ards of privacy and the emergence of print culture," and yet the structural similarities between pornography and hagiography cannot be ignored: both are intended to call forth further action in the imaginations of viewers and readers.[56] An image of Mary Magdalene naked but for her hair or the Vir-gin Mary exposing her breast is meant to arouse devotion, but is that all it would have aroused? In the image of the lactation of St. Bernard from an altar shelf from Palma de Mallorca around 1290 (see Figure 2.5), Mary's breast is exposed and full as she squirts milk into the saint's mouth. Medi-eval people were not meant to imagine that Bernard had a nursing fetish, but that he received miraculous spiritual nourishment.

Certainly one can imagine adolescent boys, in the monastery or outside it, looking at these images for sexual titillation, the way twentieth-century youths did with medical illustrations or lingerie catalogs before more explicit

Figure 2.4 Torture of St. Agatha. Sano di Pietro, Miniature, cut from an antiphonary, Robert Lehmann Collection, Metropolitan Museum of Art.

© The Metropolitan Museum of Art. Image Source: Art Resource, NY

pornography became widely available to them online. We can guess, however, that the images would have elicited quite different reactions from most viewers. It is possible to identify with the torturers of St. Barbara but the religious purpose is the identification with the suffering of the saint (which in turn is identified with the suffering of Christ through the context of the image); one may look at Mary's breast in a sexualized way but the religious purpose is contemplation of her motherhood of devout believers.

One way of determining whether it distorts the medieval past for us to label discourses or images as "erotic" is by asking whether anyone at the time did so. In fact, medieval sources not infrequently express concern over this. Jean Gerson, in the early fifteenth century, wrote extensively of the need to discern

Figure 2.5 Mary feeds St. Bernard from her breast. Detail from Retable of St. Bernard from Capella dels Templers, Palma, Museu de Mallorca.

© Museu de Mallorca, DA05/09/0028

whether women's visions were really divine or were sent by the devil. If from the devil, the purpose of the visions may be to lead people into carnal temptation. Even the wise are not capable of judging. As Gerson wrote in a possibly autobiographical account:

> I know a man who out of a devotion and a wisdom that were clearly praiseworthy took into the embrace of familiar friendship in the Lord a certain virgin living the religious life. At first there was present no trace of carnal love. Finally, through frequent contact, love slowly grew, but not wholly in the Lord, until the man could scarcely be separated from the woman, if she went away, without trying to visit her or thinking constantly about her. At that time he nonetheless thought that there was nothing carnal, devious, or indicating diabolical deception in the matter, until one time he had to be apart from her for a longer period. Then the man felt for the first time that this love was not pure and completely sincere and chaste. . . . All passionate feeling is a most dangerous companion for virtue, as it is in love, zeal, correction of behavior, or similar matters.[57]

74

Gerson clearly recognized that it could be difficult for medieval people to separate the spiritual and the carnal, as it is for moderns.

Chastity formed a beautiful ideal for medieval Christians: self-control that allowed one to focus on spiritual matters and approach the divine. It also formed an ugly one: a rejection of contact with anyone who might tempt one, and blame unfairly placed if one violated one's vow. In both its positive and its negative aspects, it defined people's lives, constituting a sexual orientation different from any that is common in the modern west.

This chapter has dealt mainly with Christianity because it is Christian ideas of chastity that have had such a great influence on modern Western ways of thinking about sex as inherently sinful. To tell as complete a story of attitudes among Jews or among Muslims would require additional chapters. However, it may be noted here that within both religions there were groups that practiced an asceticism that held that sexual activity was distracting, unhealthy, or polluting. In both religions clerics were set apart by their degree of learning, not by ordination or by sexual status. Yet there are certainly aspects of sexual activity as ritually polluting in both religions, notably the idea of semen as a substance that requires cleansing from the body or clothing before prayer, and the prohibition on sex during a women's menstrual period. Christianity took a squeamishness about bodily functions and fluids that could be found in many cultures, and made of it a factor that controlled many people's lives.

Notes

1 Eusebius, *Church History*, 6:8, trans. Paul L. Maier (Grand Rapids, MI: Kregel Publications, 1999), 212.
2 Tertullian, *De virginibus velandis*, ch. 14, in *Opera, vol. 2*, Corpus Christianorum Series Latina 2 (Turnhout: Brepols, 1954), 1224.
3 "Gospel of Thomas," 114, in *The Nag Hammadi Library in English*, ed. James M. Robinson, trans. Thomas O. Lambdin (San Francisco: Harper and Row, 1981), 130.
4 *The Passion of St. Perpetua*, trans. R. Waterville Muncey (London: J.M. Dent, 1927), 32–3, 41.
5 *Contra Jovinianum*, 1:39, trans. W.H. Fremantle, in *The Principal Works of St. Jerome*, A Select Library of Nicene and Post-Nicene Fathers of the Christian Church, 6 (Grand Rapids, MI: Eerdmans, 1983), 377.
6 *Contra Jovinianum*, 1:13, p. 357.
7 Ambrose, *De virginibus*, 1:8:52; *Patrologia Cursus Completus*, ed. J.P. Migne, 221 vols. (Paris: Migne, 1844–64) [henceforth *PL*], vol. 16, col. 214.
8 Ambrose, 1:5:21, col. 205.
9 Peter Damian, *De coelibatu sacerdotium*; *PL*, 145:380.
10 Augustine, *The Good of Marriage*, 8, in *St. Augustine on Marriage and Sexuality*, ed. and trans. Elizabeth A. Clark (Washington, DC: Catholic University of America Press, 1996), 50.
11 Augustine, *Holy Virginity*, 1, in Clark, 61.
12 Augustine, *De sancta virginitate*, 5; *PL*, 40:399.
13 Augustine, *Confessions*, 8:7, trans. R.S. Pine-Coffin (Harmondsworth: Penguin Books, 1961), 169.

14 Ammianus Marcellinus, *Historia*, 25:4:2, trans. John C. Rolfe (Cambridge, MA: Harvard University Press, 1937), 502–3.

15 *The Desert Fathers*, trans. Helen Waddell (Ann Arbor: University of Michigan Press, 1957), 86.

16 Athanasius, *Life of Antony*, 5, trans. Caroline White, *Early Christian Lives* (Harmondsworth: Penguin, 1998), 12.

17 Waddell, 137.

18 Palladius, *The Lausiac History*, trans. Robert T. Meyer, *Ancient Christian Writers Series 34* (Westminster, MD: Newman Press, 1965), 36–7.

19 Abelard, "Sixth Letter," in *Abelard & Heloise: The Letters and Other Writings*, trans. William Levitan (Indianapolis: Hackett, 2007), 150.

20 Caesarius of Heisterbach, *Dialogue on Miracles*, 4:97, trans. H. von E. Scott and C. C. Swinton Bland (New York: Harcourt Brace, 1929), 302–3.

21 Caesarius of Arles, *Sermons au peuple*, 6:7, ed. Marie-José Delage (Paris: Editions du Cerf, 1971), 1:332.

22 Venantius Fortunatus, *Life of the Holy Radegund*, ch. 5, in *Sainted Women of the Dark Ages*, ed. and trans. Jo Ann McNamara and John H. Halborg with E. Gordon Whatley (Durham, NC: Duke University Press), 73. "Monacha" is the feminine form of the Latin word for "monk," but it is not the word usually used for "nun."

23 *Life of Balthild*, ch. 3, in McNamara and Halborg, 269.

24 Jacobus de Voragine, *The Golden Legend*, trans. Granger Ryan and Helmut Ripperger (New York: Longmans Green, 1941), 196.

25 Theodore of Stoudios, *Magna Catechesis*, trans. Peter Hatlie, "The City a Desert: Theodore of Stoudios on Porneia," in *Desire and Denial in Byzantium*, ed. Liz James (Aldershot: Ashgate, 1997), 70.

26 Aldhelm, "De Virginitate," 48, in *The Prose Works*, trans. Michael Lapidge and Michael Herren (Totowa, NJ: Rowman and Littlefield, 1979), 129.

27 Damian, Letter 112, in ed. Kurt Reindel, *Die Briefe des Petrus Damiani*, 4 vols. (Munich: Monumenta Germaniae Historica, 1983–93), 3:278–9.

28 Paris, Archives Nationales, Z/1o/20, fol 173r.

29 Gérard of Cambrai, "Acta synodi Atrebatensis in Manichaeos," 10, *PL*, 142:1299.

30 Ralph of Coggeshall, *Chronicon Anglicanum*, ed. Joseph Stevenson, *Rerum Britannicarum Medii Aevi Scriptores 66* (London: Her Majesty's Stationery Office, 1875), 121–4.

31 *The Book of Blessed Angela of Foligno*, 1:1, in Angela of Foligno, *Complete Works*, trans. Paul Lachance (New York: Paulist Press, 1993), 126.

32 William of Tocco, *Ystoria sancti Thome de Aquino*, ed. Claire le Brun-Gouanovic (Toronto: Pontifical Institute of Medieval Studies, 1996), ch. 11:112–13.

33 Jocelyn Wogan-Browne, *Saints' Lives and Women's Literary Culture c. 1150–1300: Virginity and Its Authorizations* (Oxford: Oxford University Press, 2001), 47–8.

34 "Vida de Sancta Delphina, Vergis," 4:3, in *Vies Occitanes de Saint Auzias et de Sainte Dauphine*, ed. P. Jacques Cambell (Rome: Pontificum Athenaeum Antonianum, 1963), 160–3.

35 Étienne de Bourbon, *Anecdotes historiques, légendes et apologues, tirés du recueil inédit d'Étienne de Bourbon, Dominicain du XIIIe siècle*, ch. 502, ed. A. Lecoy de la Marche (Paris: Librairie Renouard, 1877), 432.

36 This idea that women cannot conceive without orgasm and therefore that any woman who conceives has not really been raped surfaced in the 1980s in abortion debates in at least two US state legislatures, as legislators argued that no rape exception to a ban on abortion was necessary. Stephen Freind, of Delaware

County, Pennsylvania, claimed in 1988 that women could not become pregnant as a result of rape, because when raped a woman has "a certain secretion" that prevents conception. Henry Aldridge, of Pitt County, North Carolina, claimed in 1985 that women could not become pregnant if truly raped because "the juices don't flow." Todd Akin, a member of the US House of Representatives and a candidate for US Senate in Missouri in 2012, claimed that "if it's a legitimate rape, the female body has ways to try to shut that whole thing down." The voters could be proud that their legislators were on the cutting edge of fourteenth-century science.

37 Waddell, 76.
38 Waddell, 74–6.
39 Aelred, *A Rule of Life for a Recluse in Treatises: The Pastoral Prayer*, trans. Mary Paul McPherson, vol. 1 of *The Works of Aelred of Rievaulx* (Spencer, MA: Cistercian Publications, 1971), 64–5.
40 *Ancrene Wisse*, in *Anchoritic Spirituality*, trans. Nicholas Watson and Anne Savage (New York: Paulist Press, 1991), 68.
41 *Speculum Virginum*, 7, ed. Julia Seyfarth, Corpus Christianorum Continuatio Medievalis 5 (Turnhout: Brepols, 1990), 211.
42 *Ancrene Wisse*, 134.
43 Margery Kempe, *The Book of Margery Kempe*, 1:22, trans. Lynn Staley (New York: W. W. Norton, 2001), 39.
44 Alcuin to Charlemagne, "Epistle 121," in *Monumenta Germaniae Historica, Epistolae 4, Epistolae Karolini Aevi 2*, ed. Ernest Dümmler, 2nd edition (Berlin: Weidmann, 1974), 176; translation in C. Stephen Jaeger, *Ennobling Love: In Search of a Lost Sensibility* (Philadelphia: University of Pennsylvania Press, 1999), 48, except that I have omitted the word "sacred" before "love" to make my point.
45 Sally N. Vaughn and Christina Christoforatou, "Introduction," to *Desire and Eroticism in Medieval Europe, Eleventh to Fifteenth Centuries: Sex without Sex*, special issue of *Journal of the History of Sexuality*, 19 (2010), 1–16.
46 *Life of Christina of Markyate*, ed. and trans. C.H. Talbot (Oxford: Oxford University Press, 1959), 116.
47 *Life of Christina*, 118.
48 Aelred of Rievaulx, *Rule for a Recluse*, in *The Works of Aelred of Rievaulx, vol. 1*, trans. T. Berkeley, Cistercian Fathers Series 2 (Spencer, MA: Cistercian Publications, 1971), 96.
49 *þe Wohunge of ure Lauerd*, ed. W. Meredith Thompson, Early English Text Society Original Series 241 (London: Early English Text Society, 1958), ll. 18–20; trans. in Susannah Mary Chewning, "The Paradox of Virginity within the Anchoritic Tradition: The Masculine Gaze and the Feminine Body in the Wohunge Group," in *Constructions of Widowhood and Virginity in the Middle Ages*, ed. Cindy L. Carlson and Angela Jane Weisl (New York: St. Martin's, 1994), 113–34 (at 115).
50 Osbern Bokenham, *Legendys of Hooly Wummen*, ll. 4172–6, ed. Mary S. Serjeantson, Early English Text Society Original Series 206 (London: Oxford University Press, 1938), 114–15.
51 *The Book of Margery Kempe*, ch. 36, trans. Staley, 66.
52 Moshe Sluhovsky, "The Devil in the Convent," *American Historical Review* 107 (2002), 1399.
53 *The Book of St. Gilbert*, 3, eds. Raymonde Foreville and Gillian Keir (Oxford: Clarendon Press, 1987), 16–17.
54 Jeffrey F. Hamburger, *Nuns as Artists: The Visual Culture of a Medieval Convent* (Berkeley: University of California Press, 1997), 219.

55 Bernard of Clairvaux, *On the Song of Songs*, 3:3:5 and 1:6:12, trans. Kilian Walsh, vol. 1, Works of Bernard of Clairvaux series, vol. 2 (Spencer, MA: Cistercian Publications, 1971), 19, 7.
56 Robert Mills, *Suspended Animation: Pain, Pleasure, and Punishment in Medieval Culture* (London: Reaktion Books, 2005), 110–11; "icon of invincibility" phrase on p. 138.
57 Jean Gerson, "On Distinguishing True from False Revelations," in *Early Works*, trans. Brian Patrick McGuire (New York: Paulist Press, 1995), 357–8.

3

SEX AND MARRIAGE

The conception of children within marriage justified, for medieval authors, the potentially sinful and at best dangerous activity of sex. Marriage was a central expectation in medieval societies. It is true that there were many people who never married – in northern Europe perhaps as many as 15 percent. Some (if Christian) entered a life of religion, some could not afford a dowry or the expense of a household, some were not permitted to marry because their parents' strategy for keeping property intact involved having only one son marry, some never found a marriage partner, some were not attracted to the opposite sex, and some chose not to marry, for whatever reason. Marriage, however, was still what we today might call the default. In terms of the divisions of medieval Christian society by sexuality, the distinction between the sexually active and the sexually abstinent could be expressed as the distinction between the married and the virgin. There was little accepted conceptual space for someone who was neither, even though in practice there were undoubtedly many unmarried, sexually active people.

Because the church ranked chastity as preferable to marriage some scholars deny that marriage was normative for medieval society, even going so far as to say those who were married were "queer" in medieval terms. But it is difficult to see how one can really say that a behavior that close to nine-tenths of all people engaged in – more in many areas – can be considered so transgressive. True, Christian theologians preferred chastity to marriage, but they recognized that not everyone was called to chastity, and marriage was certainly the expectation for the vast majority of people. Although it was denied to the most devout, who remained celibate as priests (if male) or took vows of chastity under a rule, as with nuns or monks, or chose other forms of religious life, it also structured religious thought. Marital metaphors were found throughout medieval religious teaching, whether to describe the relationship of Christ to his church, a theme common in medieval preaching, or to describe holy women's relation to the divine. Within Jewish and Muslim communities marriage was also central to both social life and religious obligation. Neither placed much value on lifelong virginity.

Unlike in Judaism and Islam, the vast majority of texts about Christian marriage and the sexual behavior appropriate to it – medical, theological, legal – were written by people who were not themselves married. It is not always easy to know how ideas about how married people should behave were actually transmitted to those married people. Preaching, certainly, was one method, especially from the thirteenth century onward; another was advice given in the confessional. But again, we know about this advice from handbooks written for confessors, not from married people reporting what they were told. We do not know what version of the church's teaching on issues like contraception or forbidden days married people actually learned and took to heart. A second irony is that although marriage was indeed expected for most people and the only legitimate sexual outlet, the same institution that told people how they should behave within it also denigrated it as, at best, a second choice. But despite the church's emphasis (stronger at times than others) on chastity as the preferable alternative, marriage was far more common, and could be used metaphorically to structure even the lives of the unmarried (the soul as the bride of God, for example).

"Marriage" may seem like a completely straightforward concept. If two people participate in a particular ritual prescribed by the jurisdiction in which they live, they are married. If they don't, they are not married. This feature of modern Euro-American society is a legacy of the high medieval church, which set out clearly defined rules about marriage. Many people in contemporary society find acceptable other forms of relationship, but society as a whole still privileges marriage. However, just because the system of legal marriage goes back to the Middle Ages (and some aspects of it back even farther), this does not mean that medieval people did not have other sorts of long-term sexual relationships. If we try too hard to classify relationships as marriages or not marriages, we will be importing categories that simply do not apply. This chapter includes discussion of long-term partnerships, particularly in the early Middle Ages, that some scholars have defined as forms of marriage, but that the high medieval church might not have recognized as such.

It is important to re-emphasize here that saying that marriage was central or normal in medieval culture is different from saying that heterosexuality was the norm. Procreative sex was privileged over non-procreative sex, whether the parties were married or not: indeed, St. Augustine had written that for a man to have non-procreative sex with his wife was worse than having it with a prostitute. Procreative non-marital sex was less sinful than non-procreative marital sex, in the view of Christian theologians. Between two partners of the same sex there could be no procreation, and hence everything that they might do was suspect in the view of the church. But that does not mean that everything that two partners of opposite sexes, or even two married partners, might do was acceptable, nor that society understood them as "heterosexual."

Marriage and law

The question "Is this a marriage?" can be a difficult question to answer in the Middle Ages, considering how dependent it is on whose definition of marriage one uses. "What rights and obligations characterized this relationship, and what status did it confer in the eyes of contemporaries?" is perhaps a better question. Did a relationship result in the transfer of property, or control over a woman's person, between families? Did it confer rights of inheritance upon the offspring? How permanent was it, and how could it be dissolved? Did it allow both parties to engage in sexual relations without accusations or insinuations of impropriety?

In the Hebrew Bible it is difficult to distinguish between a wife and another woman who is part of a man's household, because whether the same term is translated as "woman" or "wife" depends on context, as does whether another term is translated as "took" or "married." Biblical patriarchs and kings had children with multiple wives and other women. Similarly, the Arabic legal-technical term for marriage had as its original meaning "sexual intercourse." In the Roman period it was not at all uncommon for an elite man to form a long-term relationship with a woman of lower social standing who was called a concubine. Children from such relationships were not considered legitimate. St. Augustine, in his pre-sainthood days, had such a concubine. The Merovingian Frankish kings of the early Middle Ages practiced polygyny (multiple long-term sexual relationships), even if the church did not recognize them all as marriages. In addition to relationships formed by negotiation among families and involving the transfer of land or other wealth, there were also relationships formed by the abduction of a woman, or by her consent rather than that of her family.

In the early Middle Ages, when we see in our sources a system in which an elite man has multiple sexual partners, one woman is labeled the legal wife, but the other(s), called concubine(s), have some customary privileges and recognized status. This contrasts with a later situation in which the church tried to deny any legal recognition at all to concubines, and perhaps also with an earlier situation in which the line between concubine and legal wife was not sharp. Some scholars have identified a status in early medieval Europe known as *Friedelehe* or quasi marriage, in which a woman contracted matrimony on her own, without the family and property arrangements that usually accompanied it. But although such a woman may have had a recognized status above that of a concubine, she did not have the legal protection of a formal marriage. Her husband could repudiate her and pay a much lower level of compensation than he would have had to pay to her parents in a more formal marriage. Such a woman would likely be of lower social status than her partner (Charlemagne's daughters, whom he did not want to marry, were an exception). Though some historians have romanticized *Friedelehe* as a love match, it clearly provided more benefits to husband than to wife.

Over the course of the early to central Middle Ages, the church effec-
tively asserted its control over marriage among Christians, its definition and
its formation. Whereas aristocrats and presumably also those lower on the
social scale saw marriage as a way of linking families and acquiring children, the church understood it as a spiritual relationship as well, a sacrament instituted by Christ, and a calling. Early medieval churchmen asked
and encouraged – although they did not officially require – that marriages
be accompanied by a priestly benediction. The Talmud contains blessings to
be said on the occasion of a marriage; to the extent they are a reflection of an
older tradition, that tradition may also have influenced Christian practice.

The church succeeded by the twelfth century in imposing its own view of
marriage on Christians to the extent that it made a great difference, as it had
not before, whether a potential heir was born in or out of church-sanctioned
wedlock. It might be acceptable for a man to have illegitimate children, but
it was understood that they could not inherit. This had the effect of creating
a sharp distinction between the wife and the concubine, casting one set of
women as virtuous (while at the same time emphasizing their role as vessels
for childbearing). By the twelfth century the church was also successfully
exerting its control over which marriages were acceptable. Since the ninth
century the church had decreed as incestuous any marriage within seven
degrees of relationship. This prohibition held both for consanguinity (blood
relatives) and affinity (relatives by marriage). The rules about degrees of
relationship may sound a bit technical, but it is important to explain them
here because they governed a decision so central to people's lives as the
choice of marriage partner. They also seemed technical to medieval people,
who were not always sure (or who at least claimed not to have been sure)
whether a marriage to a distant relative was in fact valid.

The Roman method of counting, which was used when the rule about
seven degrees was first promulgated, counted each sexual act involved in creating the relationship as a separate degree. I am related to my brother in
the second degree (my conception and that of my brother); to my cousin in
the fourth (the conceptions of my cousin, his or her parent, myself, and my
parent); and I may marry someone with whom I share a great-great-grandparent, because we are related in the eighth degree. However, by the eleventh century the seven-degrees rule had been combined with the Germanic
method of counting, which counted each generation back to the common
ancestor as one degree. I am related in the second degree to my grandfather,
my aunt, and my first cousin (counting back two generations to my grand-
parents), and I may only marry someone with whom I share a great-great-
great-great-great-great-grandparent. If medieval people had adhered strictly
to this rule, the pool of possible spouses would have been very small, and
most people would have lived in uncertainty as to whether they were in fact
related to their spouse. The church did not attempt to enforce this rule in its
extreme. If a relationship was known, the couple could ask the church for

a dispensation before the wedding. The relationship could also be "discovered" later and become a ground for annulment of a marriage from which one partner wished to escape, and some famous couples made use of this possibility (notably Louis VII of France and Eleanor of Aquitaine in 1152, despite a previous dispensation).

The church regularized the situation at the Fourth Lateran Council in 1215. Since the Germanic method of counting degrees had become firmly established, the Council limited the prohibited degrees to four. Thus, I may not marry someone with whom I share a great-great-grandparent, but I may marry anyone to whom I am more distantly related. This reform seems to have been effective. Evidence from England, at least, in the later Middle Ages shows that people who tried to dissolve a marriage most often did so on the basis of other impediments, like previous marriage contracts, rather than on the basis of consanguinity, suggesting that people did not commonly marry within the prohibited degrees. The church had successfully claimed the right to dictate who was a legitimate sexual partner and who was not. The incest prohibition, which greatly restricted the pool of available spouses especially for the highly intermarried aristocracy, meant that young people could not marry whom they wished; in order to get the required dispensations they had to have the backing of their families.

The church also made its influence effective on the issue of indissolubility. A marriage could be dissolved only if it were shown never to have been a valid marriage in the first place. Spouses were allowed to separate only to take up the monastic life, or very rarely in cases of the woman's adultery or the man's extreme cruelty; but these separations did not permit remarriage, even for the "innocent party." Eleventh- and twelfth-century kings and aristocrats, in particular, accustomed to a system where they could repudiate an unwanted or barren wife and take another, found themselves blocked by the church's disapproval, which was made effective by the threat of excommunication and the threat of a cloud over the legitimacy of their heirs. It was Innocent III in the thirteenth century, in the *cause célèbre* of Philip Augustus of France and his wife Ingeborg, who made papal decisions in such cases definitive and enforceable.

By the thirteenth century the canon law rules about the formation and dissolution of marriage were well established and uniform across Europe, as collections of papal decretals became universally accepted as normative. Nevertheless, these general guidelines were put into specific practice by synods in different regions, and the machinery of the laws' implementation varied. For example, canon law held that no one could remarry while the first spouse was alive; but jurisdictions varied as to the level of proof they required of a spouse's death. The patterns of litigation brought by people (mostly women) who sought to claim they were married when their partner denied it, people (both men and women) who sought to dissolve a marriage on the grounds that it had never been valid in the first place, or church officials who sought to discipline people who formed their marriages in an irregular manner varied. Yet all remained, until the reformations of the six-teenth century, within a common framework that held that the consent of the two parties made a marriage permanent and binding, even if it had not been conducted at a church or blessed by a priest, or carried out with the consent of the partners' parents.

Although the church succeeded by the eleventh century in imposing mo-nogamy and indissolubility on Christians, these rules did not apply to Mus-lims and Jews. Muslim law allowed men to marry up to four wives, and to divorce their wives; as the law developed, however, unilateral divorce became rarer within the Mamluk empire, for financial reasons. The Talmud also permitted Jewish men to marry more than one wife and to divorce their wives. For Jews living under Muslim rule these marriage rules continued in force, although bigamy does not seem to have been common, based on extant documents from the Cairo Geniza (a great collection of discarded docu-ments of all sorts). From the eleventh century onward in Spain, although Jewish men retained the right to divorce their wives, those who did without good cause were fined. Sometimes the husband promised in the *ketubah* (marriage contract) not to marry another wife. In western Europe, however, an ordinance attributed to Rabbi Gershom ben Judah of Mainz in the elev-enth century forbade polygamy, and another prohibited divorce without the wife's consent. The ban on polygamy was evidently not intended to apply in cases where the couple had no children in ten years of marriage (because the husband needed to obey the commandment to procreate), or where a man was obliged to marry his brother's childless widow (the levirate). Whether or not the provision against plural marriage was in fact issued by Gershom, and whether it reflected existing practice or represented a new development, it is likely to have been influenced by the Christian culture within which the Ashkenazic Jews lived, which taught indissolubility. Women did not have the right to divorce their husbands; only the husband could give a divorce, although the community could put pressure on him to do so. Husbands' legal ability to divorce their wives was also limited by community attitudes and by the economic support granted to a wife in her *ketubah*, which she would retain in case of divorce unless she were found to be at fault. There were also circumstances under which rabbis would compel a man to give his wife a divorce – for example, in thirteenth-century Ashkenaz, his habitual recourse to prostitutes.

Muslim marriage was less influenced by Christian ideas about indissolu-bility. Men could marry up to four wives and have additional concubines, although the law forbade a man from marrying more women than he could support, and in practice it was probably mainly wealthier men who prac-ticed polygamy. (Although "polygamy" can be imagined as a gender-neutral term, it refers here only to men taking plural wives; at no point in Jewish or Muslim history was a woman allowed to have more than one husband.) Divorce was possible (for a man) at any time. Some women had written into their marriage contracts their right to compel their husbands to divorce them if they so wished, or the right to forbid their husbands to take another wife or concubine. Indeed, divorce was common enough in the cities of the Mamluk empire, and the problems of divorced or widowed women unable to earn a living on their own serious enough, that authorities established houses for them known as *ribats* where they could lead a communal and pious life, somewhat analogous to the beguines and tertiaries that one would see in western European cities several centuries later.

The possibility of marital dissolution affected the nature of marital sexuality significantly. Marital sex did not need to be for reproductive purposes to be religiously acceptable. For example, contraception was acceptable in Muslim society as it was not in Christian, and one reason given was that if a man has in mind the possibility of divorcing his wife, he should avoid begetting children with her; another was to avoid having to free a slave who bore a son. The general Christian attitude was that if one did not want to beget children, one should avoid sexual intercourse.

It is within these systems of rules about marriage generally that marital sex in medieval Europe was practiced. The question of who initiates sex and who has the right to consent or refuse, whose desires it serves and who has a choice, depends only in part on how the partners feel about each other. It also depends on the systems of laws and norms governing marriage. The nature of marital sexuality may have a great deal to do with the degree of choice the parties had in entering into the marriage in the first place, as well as with unequal relations of power between men and women in the Middle Ages.

Power within the marriage

The dynamic within an individual marriage will always depend to some extent on individual personality. Some people will be more respected and taken more seriously by their spouses than others. However a number of structural factors also help to determine relations between spouses. A woman of strong character may behave very differently in her marriage depending on whether the culture in which she lives treats strong character in a woman as something to be respected or something to be beaten out of her.

Medieval church teaching, and indeed writing in all genres, generally agreed that the man was the head of the household and the woman should obey him. Even proto-feminist writers like Christine de Pisan in the fifteenth century did not disagree with this fundamental premise, although Christine argued that women could exert influence over their husbands: a princess, for example, "will speak to her husband well and wisely, calling in other wise persons if necessary, and will very humbly petition him on behalf of the people." Still, whether or not she agrees with him, she must "love her husband and live in peace with him," and "to show this she will humble herself, in deed and word and by curtsying; she will obey without complaint; and she will hold her peace to the best of her ability." If he misbehaves or mistreats her, "she must put up with all this" or "take refuge in God."[1] Women who did not marry also bought into the idea of the submissive woman: the writings of medieval religious women almost invariably included statements of humility like "I, although an unworthy woman." This was a convention and may not have been heartfelt; nevertheless, it is clear that even a woman like Hildegard of Bingen, scientist as well as theologian, or Catherine of Siena, advisor to popes, knew she was supposed to appear subordinate to men.

Wives were subordinated by legal enactments as well as by church teaching. Inheritance laws varied widely across Europe, but in some places women could not hold land, and in others they inherited only if they had no brothers (and even then the control over the land was vested not in them but in their husbands). Across most of Europe, though, those women who achieved political power through landholding tended to be widows; Ermengarde of Narbonne in the south of France, where women had more inheritance rights, was an exception, although not a unique one. Again, in some parts of Europe married women could not enter into business contracts on their own unless they were trading as "femmes soles," a status that allowed a married woman the same economic independence and legal rights in her business as though she were single. Husbands who valued their wives' advice and help might treat them as equal partners in landholding or business, but the law placed them under no obligation to do so. In most places there were no legal sanctions against men beating their wives, as long as they did not do so excessively (which in some places meant that anything short of beating to death was permissible).

Medieval literature gives us a great many examples of women who did not behave in a subordinate manner, who talked back to their husbands. Sermon literature is full of exempla of disobedient and nagging wives. These exempla draw on common misogynistic stereotypes and are clearly meant to teach women to behave. For example, a woman is in the habit of always disobeying or contradicting her husband. Her husband places a table next to a river bank and tells her to sit near the table; to spite him she moves farther away from the table and falls in the river. The husband then runs upstream to try to pull her out. When his companions tell him that he should be looking for her downstream, he says, "Don't you know that my wife always does the contrary thing and never the right way? I believe that she will go up against the current, not downstream as others do."[2] A woman who gets into trouble because of her disobedience, the story warns us, should not expect to be rescued.

On the other hand, this genre also includes stories where the wife is wiser than the husband. In one story a woman scolds her drunken husband. He replies that he insists on having his will in his own house. He subsequently falls into the fire and she refuses to let anyone pull him out, saying that she is letting him have his will.[3] The man, of course, is burned to death. We might think that we are supposed to read this story as an example of the cruelty of women, or as an example of how a mistreated woman will turn on her husband. However, the moral that John of Bromyard in his preaching handbook takes from it puts the woman in a much better light. The woman stands for God, the man for Man in the sense of "human being" (*homo*). If man insists on being master and doing as he pleases, God will not pull him out of the fire but will allow man the free will to damn himself. People who heard the story interpreted in this way might come away with the idea that a man who mistreats his wife will get his just deserts, or that a scolding wife may have her husband's best interests at heart.

Medieval literature is rife with representations of insubordinate or unruly wives – Chaucer's Wife of Bath and some of the women in the French fabliaux are good examples. It is very difficult to draw conclusions about medieval attitudes from literary characters like these. If a woman in a story outsmarts her husband, modern feminist critics may applaud the text as subversive of medieval values, but perhaps the text would have told medieval people not that women are cleverer than men, but that peasant men are so stupid that they can even be outsmarted by women. The Wife of Bath may be a positive example to us, but medieval readers may not have read her that way. The most reasonable conclusion to draw from literary depictions of married couples is that the ambiguities would have been there for medieval readers as well. Just as some critics today read the Wife of Bath as a positive portrait of a strong woman and others read her as a misogynistic critique of women, some medieval people may have read the text each way. Women may have appreciated strong female characters, while men were appalled by them and glad to see their comeuppance (for comeuppance they often got).

To read literary texts in this way, as full of ambiguities, leads to conclusions supported by depictions of couples in hagiography, in surviving letters, and in chronicle accounts of aristocratic couples. Men were certainly in the dominant position in marriage. However, despite the legal superiority of the husband, medieval Christian society did not expect or want women to be doormats. The marital relationship was not generally one of equal partners, but it was not generally one of master and slave either. We must keep the nature of this relationship in mind when we think about marital sex in the Middle Ages. The husband was in charge and the wife was expected to obey him, but people would expect that he would not make demands that were excessive or repugnant to her, and that he would not disregard her needs.

Jewish tradition, like Christian, insisted that the woman was subordinate to her husband, and had a special term for the rebellious woman: *moredet*. It usually applied to a woman who refused to have sex with her husband. The husband of such a woman was required according to some rabbis to divorce her, and women may have deliberately withheld sexual relations or other household obligations in order to pressure their husbands into divorcing them. Over the course of the early Middle Ages, however, rabbis moved away from compelling the husband of a *moredet* to divorce his wife; on the other hand, they increasingly began to encourage Jewish men to grant their wives a divorce if they wanted one. The fear may have been that women would turn to non-Jewish courts if they were forced to remain in failed marriages. Several twelfth-century rabbis including Maimonides tried to combat the possibility of women using rebelliousness to obtain a divorce by insisting that the woman should not be granted the financial rights specified in her marriage contract (*ketubah*) if she were divorced as a *moredet*.

Marriage, reproduction, and sin

As we saw in the previous chapter, many medieval Christian writers' attitudes toward marriage were profoundly ambivalent, and they considered it at best a decidedly lesser good, at worst a necessary evil for those who were unable to live up to the ideal virtue of chastity. What emerges most clearly from all medieval writing about marriage, across religious cultures, is how closely it was tied to sex and reproduction. People today get married for love and companionship and to create an economic unit, the household, together, as well as to have children and to have a legitimate outlet for their sexual urges. People in the Middle Ages got married for those reasons too, probably for the creation of an economic unit more than anything else. Most writing about marriage, however, downplayed the other reasons, and focused on the legitimization of sex and reproduction. As a Frankish church council put it in 829:

> [Lay people] should know that marriage is ordained by God and should be sought not for the sake of lust but rather for the sake of offspring. . . . Carnal connection with wives must take place for the sake of offspring, not pleasure, and a man should abstain from sex with his pregnant wife.[4]

The significance of offspring, and their legitimacy, meant that husbands' control of their wives' sexual activity was very important. The fact that many medieval people thought of sex primarily or at least partially as a reproductive act meant that their attitudes toward it were shaped by the biology of reproduction, as they understood it. Medieval theories of reproduction, especially in Christian society from the thirteenth century on, relied heavily on Aristotle, who, as they understood him, held that the man provided the seed for conception, and women the material. Not everyone adhered to this view – early Arabic medical writing had relied heavily on Galen, rather than Aristotle, and many medical writers, Muslim, Jewish, and Christian, kept to the two-seed theory, that both men and women provided seed – but it was widespread. Women's contribution, in the Aristotelian view, was not negligible; they were not just vessels, but provided the matter that became a fetus.

Men, however, provided the form. The conception of girls, or of children who resembled their mothers, was attributed to the weakness of the man's seed (though that did not prevent people from blaming the mother when a daughter was born instead of a son). The idea of the woman's contribution to conception as inert matter waiting to be shaped by the man's contribution gave a scientific justification (though a far from universally accepted one) to the common cultural view of women as passive in intercourse, people who have something done *to* them.

The idea of the reproductive purpose of marriage also meant that a great deal of effort went into promoting marital fertility. Handbooks for medical practitioners and books of advice for husbands focused on ways to make women conceive. Historians once took some of the advice about fertility in these texts as being coded advice about contraception: because contraception was illicit, instructions for it had to be given surreptitiously. The book would tell you how to conceive, and if you did not want to conceive you could do the opposite. Monica Green has persuasively argued, however, that advice about fertility is, in fact, just that. Of course, there were unmarried couples who did not want children, and some married ones who could not afford any more or feared for the woman's health if she bore them; but for the majority of married couples children were desired and yearned for, or at worst tolerated. Some handbooks did give advice on contraception. The "Trotula" compilation advised: "Take a male weasel and let its testicles be removed and let it be released alive. Let the woman carry these testicles with her in her bosom and tie them in goose skin or in another skin, and she will not conceive."[5]

Although infertility was considered in ancient and early medieval medical texts, it became a major concern beginning in the twelfth century, and by the fourteenth century a great number of texts on infertility were produced in the major medical school of Montpellier. They identified medical conditions in both men and women that could impede conception. Infertility was caused by imbalance: one of the partners was too hot or too cold, too moist or too dry. Baths, diets, lotions, and fumigations might remedy the situation, as well as sexual techniques (what might today be called foreplay) that would promote the release of female seed, believed necessary for conception. By the fifteenth century medical texts reveal that male physicians' practice of gynecology was becoming increasingly hands-on rather than mediated through female empirical practitioners. At the same time, another genre of text, called the "Secrets of Women," also dealt with issues of fertility as well as embryology and reproductive anatomy; these texts were not intended to teach practitioners how to treat women, but rather were speculative in nature and often drew on misogynistic commonplaces about female unchastity as well as on medical knowledge.

Marriage was necessary to society for the reproduction of the species, but some doubt remained within Christian culture about the moral status of any sexual activity. The tension between valuing virginity and valuing marriage persisted from the earliest period of Christianity through the entire Middle Ages (and indeed into the modern era). The same arguments were used by writers from different periods. Yet the balance shifted over time depending on a number of factors: the demographic situation and the perceived population needs of Christendom, or a particular part of it; the nature of the particular heresies that were most prevalent at any given time and the arguments that needed to be made to combat them; and other aspects of the political and social context. Even for those who did marry, attitudes toward the role of sex within that marriage shifted over time. Chastity within marriage, for example, was more valued among the Orthodox Slavs than it had been in the earlier Byzantine Empire, and saints were depicted as miraculously bearing children in chaste marriages.

While the arguments against marriage and in praise of virginity discussed in Chapter 2 never disappeared entirely, there were several points in medieval history where the church and society generally put a greater value on marriage than at other times. One such point was the late eleventh to twelfth centuries. This was also the point at which the church was enforcing clerical celibacy and downgrading what had previously been the priest's wife to a "concubine" or "priest's whore." At the same time, however, other voices were speaking of marriage in a new way, stressing its role as a sacrament and the role of love (though this was meant to be spiritual love rather than carnal passion). The emphasis on marriage as a sacrament could outweigh the petty sin involved in the sex act.

The reasons behind this shift in the understanding of marriage were not purely theological, they were substantially political. One aspect of the church reform of the eleventh century was a claim by the church to control over many aspects of lay life, from the selection of priests and bishops and their investiture with the insignia of their office (which many secular rulers considered their prerogative) to intimate decisions about family matters. Marriage politics were critical to secular lords, who wanted sons to carry on their line of succession. If a couple did not have sons, the woman was usually blamed (especially, as often happened, if the husband had fathered sons out of wedlock). In the early Middle Ages, the husband had often been able to repudiate the infertile (or fertile-with-girls-only) wife and marry another more to his liking. By the eleventh century, however, the church had decided to assert its control over marriage, and refused to allow secular lords to repudiate their wives, excommunicating them if they did so.

The fact that the church did allow some marriages to be dissolved – most famously, that of Louis VII of France and Eleanor of Aquitaine – indicates that the principle at stake was not so much the indissolubility of marriage as the prerogative of the church to decide. In support of their claim that marriage was a matter for the church and its courts, however, writers had to stress the sacramental nature of marriage, and this resulted in a downplaying of the critique of even marital sex as sinful. Of course, it was the sacramental aspect – the fact that the marriage partners were participating in a ritual instituted by Christ himself, one sanctioned and even commanded by God – that was emphasized, not the sexual aspect. And yet sex and reproduction were such an essential part of marriage that any stress on the value of marriage worked to legitimate marital sex.

The church in the twelfth and thirteenth centuries may also have downplayed the idea of marital sex as sinful because of the attack from the Cathars. The Cathar religion, labeled a heresy (also known as the Albigensian heresy) by the church, was dualist, holding that the soul was a creation of God but the body was evil. Reproduction, therefore, was evil as well, and sex was too because it promoted reproduction. Cathars argued that sex within marriage was no less sinful than sex outside it, and that in instituting marriage the Catholic Church had made itself into a pimp. Indeed, marital sex could be worse than extramarital in that people were not ashamed of it. This argument could be twisted by some Cathars to justify extramarital sex, as Pierre Clergue used it to seduce Béatrice de Planissoles (see Chapter 4), but it could also be used to promote chastity in a way that spurred the orthodox Catholics to valorize marital sex in response.

The later Middle Ages saw another wave of valorization of marriage. One reason may have been the demographic crisis of the fourteenth century. After centuries of population growth, the number of people in western Europe was beginning to approach the carrying capacity of the land (at least given the agricultural techniques then known). More and more marginal land had been brought under cultivation; grain prices were high. One season of bad harvests could devastate the poor rural (and urban) population, and when a prolonged period of famine occurred, as in 1315–1322, all of society was disrupted. A population weakened by undernourishment was also especially vulnerable to disease, and the Black Death that swept across Europe in 1348–1350 (with recurrent outbreaks through the next century) wiped out about a third of the population. In some ways the lower population following the plague was an advantage; there were fewer shortages. Employers, though, found the lack of cheap labor a problem, and governments, concerned about low population levels, attempted to promote marriage.

In Florence, Italy, for example, the low birth rate was one reason given for the establishment in 1403 of the Ufficiali dell'Onestà (Office of Honesty) to set up and regulate a municipal brothel. This was, ironically, seen as a pro-marriage measure: too many men, according to the authorities, were never marrying because they preferred sodomy. "Abhorring the filthiness of the horrible crime which is the vice of sodomy, and wishing to uproot it," they recruited non-Florentine women to staff the brothel.[6] If, by giving them easy access to attractive female prostitutes, the city could persuade them to prefer women to men, they might marry and replenish the population.

Population size, however, was not the only issue. In the later Middle Ages the church was in trouble in a number of ways. Anticlericalism was rife; people resented the tithe money that went to the church, and stories of greedy and lecherous clerics were popular. Anticlerical heresies, like that of the Lollards in England, appeared in some areas, while in others movements like the Brethren of the Common Life or individual mystics remained orthodox but nevertheless managed to operate with minimal reference to the church hierarchy. The church at this time tended to be governed by administrators and lawyers rather than theologians or spiritual leaders. One result of all these factors was that the celibacy of the clergy no longer commanded the great respect it once had.

Lay people were assuming a more central position within the church; more and more works were being written in the vernacular for the use of lay men and women. And, as the audience changed and the attitudes toward the clergy changed, religious writing placed a higher value on marriage. This does not mean that it praised sexual intercourse within marriage per se; rather, its focus was on finding ways to be a good Christian within marriage, and those ways did not have to mean giving up on sex. The family came to be seen as a microcosm of the divine order, and valued as such. More married people came to be venerated as saints; exempla stories about virtuous married people became more common. These positive attitudes toward marriage and the family are often associated with the Protestant Reformation but in fact had their origin in the later Middle Ages.

Although reproduction was central to medieval ideas about marriage, to have made it the only focus of marital sexuality would have been problematic. Some marriages were infertile; some married couples were past the age of childbearing. There had to be some other justification for marriage in order to make such unions valid. Theologians tended to follow Augustine's formulation of the three goods of marriage: "proles, fides, sacramentum," or "offspring, faithfulness, and the sacrament."[7] Marriage was a good because of the love and loyalty it promoted between the two spouses, and also because it allowed them to participate in one of the sacraments of the church. By the twelfth century, when the concept of the sacramentality of marriage was defined, Christ himself was held to have established the sacrament of marriage by his participation in the wedding at Cana (John 2). Yet, although love was one of the purposes of marriage, marital love that was too strong could lead to excessive, sinful pleasure. The canonist "Gratian" (the text attributed to him is now known to have been composed in several stages, probably by different people) labeled people who married for the sake of sexual pleasure as fornicators, though he argued that people could marry in order to avoid sexual temptation.

Marriage without offspring: chastity and contraception

While it was clear that a marriage could be considered valid even if it did not lead to offspring, it was not so clear whether it was valid if it did not permit the possibility of offspring. During the twelfth century there was a heated dispute over what made a valid Christian marriage, with two of the greatest medieval thinkers taking opposite sides. The canon law text attributed to "Gratian" held that marriage was not completed and binding until consummated. To the objection that this meant that the Virgin Mary was not legally married to Joseph, since their marriage was never consummated (as medieval theologians believed, arguing that those whom the Bible calls Jesus's brothers were his cousins), he replied that theirs was indeed not a complete marriage. As evidence for this, he cited Jesus's commendation of Mary to the protection of John at the death of her son. If she were validly married, it would have been her husband who consoled her. The theologian Peter Lombard, author of a book called the *Sentences*, which became the leading theology textbook in the medieval universities, argued that it was consent, not consummation, that made a marriage. It was Lombard's view, held also by many others, which prevailed; thus Mary and Joseph's marriage, though never consummated, was the perfect marriage (and, as the fifteenth-century writer Jean Gerson believed, Joseph did not comfort Mary at the time of the Crucifixion because he was already dead).

As canon law developed and was applied in practice during the subsequent centuries, however, canonists increasingly argued that sexual relations did play an important role in the making of marriage. As early as the eleventh century, Ivo of Chartres held that if a man treated his concubine as his wife, the relationship could be deemed to be a marriage. Consent between the parties could create a valid marriage even in the absence of intercourse. However, consent could be given in two different ways, a distinction clarified in the later Middle Ages. Words of present consent – "I take you as my wife" – created a valid marriage immediately. Words of future or conditional consent – "I will take you as my wife," or "I take you as my husband if my father agrees" – did not. If, however, words of future or conditional consent were followed by sexual intercourse, the marriage immediately became valid; the parties were assumed to have dropped the condition. This meant that a promise of marriage given to seduce a woman into sex – "If you get pregnant, I will marry you" – was not merely enforceable but actually self-fulfilling. It might or might not be enforceable, depending on whether or not there were witnesses, but according to canon law even if performed without witnesses and an officiant, the marriage was valid; they were married in the eyes of God, even if there was no evidence to convince a church court. This was not the case, however, in the eastern church.

Although a marriage did not have to be consummated to be valid, the non-consummation had to be voluntary. If either party were incapable of sexual intercourse, the marriage could be dissolved. A jury of matrons might be called to examine the woman to see if she were physically incapable of intercourse. From some of the English cases where a group of women were called to examine the man, we know that these were not always respectable matrons but in fact prostitutes, who were in a sense acting as expert witnesses. In one case, a witness testified that she had

> exposed her naked breasts, and with her hands warmed at the said fire, she held and rubbed the penis and testicles of the said John. And she embraced and frequently kissed the same John . . . the whole time aforesaid the said penis was scarcely three inches long, . . . remaining without any increase or decrease.

The witness and her companions cursed the man "for presuming to marry a young woman, defrauding her if he could not serve and please her better than that." In another case, however, witnesses testified that the man's penis was "large enough for any woman living in this world."[8] An image from a manuscript of "Gratian's" *Decretum* (see Figure 3.1) illustrates a group

Figure 3.1 Examination for impotence. Gratian, *Decretum*, Baltimore, Walters Art Museum, Ms. 10.133, fol. 277.

of women examining a man's genitals before a judge in just such a procedure. It is not possible to tell from the image what the social status of the
women is meant to be. They are not obviously prostitutes but they are also
not obviously respectable matrons (some other representations of medieval
prostitutes show them fully coiffed, so we cannot take the headgear as an
indicator of respectability).

Sometimes the inability to consummate a marriage might not be due
to anything inherent to either partner, but to magic. Although patristic
and early medieval writers occasionally refer to temporary impotence from
unknown causes, the idea of impotence caused by harmful magic (*malefi-
cium*) became common beginning in the twelfth century in legal, medical,
and theological writing. The notion of magically caused impotence as it
developed from the ninth century onward probably originated in folk belief
in a variety of types of love magic (there was not a strong line between a
woman's use of magic to get a man to love her and to make him impotent
with other women), but it was then interpreted and systematized by scholars, who had to deal with it because impotence was grounds for annulment of marriage. Finally, in the later Middle Ages scholars connected it
to the activities of witches. In Jewish culture, too, impotence could be seen
as caused by magic, and there it could be a ground for divorce, as could
infertility.

A belief in impotence magic was not limited to Christian scholars in the
central to late Middle Ages, however. It also appeared in literature. *Njal's
Saga*, written in thirteenth-century Iceland, presents an example from the
pre-Christian period. Hrut Herjolfsson, an Icelander, has been in Norway,
where he has had an affair with the dowager queen Gunnhild. When he is
to return to Iceland, she tells him, "I place this spell on you: you will not
have any sexual pleasure with the woman you plan to marry in Iceland,
though you'll be able to enjoy yourself with other women." He marries
Unn, who eventually tells her father she wants a divorce (permissible under
Icelandic law):

> He is not able to have sexual intercourse in a way that gives me
> pleasure, though otherwise his nature is that of the manliest of
> men. . . . When he comes close to me his penis is so large that
> he can't have any satisfaction from me, and yet we've both tried
> every possible way to enjoy each other, but nothing works. By the
> time we part, however, he shows that he's as normal physically as
> other men.

The saga presents Hrut's problem in a way flattering to his masculinity:
his erection is too large, though apparently he is able to ejaculate normally
outside of his wife's vagina. The incident is noteworthy for the way Unn
expresses her own sense of entitlement to sexual pleasure.[9]

In the view of most canonists, a marriage that could never be consummated because one partner was permanently impotent was invalid and should be annulled, with the healthy spouse able to remarry. However, if one of the parties was incapable of intercourse only with his or her spouse, it might be a temporary effect of magic, and the marriage was valid and binding. The parties had to attempt to remove the spell by confessing and doing penance for the sins for which God had punished them by allowing a demon to disrupt the marriage. Confession and prayer accompanied other potential cures, both medical and magical, and a period of three years was a typical time used to determine whether the situation was permanent, although canonists disagreed over whether an impotence caused by magic could ever be permanent. Canon lawyers were thus, in their own way, addressing the problem of marital infertility that medical experts also considered and that Jewish or Muslim communities could solve by divorce or polygyny.

The monastic writer Guibert of Nogent recounts that his parents were unable to consummate their marriage for seven years. This marriage had not been popular with the husband's family in the first place, and they did their best to challenge it, urging the husband to take a lover and the wife to return to her family. Men also attempted to seduce her. She, however, refused, and Guibert presents this as outstandingly virtuous on her part: "when enticements from without were added to those impulses common to our human nature, like oil poured upon the flames, yet the young maiden's heart was always under her control and never won from her by any allurements."[10] She respected the sanctity of marriage even when there were good social reasons not to. Eventually the spell, cast by a jealous stepmother, was removed, and the couple was able to consummate their marriage.

A marriage had to be open to the possibility of sexual intercourse in order to be valid, but that did not mean there was substantial agreement as to the sinfulness of marital sex. The most rigorous writers held that sexual intercourse was always sinful, even in marriage, but others held that it helped build love between the partners. The idea that it was always sinful fell by the wayside by the thirteenth century, as the necessity of combating the Cathar heresy, which held that all flesh was evil, led theologians and canonists to put a new valuation on marriage and reproduction.

The Christian consensus eventually held that individual sex acts had to be open to the possibility of conception in order not to be sinful. This didn't mean that an infertile couple could not have sex, it simply meant that a fertile couple couldn't do anything to prevent conception. They did not actually have to seek to have children with every sex act, but they had to accept the possibility, and were forbidden to use contraception. In fact, Augustine had suggested that sex acts that did not lead to conception might be worse within marriage than without, although their sinfulness did not necessarily lie in their contraceptive nature.

> That use which is against nature is abominable in a prostitute but more abominable in a wife . . . when the husband wishes to use the member of his wife which has not been given for this purpose, the wife is more shameful if she permits this to take place with herself rather than with another woman.[11]

The implication was that a prostitute was already corrupt, whereas if the man compelled his wife to participate in unnatural acts he would be corrupting her also. "Gratian," the great twelfth-century compiler of canon law who cited this passage from Augustine, also thought that the harm in those acts was simply that they were unnatural; he did not criticize vaginal intercourse without procreative intent in the same way. He cited with approval a statement by Ambrose that "natural" sex acts, even incest, were preferable to unnatural.

The definition of what constituted an unnatural act or what it was impermissible to do with one's spouse could vary, but might include even vaginal intercourse with the woman on top, which medieval writers like Albert the Great (1206–1280) thought impeded conception. Albert, however, did not consider other positions besides male superior to be mortally sinful, only questionable. Other non-reproductive sex acts – both oral and anal – were condemned as unnatural, while the use of contraceptives came in for slightly less, although still serious, criticism.

The fact that contraception was so often vilified by theologians and preachers testifies to its use (or at least attempted use). These handbooks often presented this information as for the use of married women whose lives would be endangered by pregnancy. Some handbooks, however, told in so much detail what you should *not* do if you *want* to conceive that some suspect that they were giving surreptitious instructions for contraception.

> John [of Gaddesden] is not aiming to help a doctor whose patient is mysteriously sterile because she has blundered by wearing the heart of a mule; Magnino [of Milan] is not visualizing a patient who has inadvertently used a cabbage-seed pessary or hung saxifrage over her bed.[12]

These amulets may not have been especially effective, but some herbs may have been. Medieval women used "asarum, *ferula*, birthwort, artemisia, century plant (both the greater one and the lesser one), lupine, pepper, Queen Anne's lace, myrrh, licorice, pennyroyal, rue, peony, parsley, and cypress."[13] We do not know how these herbs worked in combination or how effective were the doses medieval women took, but some scholars have suggested that birth rates in the Middle Ages were low enough that some effective artificial birth control must have been practiced. Some of these herbs are known to produce early-term abortion if taken in high enough doses, but such high doses are also toxic to the women involved. There were also primitive barrier methods like sponges inserted into the vagina, or pebbles into the mouth of the uterus to function like an IUD. There were also some herbal methods of contraception for use by men. Some of these, however, like "chaste tree," coriander, or lettuce seed, were actually anaphrodisiacs, intended to decrease men's desire for sex or ability to maintain an erection. These might well have been slipped into a husband's food by married women who did not want to become pregnant again.

Islamic thought was much more open to the possibility of non-reproductive sex. For the eleventh–twelfth century jurist Ghazali, coitus interruptus was no more or less lawful than abstaining from sex. Marriage and reproduction were valued above chastity, but avoiding reproduction through artificial means was no worse than avoiding reproduction through chastity – nearly the opposite of the Christian view. *Hadith* – sayings attributed to the Prophet – emphasized that not all intercourse leads to pregnancy and that God controls whether a woman will become pregnant: "Practice coitus interruptus or do not practice it. If God wanted to create a human life he will anyway."[14] Muslim writers pointed out that, since coitus interruptus is not foolproof, God determined in which cases it would work. A man could not, however, practice withdrawal from a free woman without her consent: she had a right to children if she so desired, and to sexual pleasure, which the jurists believed was stimulated by male ejaculation. Jurists did not talk much about other kinds of contraception but medical and literary texts indicate that it was widely accepted and practiced; most of the medical methods, suppositories, oral medications, and fumigations, were to be used by women, who thereby had some measure of control over their fertility.

Jewish attitudes toward contraception were also somewhat more lenient than Christian ones. Destruction of the seed was a serious moral offense, but some rabbis held that the commandment not to waste one's seed was binding on men but not on women, so anything the woman did to prevent conception was acceptable. The Talmud held that, despite the commandment to multiply, a married couple might legitimately use contraception if pregnancy would threaten the woman's life. Some commentators permitted it if the wife was too young to bear a child, was pregnant, or was nursing – all situations in which Christian writers would forbid intercourse. However, the fact that serious economic hardship would result from a pregnancy was not sufficient reason to permit contraception. And of course Judaism, perhaps even more than Christianity and Islam, placed great emphasis upon reproduction as the main purpose of marriage.

One contributing factor in low medieval birth rates, besides a possible illicit use of contraception, may have been breastfeeding; particularly among undernourished populations, lactation tends to inhibit ovulation, and the medieval habit of breastfeeding boys until the age of two or more (and girls for slightly less time), coupled with a belief that sexual intercourse caused a woman's milk to become unhealthy, may have inhibited conception. Wealthier people paid wet nurses, presumably because husbands wanted to be able to resume intercourse with their wives, and tended to have children spaced more closely together.

In this discussion of contraception and abstinence, topics which are of great concern today, it is important not to forget that in the Middle Ages most married people would have been far more concerned with fertility than with contraception. Aristocrats concerned with the transmission of property, peasants who needed extra hands to work the land, and people of all social groups who believed in the religious obligation to be fruitful and multiply were all concerned to maximize, not minimize, the number of offspring. Although poorer people might be concerned about how many children they could support, in an era of high infant and childhood mortality there was much less desire, as well as less ability, to limit the number of births than there is today.

Marital sex and ritual purity

Restrictions that the church placed on the timing of intercourse may have contributed to a lower birth rate in medieval Europe than in many other preindustrial populations. The liturgical calendar was full of feast and fast days on which marital intercourse was forbidden; Sundays and sometimes other days of the week were taboo as well. Couples were not supposed to have sex during the woman's menstrual period, or in between the time they made a confession and the time they received the sacrament of the Eucharist. The penitentials of the early Middle Ages were particularly restrictive about the dates on which one could legitimately have sexual intercourse. Fewer than half the days in the year would have been permissible: Sundays, Wednesdays, Fridays, many holidays, and all of Advent and Lent were days for abstention, as well as women's periods of menstruation, pregnancy, and lactation. It is difficult to know how seriously these strictures about the timing of marital intercourse were taken. "Gratian's" *Decretum* made observance of the holy days dependent upon the consent of the parties, and later writers treated them as guidelines rather than absolute commands. (The Christian prohibition of marital sexual relations on Sundays contrasts markedly with the Jewish *mitzvah* or commandment of sexual relations on the Sabbath except if the wife is menstruating, stressing the contrast between these two religions over the moral status of marital sex.)

Even when sex on particular days was prohibited, a violation of the prohibition might be a lesser sin than the alternate refusal to render the marriage debt. In the Orthodox east, where the days before Easter were considered the most holy, a Serbian story tells of the consequences of too-zealous abstinence, even for a married priest:

> On Holy Saturday evening, a priest was tormented by a demon of lust. Remembering the requirement of abstinence, his wife refused to satisfy his urges. As a result, the priest went out to a barn and sought release with a cow. The next day, during the Easter mass, flocks of birds attacked the church. The priest ordered that the doors and windows be barred against the onslaught, and tearfully confessed his sin before the congregation. The priest and the congregants then opened the door and were allowed to leave unharmed. When the priest's wife went out, however, the birds descended upon her and tore her to pieces. Clearly she was seen as responsible for her husband's sin, because she had driven him to it.[15]

This story illustrates not only the expectations about sexual relations within a marriage but also the idea of masculine lust as a powerful force that could not be denied but must be satisfied one way or another.

Warnings about the consequences of marital intercourse at the wrong time were not as pervasive as warnings about the consequences of intercourse in the wrong place, notably in churches. The story of a couple who had sex in a church and became stuck together "like dogs," to the amazement and derision of the congregation who found them there the next day, was widely retold. Certainly it would have been difficult in a medieval village for a couple to find a place for an illicit liaison. The church, which was safe, dry, and deserted for much of the day, might have been the medieval equivalent of the back seat of a car. But even a married couple might conceivably seek out the quiet and privacy of a church. Medieval houses were small and married couples, except at the highest level of society, did not have their own bedrooms. The story may be more symbolic of the division between clergy and laity, between sacred and profane, than literal, but it may also reflect a real issue for medieval people.

The idea that sexual intercourse somehow polluted a place was also a basis for the custom of churching of women. Women who had given birth were not permitted to enter a church until forty days had passed, and they had to undergo a particular ritual. For a culture that made reproduction the basis of marriage it seems strange that it would have been seen as at the same time polluting, but the very conflicted relation between the medieval church and the flesh made this contradiction possible. The custom may have had its roots in the Jewish custom of ritual purification after childbirth, which the Virgin Mary was thought to have undergone. In the Middle Ages it was interpreted as a service of thanksgiving for a safe delivery, and some scholars have argued that it honored women and gave them a symbolically central place.

Even though the church taught that under the new dispensation it was the heart, and not the body, that needed to be purified, the giving of thanks after childbirth still had an element that recognized women's sexual activity as contaminating. Because of this a new mother was isolated from the community for a period of time until she could be ritually reintegrated. The ceremony was more than that, however: it underscored women's escape from danger through the intercession of the Virgin Mary. The feast of Candelaria (Candlemas in England), forty days after Christmas, celebrated the Virgin's purification with a procession of lights, and a woman seeking churching after childbirth brought a candle to church. The ritual also established the woman publicly as a virtuous wife and mother. The meaning of the ritual for the women involved, and for the midwives and other female peers who accompanied them, may have been quite different from that for the church hierarchy, and they may not have seen childbirth as impure.

Medieval Jewish society was less restrictive than Christian about opportunities for marital sex. The Talmud prohibits a man from forcing his wife to have sex with him, contrary to the Christian doctrine of the marriage debt; it permits marital sex even when not procreative. Jewish culture did have one very important, universally acknowledged taboo. A woman was considered unclean during her menstrual period; after her period was over she had to go through a ritual purification by visiting an immersion bath (*mikveh*) before she could have intercourse with her husband. Medieval Jewish writers went even beyond the Talmud in suggesting the disastrous consequences for men of women's impurity. As Rabbi Eleazar of Worms, a German pietist of the late twelfth–early thirteenth century, wrote:

> A woman who observes her state of *niddah* properly will not cook for her husband, she will not bake, she will not dance, she will not prepare the bed, and she will not pour water from one vessel to another, because she is in a state of impurity and she can transmit impurity. And she is forbidden to enter a synagogue until she has immersed in water. The saliva of a *niddah* transmits impurity. A *niddah* who has sexual relations with her husband causes her sons to be stricken with leprosy, even for twenty generations.[16]

Rabbi Eleazar clearly loved and respected his own wife Dolce; after she was killed in 1196 he wrote memorials to her in both prose and poetry. This did not, however, prevent him from blaming women for polluting men. But the rules of immersion could also be used to emphasize women's virtue: although the Talmud says that women achieve merit by managing the household and enabling men to study, medieval Ashkenazic writers also said that they achieved it by going to the *mikveh*. Only married women, however, were required to immerse: the impurity of women was only important insofar as it affected men.

The idea of women as polluting was not, of course, restricted to Judaism. The ritual purity of the clergy was one of the reasons Christian writers like Peter Damian gave for clerical celibacy. Menstruation was the "curse of Eve," women's punishment for original sin, so much so that theologians wondered why the Virgin Mary, who had been cleansed from sin in the womb of her mother, menstruated (the answer was that she voluntarily took the punishment on herself out of humility, even though she did not deserve it). But Christianity did not connect women's ritual impurity with the flux of blood as directly as Judaism did; women were not impure only because of, or only during and immediately after, menstruation, and they could not be cleansed by a ritual bath.

Spanish responsa speak of women refusing to go to the *mikveh* because they did not want to have sex with their husbands. A story from the late twelfth–early thirteenth century, in *Sefer Hasidim* by Judah he-Chasid of Regensburg, tells of a woman spurring her husband to charity by refusing to go to the *mikveh* until he purchased books for charitable use. When her husband complained to a rabbi, he was told, "Blessed is she for having brought upon thee pressure to perform a worthy deed. Any other way of constraining thee she knows not."[17] Nevertheless she was urged to find other ways to convince her husband, because if she refused to make herself ritually pure to have sex with him, she would not conceive a child and he might turn to other sexual activity. It was customary for a married couple to have intercourse immediately following the woman's ritual bath, as illustrated in a religious miscellany from Germany in the early fifteenth century (see Figure 3.2). On the top, a man lies in bed, apparently waiting for his wife; below, she immerses herself in the *mikveh*.

A folk belief held that what a woman saw upon coming out of the *mikveh* would determine the nature of the child conceived that night. A tradition about the second-century CE Rabbi Ishmael held that when his mother left the bathhouse, she "saw a swine. She returned, immersed herself, came forth and saw a leper. She returned, immersed and saw a camel. And so it happened to her several times, and on each such occasion she went back and immersed afresh." Finally the angel Gabriel "stood near the entrance to the ritual bath, and she saw him as she passed and proceeded home. And that night she became pregnant with Rabbi Ishmael. And in his appearance he was as fine and handsome as Gabriel."[18]

The public nature of the visit to the *mikveh* indicates a fundamental difference in medieval Christian and Jewish attitudes toward marital sex. When a woman visited the *mikveh*, anyone could see her enter, and everyone knew that she and her husband would be having sex that night (this was considered a particularly likely time for the conception of a child). This was

Figure 3.2 Wife in *mikveh*, husband waiting in bed. *Hamburg Miscellany*, Staats-und-Universitätsbibliothek, Hamburg, Cod. Heb. 37, fol. 79v, detail.

an obligation, and not considered shameful. However, Jewish culture, too, could be riven by conflicts over the value or sinfulness of sex.

Husbands, wives, and pleasure

Some Jewish writers devalued pleasure in marital sex. Maimonides held that the purpose of circumcision was to decrease sexual desire. While some suggested that letting the wife reach orgasm first would promote the conception of a son, Isaac ben Ydaiah, a thirteenth-century Provençal follower of Maimonides, suggested that circumcision reduced sexual pleasure for the woman because the man reached orgasm more quickly, and that this was a good thing:

> he will find himself performing his task quickly, emitting his seed as soon as he inserts the crown. If he lies with her once, he sleeps satisfied, and will not know her again for another seven days. This is the way the circumcised man acts time after time with the woman he loves. He has an orgasm first; he does not hold back his strength.
>
> As soon as he begins intercourse with her, he immediately comes to a climax. She has no pleasure from him when she lies down or when she arises, and it would be better for her if he had not known her and not drawn near to her, for he arouses her passion to no avail, and she remains in a state of desire for her husband, ashamed and confounded.

This contrasted with sex with an uncircumcised man, which lasted so long that the woman would derive great pleasure and demand more frequent sex, leading to the man's distraction from all other matters:

> She too will court the man who is uncircumcised in the flesh and lie against his breast with great passion, for he thrusts inside her a long time because of the foreskin, which is a barrier against ejaculation in intercourse. Thus she feels pleasure and reaches an orgasm first. When an uncircumcised man sleeps with her and then resolves to return to his home, she brazenly grasps him, holding on to his genitals, and says to him, "Come back, make love to me." This is because of the pleasure that she finds in intercourse with him, from the sinews of his testicles – sinew of iron – and from his ejaculation – that of a horse – which he shoots like an arrow into her womb. They are united without separating, and he makes love twice and three times in one night, yet the appetite is not filled.[19]

Eleazar of Mainz, who left an "ethical will" or precepts for his children in the fourteenth century, suggests that his daughters "should have sexual relations with their husbands in modesty and sanctity, not with passion and not with frivolity but in reverence and silence."[20] In general rabbinic literature was concerned with women's sexual desire or even attractiveness and the danger it posed to men. The temptation of men could disrupt the world, even the temptation of men by their own wives.

Jewish law required a man to grant his wife her right to sexual intercourse (*onah*). This doctrine resembled the Christian one of the marriage debt, except that for Jews only the man owed it to the woman. *Onah* was not only for the sake of procreation, but also for pleasure; she had the right to it even if she were pregnant or too old to conceive. The frequency of the required sexual relations depended on a variety of factors, including the status of the husband. The purpose of *onah* seems to have been to remove from a woman the possibility of sexual temptation because of insufficient intercourse with her husband. The Tosafist Rabbi Meir b. Baruch of Rothenburg held that a husband who had not slept with his wife in two years could be required by a rabbinical court to divorce her at her request, and could be fined heavily until he did so. She retained full rights to her *ketubah* (contractual marriage payment). A wife who refused to sleep with her husband could lose rights to the *ketubah* if he divorced her. She was considered a *moredet* or rebellious woman.

Perhaps the best-known rebellious medieval woman in the Christian tradition, the Wife of Bath in Chaucer's *Canterbury Tales*, does not rebel by denying her husband's sexual pleasure, although perhaps she does so by seeking her own. Although she does not enjoy sexual intercourse with her first three husbands, "suffering" their performance, she does not deny them sexual access. Instead, she fakes it:

> For winning [earning] I would all his lust endure,
> And make me a feigned appetite.[21]

She is clearly a woman of strong sexual appetites, which she exercises with her fourth and fifth husbands; her transgression, however, is her scolding and fighting, not her sexual behavior. She clearly feels that she is entitled to sexual satisfaction within her marriage.

Many medical writers held that mutual pleasure in marital sex was important because it promoted conception. This does not mean, however, that marital sex was understood as egalitarian. It still consisted of one dominant and one submissive, or one active and one passive, partner; "active" here does not mean the one who initiates the encounter, but the one who penetrates. Some manuals counseled foreplay because their authors held that female pleasure led to emission of female seed which was necessary for conception. All writers, however, agreed that the discharge of male seed within the vagina was necessary for conception. Indeed, male ejaculation was thought to contribute to women's pleasure. The Muslim medical scholar Ibn Sina (Avicenna), in a formulation widely quoted in Latin, suggested that

> because of this women's pleasure is multiplied. They receive pleasure from the motion of the seed that is in them, and they receive pleasure from the motion of the man's seed in the mouth of the womb, descending to the womb.[22]

Albert the Great wrote that in addition to their own emission of seed and the motion of their wombs, women also experience pleasure from the adherence of the man's sperm, and another scholar wrote that "women experience more pleasure than men, since women take pleasure in emitting and receiving, but men only take pleasure in emitting."[23]

Women's lust was not the desire to be held, fondled, touched; it was the desire for penetration and the man's ejaculation. From the medical point of view it was the semen, not the penetration, that caused the pleasure, but penetration was the means by which that semen was discharged within the vagina, and other genres of medieval writing stress its importance. The French fabliaux, humorous tales, illustrate the importance of the penis in marital desire. In one story a couple is magically granted four wishes, and the wife immediately blurts out that she wishes her husband's body were "all covered with pricks, so that there should be no eye, nose, head, arm or side that isn't planted with pricks." In another, a woman tells her husband of a dream in which she was at a market where all kinds of "balls and pricks" are displayed for sale, "retail and wholesale," arriving at the market in cartloads.[24] The story quoted in Chapter 1, of a wife who rejects her husband when she thinks he has lost his penis, makes the same point.

These stories, of course, were written by men. They reflect not women's desires but the way men imagined women's desires, no doubt with a fair dollop of wishful thinking in that imagination. Yet such texts could become in a way normative. Desire is shaped and channeled by culture. Women who felt desires different from those in the literature they read or heard might wonder why they themselves were different, or think that they were abnormal. This, of course, would make it even less likely that women's dissenting voices would be heard. The picture that emerges from this literature, then, is that women desire to have something done to them.

Christian religious writing also reinforced this idea that men were active and women passive. The Middle English text *Dives and Pauper*, discussing the various types of sexual sin, illustrates the way marital intercourse was understood, in its discussion of "how a man may sin in meddling with his wife." The text discusses intercourse at an improper time or place or with the wrong purpose.[25] Such texts did not talk about how the couple sins, but how the man sins. He is the one responsible, he is the one who does the "meddling." The woman might be considered less morally culpable, since she was merely submitting to her husband (a great virtue for a woman), but the flip side of this is that she is not cast as an agent in the process.

There was, then, a fundamental difference in the experience of sex for the husband and the wife. The husband desired to release his seed; while medical writers might say that the wife also desired to release seed, they also argued that the wife received pleasure from the reception of the husband's seed. Those who believed women did not emit seed, of course, found it easier to attribute all action to the male, and drew on Ibn Sina's statement about women receiving more pleasure than men because the man's ejaculation caused her pleasure.

In this situation it was obvious who was the doer, and who the done to. Not all scholars agreed. The Arab Ibn Rushd (Averroes) told of a woman he knew who became pregnant from the bathwater in which a man had ejaculated. Other medical writers, however, found this story ludicrous and unbelievable.

Passive in terms of sexual receptivity did not, however, mean passive in terms of desire. I suggested in the last chapter that, in the case of a chaste marriage, it was more likely to be the woman's choice than the man's to abstain from sex. This is because she was less likely than the man to have chosen her marriage partner, and also because she was the one to suffer from pregnancy and childbirth. It was not because medieval people thought women had less sex drive. Women could be just as lustful as men, if not more so. They were depicted exhausting their husbands. One French fabliau tells a scatological story about a couple who have a euphemism for sex, "feeding Brownie." His wife demanded sex from him so frequently, using this term, that the husband was no longer able to comply. Instead, he defecated in the bed, saying: "The grain is gone, from now on you will have to make do with bran."[26] Women, indeed, were seen as having a great capacity for desire, but it was a receptive desire.

The lustfulness of women is also reflected in medieval attitudes toward widows. The remarriage of widows, although legal, was frowned upon by some churchmen; fidelity to the dead husband, and chastity once a woman had done her duty of perpetuating her husband's lineage, were the ideal. Negative attitudes toward remarriage were even stronger in the eastern church, for both men and women; the question of whether widowed priests could remarry was highly contested, and priests' widows could do so only at the risk of considerable social stigma. But the image of the lusty widow was also very prominent in medieval culture. In a commonly repeated story from the Roman *Satyricon* by Petronius, a widow goes to the cemetery to weep over her husband's grave. There she meets a soldier who has been charged with guarding the corpse of a crucified criminal so his relatives won't be able to seize it. The widow has sex with the soldier, during which the crucified corpse is stolen. The soldier fears punishment, so the widow suggests taking her husband's body from the grave and placing it on the cross. The story suggests that even grieving widows were so lustful that they would give up their grief and loyalty for any man who came along. In addition to its appearance in collections of exempla for sermons and elsewhere, the story also appears as a fabliau under the title "The woman who got herself screwed on her husband's grave" – again, the woman as passive. In this story, the widow is weeping over her husband's grave and a man passing by tells her that his wife has died through his deed. She asks him how he caused her death, and he replies, "By fucking." She tells him she has no desire to live any longer, and asks him to release her from the world as he did his wife.[27] The lust of the widow was more of a threat than that of the virgin, because it was based on the experience of sex and not just the imagination. Marriage had awakened the capacity for lust.

Sexual practices in marriage

At this point the chapter should turn to a description of typical marital sexual practices in medieval Europe. This, however, is hardly possible. How would we identify "typical" marital sexual practices today, when they vary by socioeconomic and ethnic group among other variables? They no doubt varied in the same ways in medieval Europe. Today, however, we have interview data, which, for all their flaws, may at least give us a picture of the behavior of the population in the aggregate. For the Middle Ages we have no such surveys. Instead, I will catalogue here what we can know and what we cannot.

Frequency of intercourse is difficult to determine. Forbidden dates could at least give us a potential maximum, but it is not likely that everyone adhered to them. We can, however, say something about the physical circumstances in which sex took place. Married couples typically shared a bed. Among peasant families, they might also share that bed with several children. Among the aristocracy, servants or retainers might normally sleep in a lord's or lady's bedroom. Among high aristocrats the married couple often had separate bedrooms, so the retainers would be well aware of when the couple shared a bed. Bed-curtains, however, provided a measure of privacy even when servants remained in the chamber, which was also where important papers and valuables were kept.

It seems likely that, at least when there were not crowds of servants about, couples did retire to this bed naked. Again, this is hard to know, and the penitentials disapproved. In book illustrations that show couples in bed together, even when they are sitting up in bed and not having intercourse, they are often shown naked, at least from the waist up (the rest is covered by the bedclothes). This is true in images from medical manuals and from romances. Sometimes the woman retains her headgear; sometimes both do, as in a fifteenth-century representation of Lohengrin and Elsa in their wedding bed (see Figure 3.3). This is an artistic convention to represent social

Figure 3.3 Lohengrin and Elsa. From *Lohengrin*, workshop of Ludwig Henfflin, Ruprecht-Karls-Universitat Heidelberg, Universitätsbibliothek, Cod. Pal. Germ. 345, fol. 57v.

class and does not mean that they actually wore their headgear to bed. People lying alone in bed are also often shown wearing a hat or crown. By the same token we can't assume that people normally slept naked just because it was common to depict them that way. It could be the illustrators' way of indicating that something of a sexual nature is going on, or it could hint that when sex was intended, people got in bed naked. Even if it did reflect practice, it would be the practice only of the aristocracy, the group who had these great canopied beds that provided some privacy, and for whom the books would have been created. As weak a clue as it may be, though, it is one of the few clues we have. Talmudic texts suggest that Jews commonly slept in nightclothes. But we do not know whether medieval practice was the same, and we cannot compare two very different genres of text in two very different cultures and assume that the comparison can tell us about differences in practice.

The naked body, particularly the naked male body, is prominent in medieval literature. Sometimes running naked is a sign of madness; sometimes it is a sign of rudeness or lack of acculturation. Naked men and women appear commonly enough in later medieval art (although not with genitals exposed), often with other people in the scene, to suggest that even if these images do not represent common practice (or represent bathhouse as brothel, not as place to get clean), squeamishness was not expected from the viewer.

Even if people did go to bed naked, they would not have been able to see much of each other's bodies. We must not forget the implications of a world before electric or even gas lights. Candles would have been so expensive that most families would have blown them out immediately upon going to bed, if indeed they used them at all and did not go to bed immediately after dark. Tallow, the cheapest kind, cost about 1½ pence per pound in late medieval England, about equivalent to a quarter of a day's wage for a skilled worker. In summer, of course, it remained light for longer, but working hours both in countryside and in city were adjusted accordingly. People went to bed when there was no longer daylight enough to work, and got up when it became light enough to work. Wealthier families could afford more candles, some wealthy households using as much as a hundred pounds of tallow and wax in one night.

A frequent theme in medieval romances as well as fabliaux, however, is the man who ends up with the wrong woman as sex partner; this could imply that intercourse normally took place in the dark, although of course it could also be simply a convenient literary convention. In the story of Tristan and Iseult, Iseult's maid Brangain takes Iseult's place on her wedding night so that King Mark will not know she is not a virgin. Here the text of the thirteenth-century French *Prose Tristan* is so specific about the candle-lighting procedure that one must suspect it was a plot device that demanded explanation:

> You [Brangain] will see her to bed, as is your duty, and the candles will be extinguished. When King Mark is ready to lie down, we'll put you in the bed and Iseult will slip out. And after King Mark has had his pleasure with you, you will withdraw and Iseult will take your place. Once King Mark has found you to be a virgin, the

candles will be relit, and he'll see Iseult beside him and think he has taken her.

It is Tristan himself who extinguishes the candles and Mark demands an explanation:

> "Uncle," said Tristan, "it's the custom in Ireland that when a noble man lies with a virgin, the candles are extinguished so that the maiden is less bashful and more likely to find pleasure with her lord; and this is a very courtly way to behave."[28]

The implication is that the audience would have found the extinguishing of candles unusual. In the fabliau "The Priest and Alison," a priest offers a mother a large sum of money to sleep with her daughter, and the mother substitutes a local prostitute, with whom she splits the fee.[29] The humor of the fabliau stories resides in their plausible everyday setting, which suggests that the normal way to have sex within the lower orders – or the way the aristocratic audience would have imagined the lower orders having sex – was in the dark.

What exactly were people doing in the dark? Again the evidence is ambiguous, but it is likely that married couples did use a variety of sexual positions. The male superior position was normative. Treatises on sexual sin, whether intended for the laity themselves to read, for parish priests who were to counsel them, or for academic lawyers who discussed these questions theoretically, considered any position other than man on top to be unnatural even between a married couple. William Peraldus's influential treatise on sin, on which many pastoral works were based, distinguished between a sin against nature "according to the substance" (any intercourse other than vaginal) and against nature "according to the manner, as when a woman mounts."[30] Literary texts indicate that this man-on-top position was more or less synonymous with sexual intercourse. In one fabliau, when a man spies on his wife as she commits adultery, he sees her rear end while the priest is on top of her, suggesting that the male superior position did not have to mean that the woman remained supine.[31] Jewish tradition also took the male superior as the normative position. A text from the ninth or tenth century, the *Alphabet of Ben Sira*, told the story of Lilith, Adam's first wife, who fled from Eden and became a demon because Adam refused to have sex with her on top.

So many different kinds of texts place so much emphasis on the fact that the male superior position is the only acceptable one that we may suspect there were people out there who needed to be persuaded. One reason why married couples (or other couples) may have chosen the female superior position is that they believed it was more difficult to conceive in that position. Burchard of Worms' eleventh-century book of penances inflicted ten days' fasting – the same as for a man who masturbated or a single man who fornicated – on a husband who had sex with his wife "from behind, in the manner of dogs," or when she was menstruating or pregnant. The penalty was twice that in the case of pregnancy where the fetus had already quickened, implying that harm to the fetus may have been part of the reason, but the connection of prohibited positions with infertile times points to the main reason being the desire to prevent non-procreative sex.[32]

Of course, married couples were not supposed to be avoiding conception. But there must have been many who wanted to continue to have a sex life but did not want any more children. Margery Kempe, the fifteenth-century English mystic who fell into a deep depression after the birth of the first of her fourteen children and eventually persuaded her husband to stop having sex with her, took the more radical (but church-sanctioned) route to birth control:

> It befell upon a Friday on Midsummer Eve, in right hot weather, as this creature was coming from York bearing a bottle with beer in her hand and her husband a loaf in his bosom he asked his wife this question, "Margery, if there came a man with a sword and would smite off my head unless I should common naturally with you as I have done before, tell me the truth from your conscience – for you say you will not lie – whether would you suffer my head to be smote off or else suffer me to meddle with you again, as I did at one time?"
>
> "Alas, sir," she said, "why move you this matter, and we have now been chaste these eight weeks?"
>
> "For I will know the truth of your heart."
>
> And then she said with great sorrow, "Forsooth I had rather see you being slain, than that we should turn again to our uncleanness."
>
> And he said again "You are no good wife."

The couple negotiated: John offered to let her maintain her chastity if she would continue to share his bed, would pay his debts, and would eat with him on Fridays. She refused to give up her Friday fast, whereupon he refused to renounce his sexual rights. She prayed for guidance and was told that the reason God had commanded her to fast was as a bargaining chip with her husband. They finally agreed on chastity, and he told her, "As free may your body be to God as it has been to me."[33]

Chastity was not the goal for most couples. Yet types of sexual activity that do not lead to conception – oral and anal sex, manual stimulation – were strictly forbidden to Christians. Unlike the female superior position, however, these practices are rarely mentioned (even to be censured) in the context of marriage. Early medieval penitentials are among the very few texts to condemn oral sex, and do not mention who the participants were (or even their gender). A report of a pregnancy "in a sodomitical manner, by the dripping down of semen and not by the insertion of the instrument" (possibly but not necessarily anal sex) involves not a wife but a nun.[34] In a story that appears in the English poem *The Gast of Gy* as well as other places, a dead man returns to haunt his wife because of a sin they had committed together, a sin that may have been sodomy. Authorities seem to have found these practices rare enough, at least in the context of marriage, not to rail about them. We have no way of knowing whether this reflects an absence of the practices, or ignorance on the part of church authorities. As we will see in Chapter 5, however, people seem to have assumed that when two men had sex together, penetration would either be anal or between the thighs, rather than oral; oral sex seems a very obscure phenomenon in the Middle Ages.

Medieval people understood marital sex as being initiated by either partner. The stories about the payment of the marriage debt, and dicta about women's inability to take binding vows of chastity without the permission of their husbands, would seem to indicate that the woman was more often the reluctant partner, submitting to the needs of her husband. In Jewish law the woman had the right to sexual satisfaction from her husband, but husbands were urged to initiate intercourse because the woman was likely to be too modest to ask. Literary genres do not tell us as much as we would like to know about the inner dynamics of marital sex – among other things, such texts tend to deal much more with adultery and other extramarital relations, as lovers tend to make better stories than the long-married. However, there are enough literary references to women participating enthusiastically in marital sex – from the fabliaux where they can seem insatiable, to romances where they deeply miss their absent husbands – to indicate to us that this would not be considered abnormal or unusual.

A number of medieval texts also refer to women demanding money or gifts from their husbands in return for sex. Again, this need not reflect actual practice, but was a commonplace of misogynistic stereotypes. In Chaucer's "Shipman's Tale" a monk borrows money from his merchant friend and then gives that money to the merchant's wife in return for her adultery. When the merchant asks for the money back, the monk tells him that he gave it to his wife to give to him. To her husband's demand for the money, the wife replies that she has spent it, but that she will pay him back with sex: "score it upon my taille," she says, punning on the word for tally and slang for genitalia. She makes the exchange explicit:

You shall my joly body have to wedde [as a pledge]:
By God, I will not pay you but abed.[35]

Chaucer's Wife of Bath also reports how she extracted money from her five husbands: she has "picked out the best, both from their nether purse and from their chest." A wife should not grant her husband sexual access too easily, because "Too great a bargain is but little prized. / This knoweth every woman that is wise."[36] Even Margery Kempe tied sex to money, though in this case it was abstinence rather than intercourse that she purchased: one of the conditions that she agreed to so that her husband would allow their marriage to remain chaste was "that I will pay your debts before I go to Jerusalem."[37] This connection of women with venality, as we shall see in Chapter 4, extended from prostitution to other feminine sexual activity as well, including marriage. These are negative stereotypes of women, but they do indicate that women were accorded some power within the marriage, including the choice of whether to engage in sexual activity.

This sketch of what marital sex would have been like is deeply unsatisfactory in many ways. This is a result of the limited material we have to work with. It is not that marital sex was not discussed in the Middle Ages. Canon lawyers and pastoral leaders were quite willing to intervene and dictate what should go on in the marital bedroom. However, what they thought ought to go on and what actually went on were two very different things.

One thing we can say with some certainty, however, is that medieval people would have understood marital sex as something the husband did to the wife. Margery Kempe's husband John used the same phrase as the didactic treatise discussed above when he asked Margery if she would rather have him dead than have him "meddle with her" again.[38] When a wife in the fabliaux refuses to have sex with her husband, she expresses it not as something that she will not do, but something that she will not let him do. Married female saints, too, allow their husbands to have sex with them; this phrasing is not used of married male saints, who have sex with their wives in order to beget children.

It is notable that there are instances in which wives are seen as refusing their husbands sex, even if this is a sin or a wrongful act. What we would call marital rape seems notably absent in medieval sources. They, of course, would not call it marital rape even if it were present, because for them rape was the taking by violence of something that did not belong to the rapist. In the case of a husband, his wife's body, or at least sexual rights to it, did belong to him. But medieval people still would have seen that it was possible for a husband to compel his wife by violence to have sex with him, and we do not see this happening. There are cruel husbands in medieval stories who beat their wives, but sexual violence does not appear among the mistreatment by husbands. This hardly means that sexual violence by husbands against wives never took place, but it would seem to indicate that people did not take it as routine. The husband's unquestioned right to sexual relations with his wife, coupled with the legal and social dominance of the man within the relationship, would undoubtedly have been coercion enough.

The husband, and no one else, had legal rights to sex with the wife. A persistent myth holds that medieval custom allowed a lord to deflower his serf women on their wedding nights. This myth still appears, for example in the 1995 film *Braveheart*, even though historians have demonstrated repeatedly, for more than a century, that such a custom did not exist. The most recent (as well as detailed and persuasive) demolition of the myth, by Alain Boureau, shows how each of the medieval texts that have occasionally been interpreted as referring to such a custom has either been misinterpreted or was a fantastic explanation even in medieval times. People tended to take examples of lordship, or domination, and interpret them in folk-cultural terms as sexual. For example, a text from La Rivière-Bordet in Normandy, from 1419, which represents the lord's rights as agreed on by his tenants, stated that:

> I also have the right to take from my men and others, when they marry in my land, 10 sous tournois and a loin of pork from the whole spine up to the ear, and the tail generously included in that loin, with a gallon of whatever drink there is to be at the meals, or I can and I must, if it please me, go to lie with the bride in the case that either her husband or someone sent by him not pay to me or my representative one of the things declared above.[39]

This is presented as a local custom, not a universal usage, and it resembles many other such local customs not including the right of the first night but including other forms of sexual mockery. No doubt many peasant women were raped or coerced by their lords, and there was not a great deal that they or the men in their families could do about it. But this offense was not institutionalized. It was never an official or customary right of the lord.

Notes

1 Christine de Pisan, *The Treasure of the City of Ladies*, trans. Sarah Lawson (Harmondsworth: Penguin, 1985), ch. 7, p. 49, and ch. 12, pp. 62–4.
2 Jacques de Vitry, *The Exempla*, ed. Thomas Frederick Crane (Reprint, Nendeln: Kraus Reprint, 1967), no. 27, p. 94.
3 John of Bromyard, *Summa Predicantium* (Venice: D. Nicolinus, 1586), s.v. homo, h.1.16.
4 *Monumenta germaniae historica, Legum*, vol. 1, ed. Georg Heinrich Pertz (Hanover: Hahn, 1835), 345.
5 *The Trotula: A Medieval Compendium of Women's Medicine*, ed. and trans. Monica H. Green (Philadelphia: University of Pennsylvania Press, 2001), 97–9.
6 *Statuta populi et communis Florentiae, vol. 3* (Freiburg: Michael Kluch, 1783), 41, cited in Richard Trexler, "La prostitution florentine au XVe siècle: patronages et clientèles," *Annales: Economies, sociétés, civilizations* 36 (1981), 983–1015 (at 1008 n. 12).

7 Augustine, *De bono conjugali*, 29:32, ed. Joseph Zycha, Corpus Scriptorum Ecclesiae Latinae 41 (Vienna: F. Tempsky, 1900), 227.

8 Borthwick Institute for Historical Research, CP.F.111 and CP.F.175; part of the translation is taken from R.H. Helmholz, *Marriage Litigation in Medieval England* (Cambridge: Cambridge University Press, 1974), 89, and the rest is mine.

9 *Njal's Saga*, 6–7, in *Complete Sagas of Icelanders, vol. 3*, ed. Viðar Hreinsson (Reykjavík: Leifur Eiriksson, 1997), 9–11. The Icelandic phrase "svo að *eg* megi njóta hans" means more precisely "so that I may enjoy him" rather than "in a way that gives me pleasure" and it is possible that this is a euphemism for penetration and the possibility of conception rather than a focus on her pleasure, but it is still unusual for a medieval text to express it as the woman enjoying the man.

10 Guibert of Nogent, *Self and Society in Medieval France: The Memoirs of Abbot Guibert of Nogent*, ed. and trans. John F. Benton (New York: Harper, 1970), 64–5.

11 Augustine, *De Bono Conjugali*, 11–12, in *St. Augustine on Marriage*, ed. and trans. Elizabeth A. Clark (Washington, DC: Catholic University of America Press, 1996), 54.

12 John T. Noonan, Jr., *Contraception: A History of Its Treatment by the Catholic Theologians and Canonists* (New York: New American Library, 1965), 257.

13 John M. Riddle, *Eve's Herbs: A History of Contraception and Abortion in the West* (Cambridge, MA: Harvard University Press, 1997), 106.

14 Kasanī, *Bada'i' al sana'i'*, in Basim Musallam, *Sex and Society in Islam: Birth Control before the Nineteenth Century* (Cambridge: Cambridge University Press, 1983), 21.

15 Eve Levin, *Sex and Society in the World of the Orthodox Slavs, 900–1700* (Ithaca, NY: Cornell University Press, 1989), 166–7, based on a seventeenth-century text.

16 Excerpt from *Sefer HaRoqeah HaGadol* of R. Eleazar of Worms, translated in Judith R. Baskin, "Women and Ritual Immersion in Medieval Ashkenaz: The Sexual Politics of Piety," in *Judaism in Practice: From the Middle Ages through the Early Modern Period*, ed. Lawrence Fine (Princeton: Princeton University Press, 2001), 131–42, quote at 140.

17 *Sefer Hasidim*, 670, trans. Abraham Cronbach, "Social Thinking in the Sefer Hasidim," *Hebrew Union College Annual* 22 (1949), 1–147, at 59.

18 Micha Joseph Bin Gorion [Berdichevsky], *Mimekor Yisroel: Classical Jewish Folktales*, abridged edition, ed. Emanuel bin Gorion, trans. I.M. Lask (Bloomington: Indiana University Press, 1990), 127–8.

19 R. Isaac b. Yedediah, *Commentary on the Midrash Rabbah*, trans. in Marc Saperstein, *Decoding the Rabbis: A Thirteenth-Century Commentary on the Aggadah* (Cambridge, MA: Harvard University Press, 1980), 98.

20 Ethical Will of Eleazar of Mainz, trans. in Baskin, "Women and Ritual Immersion," 141.

21 "Wife of Bath's Prologue," ll. 412, 416–17, in Geoffrey Chaucer, *The Riverside Chaucer*, ed. Larry D. Benson, 3rd edition (Boston: Houghton Mifflin, 1987), 110.

22 Ibn Sina (Avicenna), *Liber Canonis*, bk. 3 fen. 21 tr. 1 ch. 2, trans. (into Latin) (Venice, 1507; facsimile Hildesheim: Georg Olms, 1964), fol. 362r.

23 Pseudo-Isidore, *De Spermate*, MS Bodley 484, fol. 46r, quoted in Joan Cadden, *The Meanings of Sex Difference in the Middle Ages: Medicine, Science, and Culture* (Cambridge: Cambridge University Press, 1993), 153 n. 139.

24 "Les quatre sohais Saint Martin," in *Nouveau recueil complet des fabliaux, vol. 4*, eds. Willem Noomen and Nico van den Boogaard (Assen: Van Gorcum,

1988), 213, ll. 94–8; "Le Sohait des Vez," in *Nouveau recueil, vol. 6*, ed. Noomen (1991), 269, ll. 82–97.

25 *Dives and Pauper*, ed. Priscilla Heath Barnum, Early English Text Society 280 (Oxford: Oxford University Press, 1980), vol. 1:2, ch. 6:1, p. 18.

26 "La dame qui aveine demandoit pour Morel sa provender avoir," *Nouveau recueil, vol. 9*, ed. Noomen (1996), 198–9, ll. 303–9.

27 "Cele qui se fist foutre sur la fosse de son mari," *Nouveau recueil, vol. 3*, eds. Noomen and van den Boogard (1986), 400–3.

28 *The Romance of Tristan*, 8, trans. Renée L. Curtis (Oxford: Oxford University Press, 1994), 93–5.

29 "Le prestre et Alison," *Nouveau recueil, vol. 8*, ed. Noomen (1994), 195–206.

30 Gulielmus Peraldus, *Summa de Vitiis*, 3:2:2. I am grateful to Siegfried Wenzel for the use of his draft normalized edition of this text.

31 "Le prestre qui abevete," *Nouveau recueil, vol. 8*, ed. Noomen (1994), 308, l:64.

32 Burchard, *Decretum*, 19:5; *PL*, 140:959.

33 *The Book of Margery Kempe*, ch. 11, trans. Lynn Staley (New York: W.W. Norton, 2001), 18–20.

34 *The Chronicle of Adam of Usk*, ed. C. Given-Wilson (Oxford: Clarendon Press, 1977), 120.

35 "Shipman's Tale," l:416, 423–4, *Riverside Chaucer*, 208.

36 "Wife of Bath's Prologue," ll. 44a–44b, 523–4, *Riverside Chaucer*, 105, 112.

37 *Book of Margery Kempe*, trans. Staley, 20.

38 Ibid., 18.

39 Paris, Archives nationales, no. 206, p. 307in Alain Boureau, *The Lord's First Night: The Myth of the Droit de Cuissage*, trans. Lydia G. Cochrane (Chicago: University of Chicago Press, 1998), 103.

4

WOMEN OUTSIDE OF MARRIAGE

Women's sexual activity outside of marriage did not receive anything like the same toleration or acceptance that men's did. Some medieval medical theories held that women experienced more extensive pleasure in sex than men, or greater desire. In popular discourse, as we saw in Chapter 3, women appear as more lustful than men. If women's greater lust was understood as due to biological reasons, one might expect it to be excused as natural, and expect women's transgressions to be more easily accepted. Some churchmen, indeed, did teach that men had more responsibility for their lapses than did women, either because women were weaker than men and it was therefore less surprising if they were unable to maintain the standard of virtue, or because they were the passive partner:

> Is he who does the deed more to blame,
> Or she that does it not, but suffers what men do to her?
> It is man, who does the deed.[1]

Adam could be considered more responsible for original sin than Eve, because as the man he should have resisted more strongly.

For the most part, though, the perception of women's lustfulness did not lead to toleration of their non-marital sexual activity. Rather, the church and legislative authorities saw the high risk of this activity as a threat, and as a reason to keep women under strict control. The same was true of authorities in Judaism, where the law in theory allowed a man to divorce a wife who went out in public with her head uncovered, and forbade a woman to be alone in a room with a non-Jew, and in Islam, where there developed among urban elites an ideal of women's physical restriction to the home, although these were not applied in any way consistently in practice. Stories about women's lust became not a means of recognizing women as sexual beings, but an excuse for denying women independence in other areas of life. Indeed, when plague hit Cairo in 1438, the sultan blamed women's sexual activity, and banned all women from the streets and markets, causing serious economic dislocation even after an exemption was made for slaves and old women. Yet despite the distrust of women's sexuality, as we will see, there was also some grudging sense of women's entitlement to good treatment and to loving sexual relationships.

The stricter treatment of women's non-marital sexual behavior, compared to men's, was not just due to religious beliefs about their sinfulness and lust. It was also related to their role as preservers of the family honor. Today we may think of this as being true in Islamic societies and it was true there in the Middle Ages as well, but far from limited to them. While a man's honor and virtue could derive from many sources – his honesty in his commercial dealings, his military successes, his wisdom – a woman's honor and virtue were primarily sexual. They reflected not merely on the woman herself but also on her family. A man's misbehavior did not diminish the honor of his parents or wife the way a woman's did her parents or husband.

Chapter 1 noted that scholars of medieval sexuality have tended to organize their work around different kinds of deviance, and explained why I organized this book differently. However, this chapter is organized around different types of deviance, because this is largely unavoidable in talking or writing about medieval women's sexual behavior outside of marriage. There were two acceptable roles for women: the virgin or chaste widow (discussed in Chapter 2) and the wife (discussed in Chapter 3). Everything else (sometimes even if the woman did not consent to it) fell under one or another kind of transgression.

We should not forget that behavior considered sinful by some people, or under some conditions, could be normal and expected under others. For example, fornication could be a crime under church law, and both men and women who fornicated could be treated harshly, although women usually more so. And yet, at the same time, in many medieval communities sexual intercourse was a customary, if not entirely routine, prelude to marriage. Since we often know about illicit sexual behavior from court records, and since fornicators who subsequently married each other were less likely to be dragged into court than couples whose relationship had gone sour and in some way violated community standards, the records may be silent about situations in which this behavior was normal. Law, whether secular or ecclesiastical, represented the views of the elites (sometimes the views of the elites of a previous age), and people of all social levels did not necessarily share those attitudes. Further, the same laws could be enforced with different degrees of rigor at different times, representing perhaps changes in elite or popular attitudes, perhaps changes in legal procedure and language.

Women and adultery

Adultery by women was far more serious than that by men in all three cultural traditions. The church did preach equality in this area, that it was just as bad for a married man to violate his marriage vow as for a woman to do so. In practice, however, there was a very clear double standard. Even Thomas Aquinas, along with many other churchmen both in the eastern and western church, defined adultery as illicit intercourse with a married woman. Despite the moral equivalence in the eyes of most church authorities (and under canon law), the secular view of women as under the control of their husbands dramatically affected the way even the church's courts treated them. The examples here are drawn mainly from Christian societies in the later Middle Ages, but women's adultery was one area in which medieval attitudes remained fairly consistent.

This does not mean that men were not punished for adultery. They certainly were, and the man in an adulterous relationship might even be punished more often than the woman, or more heavily. But for most men who were prosecuted for adultery, it was independent of their own marital status. Their offense was violating the marriage of their female partners. It was the female adulterer's husband rather than the male adulterer's wife who was most often the aggrieved party. Men were not free to commit adultery against their own wives and marriages, but on the whole it was not as upsetting to medieval people as misbehavior of or with a married woman.

A classic example of a man's adultery with a married woman is the Biblical story of King David, who saw Bathsheba, the wife of his general Uriah the Hittite, in her bath, and summoned her and slept with her. David's transgression was not only adultery. After Bathsheba became pregnant, David summoned Uriah home in the hopes that he would sleep with his wife and the child could be passed off as his. Uriah, however, preferred to remain on a military footing: he camped outside the city and would not go home to his wife. David then commanded that Uriah and his troops be placed in the most dangerous part of the next battle, and Uriah was killed. David then married Bathsheba. David's advisor, the prophet Nathan, preached harshly against David's transgression, and Bathsheba's child died as a consequence. However, David repented and did public penance, and the next child of the marriage was Solomon, who became a great king.

This story was very popular among Christian bible illustrators, who loved to illustrate David's peeping at the bathing woman (see Figure 4.1, from an illustration accompanying the Penitential Psalms in a late-fifteenth-century *Book of Hours*). Indeed, there was a strong connection between women's bathing and sexuality. David's peeping stood in for the whole story, which was used as an example of great penance. David was thought to have been the author of the Psalms, and a subset of them were thought to have been written specifically out of penitence for this event. Jewish texts also took this as an ideal example of repentance, although some commentators claimed that it was customary for soldiers to give their wives a conditional divorce before going into battle (so that in case they went missing in action, the wife would be able to remarry) and therefore David's action was not adultery.[2] The point here is that neither the Bible nor medieval commentators stress

Figure 4.1 Bathsheba bathes while King David spies on her from a window, from a
late-fifteenth-century Book of Hours

Harvard, Houghton Library, MS Lat 251, fol. 47r

Bathsheba's sin in committing adultery. Although in most cases the woman received more opprobrium than the man, this was not so here, possibly because she acted only at the command of the king, and a great king at that. But it was also clear that David, although married, was not transgressing against his own wives. True, he lived in a polygamous culture, but his initial relationship with Bathsheba was outside of marriage, and medieval people were reading the story within monogamous cultures. Yet his sin was clearly understood as being his acts against Uriah: taking his wife and causing his death. Thus, although the guilt was placed more on the man than the woman in this story, the double standard is quite evident.

A woman's adultery was considered especially problematic in inheritance-based medieval societies because it cast doubt on the paternity of her children. When the daughters-in-law of Philip the Fair of France were accused in 1314 of adultery with two knights, the question of legitimacy rocked the dynasty. Marguerite of Navarre's daughter Jeanne, putatively fathered by Louis X, was not permitted to inherit the throne in part because of doubts about her legitimacy, although her exclusion was justified with language prohibiting a woman from inheriting the throne. This problem had become more acute after the church's assumption of control over marriage law in the eleventh and twelfth centuries; before that time it was possible for a man to repudiate an adulterous wife and remarry, but once the indissolubility of marriage had been established, a husband who was not sure of the paternity of his wife's children did not have the option of children with a new wife.

The importance of succession is one reason why, from the twelfth century onward, a number of medieval literary genres put great stress on women's adultery. The pastoral literature of the later Middle Ages, written to help parish priests with the cure of souls, focused especially on women's transgressions. One image that appeared frequently in medieval art as a personification of lust was that of a woman in the torments of hell, with snakes or toads suckling at her breasts; in one widely told story, a priest has a vision of his mother in hell tormented in this way, and she explains to him that it is punishment for the adulterine children she bore and nursed.

In adultery cases, although the man was seen as the active partner, committing an offense against the woman's husband, the woman's passivity in allowing it to be committed did not exonerate her from blame. A case from Venice in 1383 indicates how the courts used language to place responsibility: "In contempt of God and the state and the said Venerio [the husband], she allowed herself to be known carnally by the said Marco."[3] Even though the actual sexual activity always places women in the passive voice, they could still be blamed for seeking out and initiating the adulterous relationship. In Venice, however, they were not punished as severely as men until the 1360s; the offense was that of one man against another, although facilitated by a woman.

Men's fear of women's adultery was part of a more generalized fear and distrust of feminine independence – reflective perhaps of a high medieval society in which there were substantial opportunities for women, among both the aristocracy and the bourgeoisie, to wield power. In a misogynistic diatribe, the character "Jealous Husband" in the thirteenth-century French poem *Romance of the Rose* expresses the notion that married women are all looking to take lovers, and women who want to make themselves attractive do so only for lovers.

> Is it for me that you amuse yourself?
> Is it for me you lead so gay a life?
> Whom do you think that you're deceiving now?
> I never thought to see such dressing up
> As that with which you waken the desires
> Of ribald lechers . . .
> To dances and to church alike they wear
> Their finery, which surely they'd not do
> Did they not hope the men who see them there
> Would thus be pleased – more quickly be seduced.[4]

The fear that women who go out in public put themselves on display for sexual purposes could be taken to an extreme that required women to remain in the house. Nowhere in western Europe during the Middle Ages, not even Muslim Spain, developed a purdah system in which respectable women really did not go out of doors, and indeed women, especially those below the elite levels of society, performed a variety of economic functions that required them to move about and deal with the public. Nevertheless, there was always a suspicion that they were doing it for display, as the fable of the singed cat, retold throughout the Middle Ages, indicates. A cat complains to another that his wife will not stay at home but is always roaming around, and his friend tells him to singe her fur. The point to be taken from this is that an unadorned woman will not want to go out and be seen. As Odo of Cheriton (d. 1247) drew the moral:

> Thus many men have beautiful wives, sisters, and daughters; when these women have beautiful tresses and beautiful clothing, they venture forth from their homes. . . . Hence every paterfamilias ought to knot up the hair of these women into a bun and scorch it. And he ought to dress them in skins rather than in precious garments. For thus they will stay at home.[5]

Many towns across later medieval Europe had sumptuary laws which regulated what women of different social levels could wear, with the explicit purpose of distinguishing between respectable matrons and loose women. In some cases, prostitutes had to wear certain identifying garments or were not allowed to wear particular furs or luxury fabrics. In some Italian towns, however, particular expensive types of garments were limited to prostitutes only, perhaps based on the town authorities' hope that women would not impoverish their husbands by insisting on the latest fashions if these were connected with immorality. The husbands' concerns about wives' fidelity here merged with their economic interests.

In southeastern Europe the connection between female public behavior and adultery was more explicit. Under Byzantine law if a woman slept somewhere other than under her husband's or parents' roof, attended various public events, or went to a public bath, she was deemed guilty of adultery. In commenting on this, Slavic clerics listed different sorts of public events that constituted proof of infidelity. A husband could repudiate a wife who left his home or who attended particular festivals. Ashkenazic rabbis (a Jewish culture in which women had more freedom of movement than in Sephardic) could argue over whether a woman who was raped during a journey was guilty of adultery for putting herself in such a position.

Even within medieval cultures that considered female adultery such a disruptive force within society, however, there are a few hints that people in western Europe (or at least the women themselves) sometimes thought it was excusable. Literary texts do not reflect social practice on issues like this, but they may reveal the limits of what people in the culture could imagine or sympathize with. Several of the lais of Marie de France, a French poet of the twelfth century, tell of women married to men whom they do not love and who mistreat them. In *Yonec*, for example, an old man marries a young woman and locks her in a tower for seven years:

> The lady lived in great sorrow,
> with tears and sighs and weeping;
> she lost her beauty as one does who cares nothing for it.
> She would have preferred
> death to take her quickly.[6]

She eventually takes a lover. Here the message seems to be that the husband who does not treat his wife well only gets what is coming to him if she is unfaithful. Women are entitled to love, and if they do not get it from their husbands, they will get it elsewhere.

Another high medieval literary genre often connected with a positive valuation of at least some women's adultery is the poetry of "courtly love," not a medieval term but rather one coined in the nineteenth century. This body of poetry is connected in particular with the troubadours of southern France. It often takes on the voice of a man of subordinate social position, addressed to a married woman of superior position, and seeking sexual union with her.

> In good faith, without deceit,
> I love the best and most beautiful.

My heart sighs, my eyes weep,
because I love her so much, and I suffer for it.
This love wounds my heart with a sweet taste, so gently,
I die of grief a hundred times a day
and a hundred times revive with joy.

. . .

Good lady, I ask you for nothing
but to take me for your servant,
for I will serve you as my good lord,
whatever wages come my way.
Behold me at your command, a man to rely on,
before you, o noble, gentle, courteous, and gay.[7]

Some of the poetry was written by women, and refers to married women
taking lovers.

I'd like to hold my knight
in my arms every evening, naked,
for he'd be overjoyed
were I only serving as his pillow,
and he makes me more radiant
than Floris his Blancheflor.
To him I grant my heart, my love,
my mind, my eyes, my life.
Fair, agreeable, good friend,
when will I have you in my power,
lie beside you for an evening,
and kiss you amorously?
Be sure I'd feel a strong desire
to have you in my husband's place
provided you had promised me
to do everything I wished.[8]

Some scholars took quite literally the relationships suggested by the poems
and argued that adultery was common and accepted, at least at southern
French courts. They took seriously the "rules of love" put forward by the
twelfth-century author Andreas Capellanus in his *De arte honesti amandi*,
a work translated under the title *The Art of Courtly Love*. Andreas also
spoke of "courts of love" at which noble ladies gave decisions in love
cases:

A certain lady had a proper enough lover, but was afterward, through
no fault of her own, married to an honorable man, and she avoided
her love and denied him his usual solaces. But Lady Ermengarde of

Narbonne demonstrated the lady's bad character in these words: "The later contracting of a marital union does not properly exclude an early love except in cases where the woman gives up love entirely and is determined by no means to love any more."[9]

Other scholars, however, have argued that a close reading of the poems does not indicate that the love expressed there was adulterous, or indeed corresponded to any identifiable social phenomenon. Some have treated the courtly love phenomenon as merely a literary game, arguing that given general attitudes toward female adultery in medieval society the kinds of relationships discussed in the poetry could not have been acceptable. A number of explanations have been put forward for the prominence of this sort of poetry in Occitan (southern French) society. The impetus for it seems to have come from literary genres known in Muslim Spain, where female adultery certainly was not socially acceptable. The south of France was the hotbed of the Cathar heresy, which was interpreted as teaching that adultery was no worse than marital sex, as long as conception did not take place, so the suggestion has been made that this formed the social backdrop to this body of literature. More recently Frederic Cheyette has argued that this love poetry was not simply a way of doing honor to a husband through praise of his wife (as has been suggested), but rather doing honor to the lady herself. In the south of France inheritance law allowed women to hold land, and many women were powerful lords in their own right. The expressions of love and loyalty in the poems could be an expression of political relations in the affective realm.

Adulterous love also appears prominently in other types of literature, particularly the Arthurian stories that center on the love triangles of Lancelot/Guinevere/Arthur or Tristan/Iseult/Mark. These stories, which likely originated in the north of France or in Britain, describe the same kind of asymmetric adultery (the wife of a powerful man, involved with a subordinate man) as the love lyrics. Not all these tales involving "courtly love" were adulterous. Stories like that of Erec and Enide, told in French by Chrétien de Troyes and in German by Hartmann von Aue, present love between a man and a woman that ends in marriage, although not always entirely happy marriage.

Whatever the origins of the love poetry, adultery was not widely accepted, even in the south of France. Indeed, a thirteenth-century book of legal customs from the town of Agen in Aquitaine, the region where the adulterous love lyric was born, depicts harsh punishment of adulterers (see Figure 4.2): a man and woman are marched through the streets naked, tied together at the genitals. Shame punishments like this were common across Europe for a variety of offenses; what is notable here is that the municipality, not just the church, was punishing adultery.

Figure 4.2 Punishment of adulterers. Livre des coutumes, Agen, Bibliothèque municipal, MS 42, fol. 39v, detail.

However, just as it was socially acceptable for Hollywood celebrities to
have affairs and divorces long before it became possible for other Americans
to do so without stigma, it may be that people were willing to accept that
the mores of the aristocracy were different. Even among this group, however, it cannot have been the norm. Furthermore, although this poetry seems
to place women in a position of power – the man is begging the woman for
her love – it is putting her on a pedestal and objectifying her rather than
according her any real power in the relationship. As the "court of love"
cases show, the genre considered it the woman's obligation to grant her
favors if the man was worthy:

> Another question like this came up: two men who were in all things
> absolutely equal began to pay court at the same time and in the
> same manner and demanded urgently that they be loved. Therefore
> it was asked which man's love could be chosen in such a case. We
> are taught by the admonition of the same countess [Marie of Cham-
> pagne] that in such a case the man who asks first should be given
> preference; but if their proposals seem to be simultaneous, it is not
> unfair to leave it to the woman to choose the one of the two toward
> whom she finds her heart inclining.[10]

The woman had a choice only if all other factors were equal; otherwise, according to these decisions as reported by Andreas Capellanus, love was a woman's obligation. That this was so even when it was adulterous is indicated by another case:

> A certain knight was in love with a woman who had given her love to another man, but he got from her this much hope of her love – that if it should ever happen that she lose the love of her beloved, then without a doubt her love would go to this man. A little while after this the woman married her lover. The other knight then demanded that she give him the fruit of the hope she had granted him, but this she absolutely refused to do, saying that she had not lost the love of her lover. In this affair the Queen gave her decision as follows: "We dare not oppose the opinion of the Countess of Champagne, who ruled that love can exert no power between husband and wife. Therefore we recommend that the lady should grant the love she has promised."[11]

These supposed decisions can hardly have been real advice as to how medieval women were supposed to conduct their love affairs. If the courts ever actually existed, they were a game, dealing with theoretical cases. Nevertheless, the game was important enough to influence the writing of love literature for the next three centuries, in which adulterous love was glorified.

The glorification of love, adulterous or not, is not necessarily favorable to women. Although the ascetic literature of the Desert Fathers (Chapter 2) is highly misogynistic, blaming women for men's temptations and sins, this does not mean un-ascetic love poetry cannot be misogynistic too. The woman is often cast as cruel or dangerous even when she is an object of desire. Poetry in praise of a woman's beauty does not necessarily represent respect for her as a person in the modern sense, and indeed, as in some medieval Hebrew love poetry, can stress that the beauty is deceptive:

> Balm [lies] in her face and on the thread of her lips –
> Death [lies] in her eyes and under her skirts.[12]

The idealized woman is as much a stereotype as the sinful woman, and if she is sinful (adulterous) as well as beautiful, the genre that focuses on her cannot be depicted as pro-woman. Scholars whose writing glorifies medieval love need to keep in mind the gendered nature of that love and that it expresses the feelings of men much more than women.

The frame story of the best known literary work from the Arabic Middle Ages, the *One Thousand and One Nights*, also hinges on female adultery. This compilation existed in various recensions from the ninth century on, although the versions that survive are from the later Middle Ages.

A king, betrayed by his wife, visits his brother and observes the brother's wife and her servants in the garden having sex with male African slaves. The myth of African sexual potency that haunted the era of the transatlantic slave trade can already be seen here. The brothers then go in search of a man whose plight is worse than theirs and encounter a woman imprisoned in a chest by a djinn who nevertheless had managed to have sex with a hundred different men. This sends the Persian king over the top; he despairs of ever finding a faithful woman, and he determines to marry a different woman each day and kill her after their wedding night, so that she will not have a chance to betray him. This goes on until the vizier's daughter Sharzad (Scheherezade) volunteers to marry him, and tells him such captivating stories that each morning he decides to keep her alive for another day in order to find out what happens. The bulk of the work is the stories, some of which involve sexual escapades, including jealous husbands whose jealousy turns out to be wrong. But all these stories are set within the frame of woman's sexual rapacity and unavoidable betrayal.

With the French fabliaux, a genre of the twelfth and thirteenth centuries, it is sometimes difficult to know whether the audience is meant to be sympathetic to the unfaithful wife or not. In one story, "The Bourgeoise of Orléans," a jealous husband gets beaten by his friends and relatives and is grateful for it. His niece, whom he persuades to spy on his wife, tells him that the wife has a plan to have a young scholar visit her at night when the husband is away. The husband pretends to leave on a trip, but comes back in disguise. The wife recognizes him, pretends to take him for the young man, and says she will hide him in an attic room until the household has gone to bed. She then goes to the hall and informs her husband's relatives and servants that a student has been bothering her by begging for her love, and that she has locked him in an attic room. They beat the supposed student, actually the husband, and throw him on the dungheap. She spends the rest of the night with the actual student. When the husband returns the next day, his nephews tell him that his wife had them beat her would-be lover. He is pleased with how well she handled the matter, and is never jealous again, although the wife continues to see her lover secretly. Perhaps a medieval audience would not in fact have sympathized with the wife, but they certainly would not have sympathized with the husband, who was seen as getting his deserts for his jealous behavior.

The sympathy was particularly likely to be on the side of the woman in a situation where a young woman was married to an older man, as in the fabliau literature, or as in the Arthurian love triangles. This type of story might appeal to a masculine sensibility, expressing the idea that young (and beautiful) women should not be monopolized by old men. But one can also see echoes of a sympathy toward women: the idea that they are entitled to love, which they were not likely to have in an arranged marriage (as the marriage between a younger woman and an older man was likely to be).

129

Several of Geoffrey Chaucer's *Canterbury Tales* provide somewhat sympathetic portraits of adulterous women. The story of May and January in the "Merchant's Tale" is one in which an old man makes a fool of himself by marrying a younger woman. She, understandably enough, is not attracted to him:

> God knows what May thought in her heart
> When she saw him sitting up in his shirt
> In his nightcap, and with his neck lean;
> She praises not his playing worth a bean.[13]

May takes a young lover. The pagan gods Pluto and Proserpine observe the couple having sex in a pear tree in the presence of January, who has gone blind. Pluto restores January's sight so that he can see what his wife is up to, but Proserpine grants May the wit to explain away her activity so that she gets away with it. The story was meant to be humorous and its purpose was not to license adultery by aristocratic women, but it does imply that an old man with a young wife was more or less asking for trouble – not necessarily because young women are especially sinful, but because old men who are so lascivious that they imagine they can satisfy a wife are ridiculous.

A similar situation appears in the "Miller's Tale," in which a young wife, Alison, makes a fool of her carpenter husband. Alison takes as her lover the young clerk who lodges in their home. The clerk persuades the older man that a flood is imminent, and when the time comes the three hide themselves in tubs hanging from the ceiling. Alison and the clerk, Nicholas, sneak out and spend the night together. While the cuckolded old man is clearly a figure of fun here, the young clerkly lover is as well. Another potential lover, Absolon, sings below the window and asks Alison for a kiss. She sticks her rear end out the window so that he ends up kissing it instead of her mouth. When he realizes what has happened, he goes to fetch a hot plow coulter from a blacksmith. Returning, he asks for another kiss. Nicholas presents his buttocks for the kiss this time. Nicholas ends up being burnt; the husband is injured when he hears Nicholas yelling for water and, thinking the flood has finally arrived, cuts the rope that tethers his tub to the ceiling; and Absolon has been shamed by the kiss. Alison is the only one who emerges from the adventure unscathed, except in terms of her sexual honor.

> He [the carpenter] was held mad in all the town
> . . .
> Thus the carpenter's wife was screwed
> Despite all his guarding and his jealousy
> And Absolon has kissed her lower eye
> And Nicholas is scalded on the butt.
> This tale is done.[14]

The reader is hardly meant to admire Alison, but neither does the tale moralize that adulterous women come to a bad end. She is young and pretty, and this is the kind of behavior that one can expect from her.

We do not know how much the sympathy that some literature expressed toward adulterous women extended to leniency in practice: there was much fulminating against adulterous women as well. As a mortal sin, adultery demanded confession and penance. After the Fourth Lateran Council of 1215 demanded regular, annual confession from all Christians, a great body of literature grew up providing advice to confessors and sermon stories to encourage people to confess. Although the church certainly did not condone women's adultery, priests were supposed to keep all confessions confidential. This could raise problems when a woman confessed to adultery: the confessor was supposed to impose a harsh penance for this serious sin, but could not impose a penance that would make clear to her husband that she had committed a serious offense. This demanded some ingenuity on the part of the confessor, but the fact that it was demanded indicates a real interest in repentance, which could only be promoted if the offended husband did not know. A great many exempla pointed out that the serious sin of adultery could indeed be atoned for by confession, sincere repentance, and penance. To stress the power of confession, the gravest sin made the most striking demonstration, and often that grave sin was women's adultery.

The somewhat sympathetic treatment of adultery in the confessional compared to the harsher treatment in church courts illustrates how problematic it can be to talk about "the church's position," let alone "medieval attitudes." Churchmen operated as teachers, as arbiters of sin, and as maintainers of social and moral order, but it was generally not the same individuals in these roles, and the goals could be very different.

Unmarried women and sexual activity

Restrictions on the behavior of women who were not married were not as severe as those on married women. Among some groups, the aristocracy in particular, a daughter's virginity might be important in making a good marriage, and Jewish and Muslim elites too might guard their unmarried daughters carefully. At other levels of Christian society, however, premarital sex, or what was called "simple fornication," between a single woman and a single man, was reasonably common. This is not to say it was totally accepted – much of what we know about it comes from court records from the late Middle Ages in which people were fined for it, and we have even less data from earlier periods – but it was by no means outrageous. In many instances, however, the woman involved bore the brunt of the penalty.

In England in the high Middle Ages one of the distinguishing features of villeinage (unfree status) was a payment called *legerwite* or *leyrwite*. This fine was payable by an unmarried female serf who engaged in sexual activity. There was no such fine payable by the male partner. That only the woman and not the man was fined could be related to the problem of evidence. If an unmarried woman became pregnant, that was pretty clear evidence that she had fornicated. With a man the proof was not nearly as obvious. The purpose may have been to discourage the bearing of illegitimate children, who put a burden on the community. But the fine may also reflect an attitude about the sexuality – or the fertility – of female serfs as the property of the master, to be recompensed if taken without permission. In that sense, the woman was paying for her independence of choice. Judith Bennett has suggested that in leyrwite, the lord was taking a share in what he saw as the profit of fornication. Medieval people tended to assume that women received gifts in courtship, if not outright payment for sex, and that such gifts were a motivating factor for women to participate in illicit sex. The lord may merely have been claiming his share of his serf's income. What leyrwite is *not* is a remnant of the *droit de seigneur* (or *ius primae noctis*), the lord's right to have sex with the bride on her wedding night. There is no evidence that such a right ever existed (see Chapter 3).

Leyrwite fines were levied in the manorial court. Church courts also fined people for fornication, and here the punishment for men and women was more likely to be similar. It is likely that in many instances the fornication was taken as a prelude to marriage. Cases involving disputes over the validity of marriage often include testimony about sexual relations between the partners before the alleged marriage took place. From early modern England, when we have parish registers with dates of baptisms and marriages, 10 to 30 percent of brides appear to have been pregnant at the time of marriage; couples may have been intending eventual marriage but postponing it until pregnancy forced them into it, and this pattern may well have held true in the Middle Ages as well.

The numbers may have been lower in southern Europe, where the age of marriage for women was substantially lower so that women were more likely to be living with, and more closely supervised by, their families until the time of their marriage. However, there too there is significant evidence, for example from late medieval Venice, that couples at the lower levels of society lived together in what the church courts would consider fornication until they saw the necessity to marry. Where dowries or children were not an issue, formal marriage may not have been that important. Indeed, there are examples of couples with children who were not formally married, whose situation did not occasion much concern until the man abandoned the woman and she sued for support. In one case involving a woman of "good condition" who came to Venice under a promise of marriage and bore five children to her partner, he was prosecuted for fornication, had to pay to support their children, and had to provide her a payment "for her modesty," which would have been enough of a dowry for her to marry as a non-virgin.[15] It may be that the authorities prosecuted fornication, when it came to their attention in cases like this, not to prevent it, but to make sure that it kept on the regular track toward marriage.

That fornication was considered often simply a prelude to marriage is also indicated by a penalty that was common in the English church courts, abjuration *sub pena nubendi* (on pain of marriage). According to canon law, as we have seen, marriage vows expressed in the present tense ("I take thee to my wedded husband") created a valid marriage immediately; but vows or promises in the future tense ("I will take thee to my wedded wife"), or conditional vows no matter what the condition, created a valid marriage immediately upon the occurrence of sexual intercourse. Thus, a couple who abjured each other *sub pena nubendi* would be made to exchange words of future consent. If they did have sex again, they would not just be obliged to marry each other, their marriage would already be accomplished and indissoluble. The church debated the validity of a marriage between two people who had previously committed adultery together during the lifetime of a now deceased spouse (ultimately concluding that it was acceptable as long as they had not hastened the death of the spouse), but there was little debate over turning fornication into marriage. The purpose here seems to have been to prevent concubinage or living together without marriage rather than to prevent casual sex.

Those women most likely to engage in sex as a prelude to marriage were probably wage workers, both urban and rural, who in some places probably made up the majority of the unmarried female population, and this would be true of women from all religious communities. Daughters living with their parents would have less opportunity; women of the aristocracy generally married younger. In Paris in the late fifteenth century, the women prosecuted in the church courts for sexual offenses (carnal knowledge, being maintained by a man) or who brought suits themselves to enforce alleged marriages tended to be living outside their parents' homes, whether as servants or in some other capacity. Some of these alleged marriages were claimed to have been contracted quite informally, and it may be the case that there was a deliberate gray area in which one partner considered the couple married and the other did not. For example, Colin Maillard testified that the (unnamed) woman he was with told him she would have sex with him only in the name of matrimony. Colin said he would not marry her, but they had intercourse anyway. She now sought a declaration that their marriage was valid, since a conditional promise followed by intercourse made a binding marriage, whereas he claimed that since he had made no promise there was no marriage. He may, of course, have been lying outright, but it is also possible that both parties believed they were telling the truth and even that they had deliberately left things ambiguous. She could have sincerely believed, or hoped, that his having intercourse with her meant that he had changed his mind about the conditions, or he could have believed or hoped that she had changed hers.[16]

From Venice we have a case of a woman from a higher social level whose father wanted to dispose of her in marriage but who acted on her own preference. Elisabetta Badoer, from a noble family in the mid-fifteenth century, became involved with Pirano Contarini, illegitimate son of a leading family. He claimed that she had sex with him and indeed secretly married him; her father, concerned that this story would spoil her chances of contracting a better marriage, had her examined by women who testified that she was still a virgin. In the legal case between the father and the putative lover or husband, the woman's own wishes were not primarily at issue. Yet, although Pirano lost in court and Elisabetta's father arranged another marriage for her, it was plausible enough that this young noblewoman would take a lover as a prelude to marriage that the highest court in Venice considered the case.

Wage workers or servants, who lived not with their family but with their employer or with other workers, would have more opportunity both to meet potential partners and to have sex with them. There are no statistics for the incidence of non-marital sex among wage workers, but poems and ballads like "A Servant-Girl's Holiday," from fifteenth-century England, celebrate their sexual activity:

> Jack will pay for my share
> On Sunday at the ale-feast;
> Jack will souse well my throat
> Every good holiday.
> Soon he will take me by the hand
> And he will lay me on the ground
> So that my buttocks are in the dirt
> Upon this high holiday.
> In he thrust and out he drew
> And ever I lay beneath him:
> "By God's death, you do me wrong
> Upon this high holiday!"
> Soon my womb began to swell
> As great as a bell.
> I dare not tell my lady
> What happened to me this holiday.[17]

The pastourelles, twelfth-century French poems that celebrate the seduction or rape of a shepherdess by an aristocrat (see Chapter 5), assume that she would be sexually involved with a man of her own class as well – in a number of them she calls upon her lover to rescue her.

Chaucer's *Canterbury Tales*, once again, provide us with an example that may indicate how peasant sex was regarded. In the "Reeve's Tale," a miller has cheated two clerks who brought him grain to grind. To take their revenge, while spending the night at his house and sleeping in the same

134

room as the miller, his wife, and his daughter, one of them has sex with the wife and the other with the daughter. They end up beating the miller. The story tells us a number of things. The women's consent is irrelevant; they end up enjoying the encounter, and Chaucer does not pay any attention to whether they welcomed it in the first place. This is obviously not a reflection of the actual attitudes of non-elite women but rather an indication of how women's consent gets lost because they are always perceived as passive.

But the story also tells us that having sex with the miller's wife and daughter is not as big a deal as we might expect. The clerks do not do it to shame the miller, but rather to claim some compensation for what the miller has stolen from them; they receive restitution from something that is in a sense his property.

> Thus is the proud miller well beaten
> And has lost the grinding of the wheat,
> And paid for the whole supper
> Of Alan and John who beat him well.
> His wife is screwed, and his daughter too.
> Lo, see what happens when a miller is false![18]

The women are not described as having lost anything, either virginity or fidelity. Again, of course, this story was written by a court poet as humor, and does not reflect the way an actual peasant household would have experienced the situation. It does, however, tell us that not all of medieval society bought into the notion that women's chastity was the most important value; to the upper classes the chastity of artisan or peasant women was largely inconsequential. And this would be particularly true of the lowest class of women of all: the enslaved (discussed here in the context of rape and coercion). Slavery was widely practiced in Mediterranean Europe, in both Christian and Muslim societies, and about 80 percent of the enslaved were women. Prices were considerably higher for women who were considered more attractive, and it is likely that many of them were purchased for sexual service. Sexual service could be demanded as well from women who were not purchased for that reason. In Muslim law men were permitted to have sex with women they owned; in Christian communities the penalties for having sex with someone else's slave imply that one could have sex with one's own with impunity. Enslaved women were vulnerable not only to their owners and the owner's family and friends but were also at risk because they were the ones who did much of the daily business outside the home.

One reason why slave women – cast as other by their legal status if not by their ethnic group – were in demand for daily activities was the restrictions placed on women of the slaveholding classes. In middling as well as elite families, women's chastity could be highly consequential. In southern Europe, much more so than in the English and northern French examples just discussed, a woman's chastity could be the guarantor of her family's honor, and traditionally the taking of her virginity required vengeance, which could be replaced by a court verdict. A case in Venice in 1345 is typical: Filippo di Vinzono was accused of seducing the daughter of Guidono Frami, and "had sexual intercourse with her several times with great damage and loss to the said Master Guidono."[19] In late-fifteenth-century Paris, accusations that a woman had been deflowered were among the most serious heard by the archdeacon's court, requiring detailed testimony. The records here do not mention honor but focus on the more prosaic question of dowry. Sometimes the woman who claimed to have been deflowered sought marriage with the man in question. Sometimes he was already married, or a priest; in these cases she sought from him a dowry to enable her to marry elsewhere. Not being a virgin was considered to hurt her marriage chances. The man's response in these cases was often to claim that she was not a virgin by bringing testimony about her reputation or even from men who claimed to have previously had sex with her.

Concubinage and quasi-marriage

Non-marital sex was not always a prelude to marriage. One group for whom it was not comprised those women whom people in the Middle Ages called "concubines." In the early Middle Ages, as we have seen in Chapter 3, concubinage was a quasi-marital relationship. In the central and later Middle Ages, the term could mean several different things. It could simply mean "girlfriend" or "woman whom one sleeps with," and in this case the concubine of a single man could be a potential marriage partner. Just because both partners were single, however, does not mean that they necessarily envisioned marriage, especially if they came from families of very different social standing.

A concubine could also be an enslaved member of a household, with lesser status than a wife but nevertheless a quasi-permanent connection to the owner. Under Islamic law an enslaved woman who bore her master's child was freed. Even if not free a woman in this situation could enjoy considerable status. The practice of married men keeping concubines in their home was largely limited to Muslims and to Jews in Muslim regions. However, long-term relationships with enslaved people were not unknown to Christians. The merchant Francesco Datini of Prato had a son with an enslaved woman while he was living abroad as a representative of his trading house. When Datini returned to Prato, he sent for the boy and his wife raised him; the mother was married off. It is never clear, of course, what kind of relationship a merchant like this could have with an enslaved woman slave; the disparity in status meant that it could never be fully consensual.

A concubine could also mean a free woman who had a sexual relationship with a married man, what in later times would have been called a mistress.

Sometimes these relationships were of long standing and the woman bore several children. The most famous case was probably Katharine Swynford, who eventually became the third wife of John of Gaunt, the powerful son of Edward III, uncle of Richard II, and father of Henry IV of England. Four children were born from the relationship during the lifetime of Gaunt's second wife. The children were subsequently legitimized by letters patent of Richard II (under English common law, unlike canon law, children were not automatically legitimated by the subsequent marriage of their parents, so legitimation was necessary to inherit land). The letters patent did not mention the right to inherit the throne, and Henry IV in confirming the letters explicitly excluded it; nevertheless, Swynford's great-grandson, claiming descent from Edward III through her, successfully claimed the throne in 1485 as Henry VII and founded the Tudor dynasty.

Similar situations of concubinage between a man of higher status and a woman of lower status can be found in late medieval towns, where a woman might enter a relationship with a man who was far too high in the social hierarchy to marry her, but who would live with her until he married and provided for her thereafter. She would return to the marriage pool well dowered. Carol Lansing documents a case from Bologna in 1285 in which one Zannos was accused by Divitia of raping her after promising her marriage; he said that he had promised, rather, to take her as an *amica* (girlfriend or concubine) until they had children. "When I have children from you I will have just cause to ask my father's permission to take you as my wife without a dowry and then I'll take you as my wife." The point was not to determine whether they were actually married, but rather whether he was guilty of rape. A woman without resources, as Divitia was, might have a hard time being taken seriously here in any case, but the prospect of a man getting his father's permission to marry his concubine in order to legitimate his children was apparently plausible enough that Zannos won his case. Lansing suggests that such situations, where couples married after children arrived, may have been common village practice.[20]

A concubine could also be a woman living in a domestic partnership – essentially, in the social role of a wife – with a man who was for some reason unable to marry her. Because in medieval Christianity there was no divorce as we know it (as discussed above, p. 83, what they sometimes called divorce was what we would call annulment, and required proof that the marriage was not valid in the first place), many people unofficially separated from a spouse with whom they were not happy. These people were not free to marry again. A woman who separated from her husband in this way and lived with another man would be called an adulteress if found out. An unmarried woman who lived with a man separated from his wife, however, would more likely be called a concubine.

One of the most vituperated types of woman in the Middle Ages was the "priest's concubine." In many cases these women were de facto wives, and "priest's domestic partner" probably more accurately reflects their role to a modern reader than the medieval term "concubine," which has connotations of sex only. Earlier, clerical marriage had been prohibited, but if priests married anyway the marriages were regarded as valid. From the twelfth century on, after clerical celibacy began to be enforced, many writers made a concerted effort to blame these women for polluting the church and corrupting priests. Preachers attacked them for their greed, accusing them of despoiling the goods of the church. In one popular exemplum, told by the fourteenth-century English exemplum collector John of Bromyard among others, a priest tells his concubine he must leave her because she has made him so poor he has nothing left but a cloak. She weeps, and he thinks it is because she is losing him, but in fact it is because she did not despoil him of the cloak too. Bromyard tells another anecdote in which a priest chooses to give up his church rather than leave his concubine; she, however, immediately leaves him because she can no longer profit from him.[21]

Although the concubine's greed was a common theme, her lust was important too. Bromyard placed ten of his fourteen stories about the damnation of priests' sexual partners in his chapter on lust, not greed. By treating "concubines" as gold-diggers (despite the fact that most parish priests didn't have much to despoil and would hardly be tempting targets for such women) and as whores, rather than as unofficial wives, celibate men displaced onto women the responsibility not only for their sexual desires but also for any wish they might have for a normal household and family life.

One might guess that the priest himself would be more to blame in either a casual or a long-term relationship, since he was breaking a vow while his partner was not, yet to late medieval writers the woman was more responsible. One fifteenth-century English handbook for parish priests states: "If any [priest] commit fornication or adultery with a woman through sudden chance or by the woman's manipulation and not of his own purpose or deliberation, then much less penance should be enjoined to him."[22]

One priest's concubine whose words have come down to us is Béatrice de Planissoles of Montaillou in the south of France. In 1320 her whole village was suspected of heresy and interrogated by the Inquisition. The widowed Béatrice, although a petty noblewoman, mixed socially with the less elite people of the village, and became the lover of the local priest. As she told the inquisitor (perhaps shaping her story to what he wanted to hear):

> Later, around Easter, he visited me several times, and he asked me to give myself to him. I said one day that he so bothered me in my home that I would rather give myself to four men than to a single priest because I had heard it said that a woman who gave herself to a priest could not see the face of God. To which he answered that

I was an ignorant fool because the sin is the same for a woman to know her husband or another man, and the same whether the man were husband or priest. It was even a greater sin with a husband he said, because the wife did not think that she had sinned with her husband but realized it with other men. The sin was therefore greater in the first case.

This, of course, was not a typical argument for seduction; Pierre Clergue was a Cathar heretic, although serving as the local parish priest. He told her that:

a man and a woman could freely commit any sort of sin as long as they lived in this world and act entirely according to their pleasure. It was sufficient that at their death they be received into the sect or the faith of the good Christians [Cathars].

With these arguments, she testified, he convinced her, and he came to spend the night with her two or three times a week over a period of a year and a half. "He even knew me carnally Christmas night and still this priest said the mass the next morning although there were other priests present."[23] She also had sex with him in a church. During their sexual encounters he wore an herbal amulet to prevent conception.

Béatrice also revealed that during her husband's lifetime she had been raped by Pierre Clergue's cousin Raimond, who then kept her as a concubine after her husband's death. The inquisitor, Jacques Fournier, Bishop of Pamiers, was much more interested in pursuing the heretical opinions Béatrice had learned from Pierre and others than in the sexual activity, and the Inquisition record indicates remorse only for the opinions.

Another one of the few medieval women to express herself on the question of concubinage was the famous Heloise. Heloise was the very bright niece of Fulbert, a canon in twelfth-century Paris, who believed that she had the potential to be educated. He hired as her tutor Peter Abelard, who had acquired quite a reputation as a theologian but was short of funds. The two were left alone together for their tutoring sessions – apparently Fulbert did not consider a chaperone necessary. However, as Abelard later described it:

First we were joined in one house, then in one heart. Under the pretext of study, we had all our time free for love, and in our classroom all the seclusion love could ever want. With our books open before us, we exchanged more words of love than of lessons, more kisses than concepts. My hands wandered more to her breasts than our books, and love turned our eyes to each other more than reading kept them on the page.

Abelard makes it sound as though the desire were mutual. However, he earlier describes the whole situation as part of his plan:

> Now, having carefully considered all the things that usually serve to attract a lover, I concluded that she was the best one to bring to my bed. I was sure it would be easy: I was famous myself at the time, young, and exceptionally good-looking, and could not imagine that any woman I thought worthy of my love would turn me down. . . . I was all on fire for the girl and needed a way I could get to know her on a private and daily basis to win her over. So I approached her uncle. . . . The simplicity of the man just staggered me, as if he had set a ravening wolf to watch over a lamb. When he put her in my hands not only to teach but to discipline as well, what else was he doing but giving me complete freedom, even if I never took advantage of it, to convince her by force if more gentle inducements did not prevail?[24]

For a teacher to beat his student would have been routine in the Middle Ages, and not considered abusive; Abelard's connection of the beatings to sex, however, is unusual.

The sort of relationship Abelard and Heloise had might be called sexual harassment in the early twenty-first century even if it was consensual on the student's part, because the hierarchical relationship could be seen as inherently coercive. Though Abelard was hired privately and had no institutional hold over Heloise, her uncle gave him full charge of her, with permission to chastise her physically. Given that she never claimed to have been coerced or seduced, however, the relationship must be seen as (at least eventually) consensual; she might have had a hard time avoiding it, had she wished, but she did not claim that she wished to, and to say that it was totally coercive robs her of any agency.

In any case, the aftermath of the liaison is well known. Heloise became pregnant, and the two married secretly after she gave birth. Upset about the marriage (perhaps because he mistrusted Abelard's motives for secrecy), Fulbert hired men to castrate Abelard. The couple subsequently took up the monastic life, and a series of letters between the two of them survives. The authenticity of Heloise's letters has been doubted, some scholars believing that Abelard wrote the entire correspondence, but Barbara Newman and others have convincingly argued for her authorship.

Abelard, in his autobiographical *Historia Calamitatum*, tells us that Heloise at first refused to marry him, arguing that it would take him away from his scholarship and tie him to domestic duties. "What husband could ever concentrate on philosophy or scripture and still put up with babies howling, nurses mumbling their lullabies, and a riotous gang of servants tramping all throughout the house?"[25] She said that she would rather be his concubine or whore than his wife, because then his love would be freely given rather than constrained by a bond. If we assume that the words as he reports them are indeed hers, we are left with a woman who believed that a couple can have a fulfilling emotional and sexual relationship without marriage. The highly educated Heloise (who eventually became an abbess), was hardly a typical medieval woman, but she does show us the range of possibilities for medieval views.

It may be, too, that Heloise saw a traditional marriage as limiting not only for Abelard but also for herself. If she thought being a husband would tie him down, perhaps she did not want to be tied down as a wife either, with all the domestic obligations that implied; when she spoke of the distractions of children, it may have been her own distractions she meant. Priests' concubines seem in many cases to have been wives in all but name, in effect domestic partners. However, Heloise seems to have had something else in mind, something that would free both her and Abelard from the routines of domesticity. She later expressed regret for her sexual transgression as would only be appropriate for a nun:

There were many earlier sins, I know
for which I bear responsibility –
my devotion to the pleasures of the flesh,
whose consequences have become a fitting punishment for me.[26]

But it was not a temporary lapse, but rather a real passion that she had hoped to develop in some way other than that of traditional marriage.

Prostitution

Another group of women for whom fornication did not constitute a prelude to marriage were prostitutes. The Latin word for them, *meretrix* or whore, was also used for priests' concubines; the Hebrew word, *zonah*, could be used for any sexually transgressive woman. It is often extraordinarily difficult to tell when a medieval text is referring to a woman who took money for sex and when it is simply referring to a heterosexually active single woman. Canon lawyers in the Middle Ages could not even agree among themselves as to what constituted prostitution. They generally did not make the acceptance of money the deciding factor; rather, promiscuity was key, but they disagreed as to how many men a woman had to have sex with to be considered a prostitute, some suggesting forty and some going as high as twenty-three thousand.

One reason for the conflation of the prostitute with the "loose woman" generally is that there was no conceptual space in the medieval scheme of things for a sexually active single woman who was not a prostitute. The fourteenth-century preacher's manual *Fasciculus Morum* ("Little Treatise on Morals"), for example, provides a detailed breakdown of sexual sins, again from the man's point of view. If a man has sex with a married woman, it is adultery; if with a virgin, it is sacrilege (if she is a nun) or *stuprum* (defloration) if she is not. Fornication "particularly refers to intercourse with widows, whores, or concubines. But the term 'whore' must be applied only to those women who give themselves to anyone and will refuse none, and that for monetary gain."[27] If not a wife, virgin, widow, or concubine, a woman was a prostitute; there was no other category.

That canon lawyers and theological writers found no difference between a prostitute and a sexually active woman morally does not mean that they did not recognize that the sex trade was a business. They wrote about the circumstances under which it was legitimate for a prostitute to take money. The twelfth-century Parisian scholar Peter the Chanter and his associates Stephen Langton, Robert Courson, and Thomas of Chobham said that a prostitute did not have to make restitution of her ill-gotten gains. Chobham even argued that the prostitute was entitled to a reasonable wage for her sexual services. However, this was only true if no fraud were involved. If the woman had defrauded the customer, for example by using make-up to appear younger or more beautiful than she actually was, she was only entitled to the amount he would have paid had he known her actual appearance. In the early thirteenth century depictions of the Prodigal Son begin to appear that give great detail on just how he wasted his money cavorting with prostitutes. The image from the Prodigal Son window at Chartres cathedral (see Figure 4.3) shows a prostitute driving him away from the brothel after he has spent all his money. The story is about the wastrel son and his father's forgiveness, but the prostitute who is only concerned with his money and wants nothing to do with him once it is gone emphasizes women's greed.

Recognition of the economic need that drove many women to prostitution appeared in some medieval writings, for example the story of St. Nicholas, in which the saint dropped three bags of gold down the chimney of a poor man's house so that the man's three daughters would not have to support themselves by prostitution. (The three bags of gold became the symbol of pawnbrokers, because St. Nicholas was their patron saint. The three gold balls that signify a pawnshop today derive from this story, as does the idea that St. Nicholas brings gifts down the chimney.) The legend of St. Nicholas is somewhat unusual, however, in acknowledging the economic forces that drove women to prostitution. And indeed canon lawyers, although they believed that need could excuse a man becoming a thief, did not believe that it could ever excuse a woman becoming a prostitute, although it could make the sin more understandable.

Other stories – like those of St. Mary Magdalene and St. Mary of Egypt, the two best-known prostitute saints – de-emphasize the financial aspect. Mary Magdalene is often depicted as coming from a rich family, and some

Figure 4.3 A prostitute drives away a destitute man. Chartres Cathedral, Prodigal Son window roundel.

of the French and German dramas about her explicitly tell us that she refused money when it was offered or that she gave her body without fee to anyone because she did not need the money. The story of Mary of Egypt was retold in two different versions, one of which had her refuse money from her customers "lest any should for lack of funds fail to sin with her."[28] She thus did not have the excuse of financial necessity for corrupting her customers. However, the versions that do describe her as accepting money are not more sympathetic; they merely attribute greed as well as lust to her as a motive.

If we look at the economic position of single women in the Middle Ages – particularly the later Middle Ages for which we have the best data – it is easy to understand how many were drawn or driven to prostitution. Some scholars who write about prostitution, whether in the Middle Ages or in other periods, describe prostitutes as victims, even suggesting the term "prostituted women" instead of "prostitutes" to underscore that this is something that has been done to them. Another group of scholars sees prostitution as work like any other work, and women choosing it because it pays better or has better working conditions than other occupations. This model emphasizes women's role in making their own choices. In medieval Europe the latter model is probably a bit closer to the truth – there are cases of women coerced into prostitution by their families or employers, but certainly not the majority – but we must not see prostitution as a choice among a number of desirable alternatives. It may have been the best alternative available to a particular woman because wages for women were low (which they were), because women were excluded from many of the skilled crafts (which they were), or because she had become pregnant and it was very hard for a single mother to find work. One could see prostitutes as being coerced by the economic circumstances; other women who also performed low-paying tasks were similarly coerced, but prostitution was not only low-paying but socially degrading.

The working conditions of prostitutes varied greatly. Many late medieval towns – in France, Germany, Italy, Spain, and (less commonly) England – had official brothels. Sometimes these were private institutions licensed by the local authority (the municipality, or, in some cases, the local ecclesiastical landlord). In other places, they were municipally owned, and management was farmed out to an administrator. These official brothels were often bathhouses as well. They could be closed down on particular occasions, for example during Lent or Holy Week, or, in the case of Southwark across the river from London, when Parliament was sitting at Westminster. The regulations for these brothels were supposed to give women some measure of protection, for example forbidding the brothelkeeper to beat them, but they also severely restricted aspects of their lives, for example forbidding them to have lovers other than their customers. A woodcut from fifteenth-century Germany or the Netherlands (Figure 4.4) depicts what is probably a brothel scene, where a young man cavorts with a naked woman on his lap while another looks on, in a comfortable tiled and paneled room. A man in fool's cap and bells looks on with a hand over his face, a gesture that denoted agreement with the action. The second woman's speech scroll says "Behold the enticement of youth." The point is a warning to the man, not to the women, but it is women who provide the enticement or temptation.

Most prostitutes probably operated in a much less formal setting. Women who worked in the official brothels often complained to the authorities about clandestine prostitutes who were competing with them for business, but laws were never thoroughly enforced against the latter. Some prostitutes shared houses, some operated out of taverns, some rented rooms from accommodating landladies or landlords, or indeed operated out of the

144

Figure 4.4 The Seduction of Youth. Meister der Banderollen, © Albertina, Vienna, DG1926/934.

homes of their employers. Some worked in bathhouses; indeed, although not all bathhouses were brothels, and in many places the sexes were strictly segregated, it is clear that many European towns had bathhouses that doubled as places of assignation for couples, and many of these couples included prostitutes.

Because prostitutes and non-commercial heterosexually active women were not always distinguished, it is not always possible to tell from the court records whether someone was a commercial prostitute or not; we can only guess from the frequency of accusations or the number of different partners. And, of course, most people in Europe lived in rural areas where villages might not be large enough to support a brothel, and any prostitution would have to be fairly casual.

Although the church condemned prostitution, many municipal authorities took the attitude that official brothels prevented greater sin. They provided an outlet for lust; Ptolemy of Lucca, a political theorist of the thirteenth to fourteenth centuries, used a vivid metaphor: "a whore acts in the world as the bilge in a ship or the sewer in a palace: 'Remove the sewer, and you will fill the palace with a stench.'"[29] The prostitutes themselves might not be respected,

145

but they performed an important function in the city by preventing "evil to wives and virgins."[30] Did wives and virgins appreciate the favor? If the evil that prostitutes were thought to prevent was harassment or rape, perhaps so.

Prostitutes could also serve another important function in the medieval city, particularly in multicultural regions like Spain: marking the border of who was and who was not a member of the community. Prostitutes were considered common to all men; regulations from towns in various parts of Europe prohibited them from taking particular lovers or stated that they could not be raped since they had given consent to all by their choice of profession. At the same time, however, medieval Christians were very concerned about just who constituted that community of men to whom the prostitutes belonged. In Christian Spain, a Jew or Muslim man who had sex with a Christian woman could be subject to the death penalty (though this was not consistently enforced). There was great concern over this possibility of inter-religious or inter-ethnic sexual relations. One might expect that, since prostitutes were already corrupt, it did not matter if they slept with non-Christians. However, perhaps because of prostitutes' function as markers of community, judicial authorities were very concerned about Jews or Muslims having sex with Christian prostitutes, and the prostitutes themselves sometimes refused to have sex with circumcised men and reported them to the authorities. Christian authorities were not so concerned about Christian men having sexual contact with non-Christian women; indeed, they encouraged the prostitution of *mudéjar* women (Muslims living within Christian Spain). Jews in Christian Spain debated whether it would be better to have Jewish prostitutes to prevent men from wasting their seed on gentile (presumably Muslim) women.

Although the authorities, whether ecclesiastical or secular, considered prostitutes fallen and depraved, their peers among the working people of the towns may not have adopted that attitude, especially where religious boundary-crossing was not an issue. Among people who believed that simple fornication or adultery by married men with unmarried women was not all that bad, prostitutes might be just another sort of service worker. They could be part of networks of women within towns, associating with other servant women if not with their mistresses. One London case involved a prostitute who gave other women information about the sexual prowess (or rather lack of it) of potential marriage partners, reporting "that certain young men which were in contemplation of marriage with them had not what men should have to please them."[31] One man sued her for the damages he sustained in losing the opportunity to marry a rich widow. Whether or not she actually was at fault, it is clear that a prostitute could be expected to be involved in gossip networks with respectable women.

Prostitutes were also sometimes sought out as expert witnesses in church court proceedings in the later Middle Ages. In a case of impotence, as discussed in Chapter 3, it was important to determine whether the man was impotent with all women (in which case the marriage was invalid) or only with his wife (in which case it was not). The women undertaking the examination were supposed to be respectable matrons, and they had to take oaths as to their good character. In these cases, although the oaths about character were not challenged, historian Jeremy Goldberg has identified the women involved as prostitutes on the basis of other records. Yet they were respected enough to do this sort of work that other women might be embarrassed to do.

Although contraception has been discussed in Chapter 3 because it was used by married people, it may also have been used extensively by unmarried women, especially prostitutes. (I say unmarried women, rather than couples, because with condoms unknown contraception was not in any way considered a man's responsibility.) Just how widespread knowledge of contraception was is not clear. Very few women, especially prostitutes who would tend to be uneducated, would have been able to read the gynecology handbooks that discussed it, but the information was no doubt also passed on orally from one woman to another. One indication that men may not have been all that familiar with birth control comes in a medical discussion of prostitutes by Albert the Great and why, despite the frequency with which they have intercourse, they do not become pregnant. It may be that the low pregnancy rate for prostitutes was a real phenomenon. Twentieth-century studies showed that many prostitutes were infertile because of repeated venereal infections, and this may have been a factor in the Middle Ages also. We might also assume, logically enough, that prostitutes would be among the women most likely to participate in an oral tradition about contraceptive methods. Medieval medical theorists, however, thought that prostitutes were unlikely to conceive either because too frequent intercourse made their wombs close up, or because too much seed made their wombs too slippery and nothing could adhere. The theorists simply might not have known about a tradition of contraception passed on among prostitutes.

One might expect that the most common way of avoiding pregnancy would have been coitus interruptus, or intercourse other than vaginal. Medieval texts do contain plenty of warnings against the sin of Onan, or coitus interruptus, on the grounds of infertility and the wasting of sperm. There are remarkably few references, however, to oral, anal, or manual sex between women and men. A few texts, like that of Peraldus, define sex with a woman "elsewhere than in the place deputed by nature" as sodomy; the canonist "Gratian" adopted Augustine's dictum that the worst sexual sin was "when a man wishes to use a member of his wife not conceded for this" (see Chapter 3). Literary texts may use language in which it is sometimes possible to read references to oral sex, for example in a dawn song from the late fourteenth–early fifteenth century by German poet Oswald von Wolkenstein, but even such metaphorical language as:

> The young maiden gently let him
> pour into her mouth
> the Saint John's drink of love

is relatively rare.[32]

Such references, however, are not nearly as pervasive as might be expected. This is not likely to be because church authorities or other writers thought this behavior was acceptable. Nor is it likely to be because the behavior was unknown. St. Augustine gave as one of the justifications for prostitution the argument that if a man wanted to commit a depraved sexual act, it was better for him to do it with a prostitute, who was already corrupted, than with his wife. But non-vaginal sex is very rarely mentioned in connection with prostitutes, even in discussions of the depraved and polluted nature of the latter. We must conclude that medieval people simply did not talk about it, or at any rate write about it; it fell into the category of "the unmentionable sin," along with homosexual sodomy.

Women's same-sex activity

One final group of women for whom sexual activity was not a prelude to marriage consisted of women, married or not, who had sexual relations with other women. We know excruciatingly little about such women in the Middle Ages. There were a significant number of women who never married, perhaps 10 to 15 percent in northern Europe in the later Middle Ages, fewer in other areas. Some of these were nuns, and some no doubt were women who would have chosen to marry if they could, but were unable to find a husband; some were women of low social status such that men of the same status could not support a family, leaving the women to remain in domestic service or low-waged work. Many of them must have been women who made the choice not to marry, either because they were not attracted to men or because they preferred to remain independent of a husband's legal control. Unfortunately, the sources do not tell us which of the many possible reasons was behind any given woman's decision not to marry. Women who did not marry might live together, but we do not know whether they were friends, housemates, or lovers (or all of these). It is important not to apply a double standard of evidence here: we do not require an eyewitness report of genital contact to state that a given man and woman's attraction to each other was sexual, and we should not require it for two women either. Even having said that, however, the evidence remains extremely thin. When there is evidence for love between two women – like Elizabeth Etchingham and

Agnes Oxenbridge, two fifteenth-century English women who were buried next to each other with a shared memorial brass – antiquarians and historians have often ignored it.

One reason for the paucity of evidence is that most of the sources we have for medieval sexuality are primarily concerned with men. Women's behavior is important insofar as it affects men: adulteresses deprive men of their rights to sexual exclusivity, prostitutes tempt men, and so forth. Women might be seen as aggressively lustful, but they remained passive in the sense that society expected men to remain in control and make the choices. Hence any choices that women made that did not involve men were not part of the discussion. Women's activity might be included in the confused category of sodomy, but it might not. There is no medieval term that can be directly translated as "lesbian" without a string of caveats. And yet medieval people clearly could imagine women's same-sex relationships as a parallel to men's, without the use of any phallic instrument. Figure 4.5 comes from a "Moralized Bible," one of the two earliest surviving (1220–1230). In this type of work, each illustrated scene from the Bible is coupled with another giving its moral meaning. The Bible scene which this picture illuminates is Eve being tempted by the serpent; the moralization involves devils encouraging one female couple and one male couple to kiss. Neither couple is in a bed, the traditional setting for a scene of love; the positions, rather, suggest furtiveness. The images, together with the commentary, represent temptation and sin, particularly the sins of the mouth. This is a somewhat unusual depiction in showing women as lovers at all (although there are instances when it is not possible to tell whether a figure is meant to be male or female).

Medical writers do not have much to say about women having sex with other women. The ninth-century Christian Arab physician Yuhanna ibn Masawayh thought that lesbianism (the Arabic term he used was etymologically related to rubbing behavior, but also came to refer to love between women) was the result of a mother eating certain foods that create a lifelong itch in the daughter she nurses. William of Saliceto in the thirteenth century wrote that some women had a growth at the mouth of the uterus that could protrude outside the vagina and could be used as a penis. The discussion of the enlarged clitoris that one finds in nineteenth-century investigations of women's same-sex relations is absent from the medieval discourse.

There is somewhat more evidence for loving relationships between women than there is for genital sex. There are love poems written by one woman to another, in language that clearly sounds erotic to a contemporary reader. As with men's same-sex love poetry, most of it occurs within a monastic context. It certainly makes sense that nuns might develop intense and passionate relationships with each other, but this seems rarely to have been a concern for the authorities of the women's houses. Visitations that reported sexual irregularities in these houses focus almost exclusively on heterosexual relations (and, indeed, a study of the thirteenth-century visitation

Figure 4.5 Couples embracing, the moralized meaning of Eve's temptation by the serpent. Moralized Bible, Österreichische Nationalbibliothek, Codex Vindobonensis 2554, fol. 2, detail.

records of Eudes Rigaud of Rouen shows that women were not disproportionately accused of sexual offenses compared to men). A few penitentials from the early Middle Ages, intended also for use primarily in a monastic context, have penances for women who "practice vice" together, but it is not punished as severely as adultery: in the Penitential of Theodore, a woman who "practices vice with a woman" is assigned three years of penance, as opposed to four years for a man who has sex with a married woman or ten years for a man who has sex with a man.[33] The Penitential of Bede provides three years for a married man who has sex with a married woman, four years for "sodomy" (undefined), three years for "a woman fornicating with a woman," and seven for "nuns with a nun by means of an instrument." Penances are generally higher for transgressions by monastics, so it is not clear whether it is the nuns or the instrument that make the penance higher.[34] Nearly seven hundred years later the Lollard Conclusions expressed some of the same concerns about nuns' sexual activity, including contraception, abortion and infanticide, sex with each other, bestiality, and the sexual use of objects.

Accusations of this behavior in specific cases, as opposed to general statements, are quite rare. And when a writer uses circumlocutions, as did Abbess Heloise in a letter to Abelard, can we be sure she is referring to sexual relations between women? Karma Lochrie suggests that Heloise's words talk about nuns being seduced by secular women who are given hospitality in the convent:

> Surely nothing is so conducive to a woman's seduction as woman's flattery, nor does a woman pass on the foulness of a corrupted mind so readily to any but another woman; which is why St. Jerome particularly exhorts women of a sacred calling to avoid contact with women of the world.[35]

With the passage translated in this way it is easy to see it as meaning that these secular women seduce the nuns into having sex with them. But the Latin *lenocinium* can also mean ornamentation, and if translated this way, it would mean that seeing the secular women's finery corrupts the nuns, but not necessarily into sex with them. And *lenocinium* also refers to bawdry, pimping, or procuring, suggesting that secular women might have persuaded the nuns into sex with men. Keeping an open mind means accepting the same-sex possibilities of the passage, but also acknowledging its ambiguity – an ambiguity Heloise may well have intended.

As with other kinds of sexual behavior, the more definite evidence that survives comes largely from court records. What becomes apparent there is the surprising infrequency of prosecutions: only twelve have been found by historians for the entire medieval period. This is unlikely to have been because extremely few women were sexually involved with each other. Rather, it comes from the medieval understanding that sex was something that one person did to another, by penetrating him or her. Unless the activity that took place between two women involved a dildo, it did not count as sex. Courts and judges could find it quite confusing to figure out exactly what offense two women together were committing, unless they imitated male–female intercourse.

Etienne de Fougères (d. 1178), in his *Livre des manières*, depicts sex between women as more ridiculous than sinful because of the lack of a phallus.

> These ladies have made up a game:
> with two bits of nonsense they make nothing;
> they bang coffin against coffin,

without a poker stir up their fire.
They don't play at "poke in the paunch,"
but join shield to shield without a lance.
They have no concern for a beam in their scales,
nor a handle in their mold.
Out of water they fish for turbot
and they have no need for a rod.
They don't bother with a pestle in their mortar
nor a fulcrum for their see-saw.[36]

Although Etienne may find the absence of a man ridiculous, however, he does make the point that the women are quite satisfied with the situation. Sahar Amer suggests that Etienne's phrasing here, unusual in a western European context ("shield to shield without a lance"), is found in earlier Arabic literature and that homoerotic ideas crossed cultural boundaries.

If an artificial phallus was used, there was a penetrator, and she was transgressing gender roles by being the active partner. The penitentials, referring to "instruments" used by women, indicate too that the matter was considered more serious when a phallus was involved. In addition, of course, same-sex behavior did not involve reproduction or cast doubt on the paternity of children and therefore on inheritance claims, and thus presented less of a threat than heterosexual adultery in that regard.

Those women who were condemned by the courts for their same-sex behavior, then, were not seen as having a homosexual orientation or being lesbians (a term not used in the Middle Ages). They were described as usurping the role of a man. For example, Katherina Hetzeldorfer was put to death in Speyer in 1477 for a crime unnamed in the records; women testified that she wanted to "have her manly will" with them, that she "behaved exactly like a man with women." Hetzeldorfer confessed that she used a "piece of wood that she held between her legs" and "that she made an instrument with a red piece of leather, at the front filled with cotton, and a wooden stick stuck into it."[37]

Often, besides using a dildo, the women who were condemned dressed as men. This adds another complication to the sources: in many cases where we have references to women dressing as men but not to any sexual behavior, there may have been same-sex activity involved, but we cannot assume this. When men dressed as women, it was usually for sexual reasons (or as a disguise to escape from violence). When women dressed as men, however, there could be a variety of other motives. In many medieval tales of women in men's clothing – including those of female saints who joined male monasteries, which are legendary, and that of a female university student at Krakow in the fifteenth century, which is probably true – the women disguised themselves as men to gain access to an institution that excluded women. Women who needed to travel might also find it safer to dress as men to avoid sexual violence; there are more examples of this in literary sources than in documents of practice, but there is no reason something like this would turn up in court records, and even if the men's clothing is used as a plot device, it is not at all implausible. Thus, women's cross-dressing is often found in contexts other than a sexual or romantic relationship with another woman.

When female cross-dressing for reasons other than the sexual is presented in literature, as in the French *Yde and Olive*, a thirteenth-century chanson de geste retold several times in subsequent centuries, where the heroine disguises herself as a man in order to escape from her father, it may have sexual consequences. Yde travels from Spain to Rome, where the king's daughter falls in love with him/her. They marry. On their wedding night Yde pretends to be ill, so they do nothing but "kiss and hug," which may not be as chaste as it sounds; this language could also denote a non-vaginal sexual encounter between two women. Two weeks later Olive finds out her husband's secret. Eventually it becomes public and the king investigates by having Yde disrobe publicly. At this point God miraculously transforms her into a man. In this same-sex marriage the bride does not know that the bridegroom is also a woman; the bridegroom knows, but cannot escape the marriage without gravely offending the king. Nevertheless, there is definitely an element of homoerotic attraction here and in other Arabic and western European tales with similar plot devices, and it operates along much the same love-at-first-sight lines as opposite-sex courtly love:

> Yde was much looked at and noticed,
> For Olive had seen her from the windows.
> Her entire body throbbed with pleasure
> And she said in a low voice so that no one could hear
> "He will be my friend. I want to tell him so tomorrow."[38]

The couple's initial meeting follows the conventions of opposite-sex love, and the miracle returns the women to that pattern; the same-sex marriage was a thrilling but dangerous interlude. In an Arabic tale of similar plot, from the *Thousand and One Nights*, the women also kiss and caress, although the Arabic terms used may be more sexually loaded than those in the French tale. On the third night after the wedding, after threats of banishment or even death if s/he does not consummate the marriage, the cross-dressed Princess Budur tells her/his wife, Hayat al-Nufus, her entire story. Hayat al-Nufus fakes her defloration with chicken blood and shares in Budur's secret. Budur rules Hayat al-Nufus's father's land until her husband, Qamar al-Zaman, appears.

Finally the secret is revealed and Qamar al-Zaman marries Hayat al-Nufus as well. The possible eroticism between the women is a small part of an extended tale focusing mainly on men's exploits; the two women later

have affairs with each others' sons, indicating some sort of continued familial intimacy, but hardly a long-term lesbian union.

An example of institutionalized female cross-dressing, from the Ummayad
court at Baghdad in the ninth century, shows that it was not equated there
with same-sex relations. (Actually, it was connected with male same-sex
relations, not female!) Slave women were dressed as boys; as one historian
put it, "this attire gave them a svelte carriage, and emphasized their buttocks."[39] Known as *ghulāmīyāt* (boy-like), these women were apparently
sexually appealing to men of the court who were otherwise attracted to
boys; indeed, the story goes, the mother of the caliph al-Amīn first had the
slave women dress as boys to remedy her son's exclusive taste for sex with
eunuchs. Poetry written to these *ghulāmīyāt* indicates that their appeal lay in
their gender-crossing, the fact that they allowed men to have sex simultane-
ously with a woman and a boy. But these women mainly became *ghulāmīyāt*
by the choice of their owners, not by their own desires. There is no evidence
for their having sex with other women, and they serve to underscore the
equation of all "passive" partners – that is, those who were penetrated – in
the active men's eyes.

Gynecological handbooks give us some information on women's sexual
relations with other women, if only very obliquely. Many medieval medical
writers thought that moderate, regular emission of seed (through orgasm –
women were thought to emit seed too) was necessary for good health. A virgin or widow – a woman who did not have a legitimate sexual partner,
but was still considered respectable – might become ill because of lack of
orgasm. In this case, the handbooks suggested, the midwife should use manual manipulation to relieve the congested condition of the genitalia. This
suggestion seems a long way from modern lesbianism; the manual stimulation is to be done by a medical practitioner, and would not have been
considered a sex act. Nevertheless, the idea that it was one woman's profes-
sional duty to give another woman the stimulation necessary to her health
is surely relevant to the history of women's same-sex sexual activity. One
medieval medical writer talked of the "sodomitic" practices of the wives of
Italian merchants, who used dildoes with each other while their husbands
were away, because they did not want to take a male lover and risk becoming pregnant.[40]

Scenes of women fondling other women also occur in literary texts. In
these scenes the woman doing the fondling puts herself in the place of a
man, even if she is not dressed as one, and the scene was probably written
(as with much contemporary pornography involving two women) for the titillation of men rather than women. In the Catalan romance *Tirant lo Blanc*,
for example, the hero is in love with a princess whose maid hides him in her
room. He then watches from his hiding place while the maid helps the princess take a bath, fondling each part of her body and saying: "See her eyes
and mouth? I kiss them for you. See her delicate breasts, one in each hand?

I kiss them for you. . . . Only Tirant's hands deserve to touch what mine are touching."[41] The romance does not present the maid as "a lesbian" – she has her own romantic intrigues with men – and she is performing for the gaze of the male within the text as well as the male reader. Nevertheless, the fact that the princess does not object to the fondling may tell us something about the level of physical, even sexual, contact that was considered normal or acceptable between women; or it may tell us about nothing more than male fantasies. In the same text, the maid wears a Moorish mask and mimes fondling and having sex with the princess; Tirant, seeing them, thinks it is the black gardener with her. The princess and her ladies, however, are aware that it is a woman, and they find it quite amusing.

Violence and coercion

The women involved in all the various types of non-marital relationships this chapter has discussed were seen differently by different groups of people. Nearly all the sources that tell us about them were written by men, and women may have understood their relationship or their own behavior quite differently from how it is described.

Nowhere does this difference in perception between the women themselves and the men whose writings we have hold more true than in the case of rape. If we think in terms of modern categories, rape does not belong in a chapter on women's extramarital sexual behavior. It does not involve any sexual behavior on the part of the woman; she is the victim of an act of violence. Yet men in the Middle Ages would surely have considered rape as an appropriate part of a chapter on women. Indeed, in many kinds of sources, they drew very little distinction between rape and heterosexual intercourse generally. The woman's consent really did not matter. The implications of this for male sexual behavior will be discussed in Chapter 5; here we look at rape in the context of women's sexual behavior.

Many medieval medical theorists believed that conception could not take place unless both parties emitted seed, and thus that a woman could not become pregnant without experiencing pleasure, as we saw in Chapter 3. Therefore, a woman who became pregnant must have given her consent to the act of intercourse, because she enjoyed it. Some medical writers, however, drew a distinction between the body and the mind in this regard: it was possible for the body to experience pleasure even if the mind was unwilling. While still based on erroneous scientific knowledge, this view at least avoided making women complicit in their own rapes.

Many depictions of rape do not so much make women complicit as make women's consent irrelevant. The man takes what he wants, and the sources do not really care whether or not the woman gave it willingly. Sometimes they depict her as being initially unwilling but coming to enjoy it. In the thirteenth-century Icelandic *Grettir's Saga*, the hero is outlawed and on the run, and takes

155

refuge in a barn. The farmer's daughter and servant find him there, asleep and naked. The servant comments that for such a big man, who has done such great deeds, he has an awfully small penis. He awakens and composes a verse in proper meter, in which he tells her that although it seems small now, it can be large when aroused. He then rapes her and, the saga tells us, "when she left Grettir she did not taunt him again."[42] Significantly, it is the servant who is raped in this story (the farmer's daughter runs from the room when Grettir seizes the servant). As in the pastourelles (discussed in Chapter 5) and as in what legal documents tell us about medieval servitude, women of the lower class are available to men of the upper, and have little to say about it.

The lack of attention paid to whether or not the woman consents is perhaps not surprising given the role of consent (or lack thereof) in other aspects of life. Although according to canon law a woman had to consent to her own marriage, in practice the choice was often made by her parents, at least in areas and among social groups in which girls were married off in their early teens (in general, the aristocracy across Europe as a whole, and all social and religious groups in southern Europe in the later Middle Ages). Consent takes on a very different meaning, too, in a society that did not place a high value on individual autonomy. Ties of dependence were crucial in medieval society, and it was difficult for anyone to say no, about sex or anything else, to someone on whom s/he was dependent. There was no *droit de seigneur* as a right, but there was a good deal of what today might be considered *quid pro quo* sexual harassment, except that it was not illegal in the Middle Ages. Even when it was a long-term relationship in which a servant bore more than one child to her master, we do not know how voluntary it was; as with slaves in the antebellum southern United States, the decision to agree to become one's master's mistress might be based on both physical coercion and economic necessity, as well as the desire to achieve a better life for one's children. An element of choice might be involved, and yet coercion remained the basic condition.

There are no statistics as to the prevalence of rape in medieval society. We have some court cases, but we can assume that the crime went unreported even more often than it does today, so the number of cases is not a good indication of the incidence of the offense. And there were many more instances that were not merely unreported but also unperceived as rape, because the coercion was other than physical.

Rape could also be understood in the Middle Ages, as it is today, as a crime primarily of violence against women, rather than of sex. In England in the late twelfth and early thirteenth centuries, for example, both legal treatises and actual cases emphasize not the lack of consent on the part of the woman, but the physical violence she suffers: "Sibba daughter of William appeals William son of Hugh of Bolton that in the king's peace he took her outside the village of Wheldrake and lay with her by force and made her bloody."[43] Later, however, the language of both treatises and rape cases focused on the loss of virginity, and from the late thirteenth through the fifteenth centuries it came to focus on the question of a woman's consent. These changes reflected changing political conditions and the way those who made and enforced law thought about sex and power. Kim M. Phillips argues that a focus on violence against women was more favorable to the women themselves, because it is more likely to have protected their safety. It is true, too, that a focus on consent, in the Middle Ages as today, could lead to a "he said/she said" argument in which a woman's reputation could be dragged through the mud. However, to focus only on the evidence of violence and not on consent could mean that if the means of coercion were merely a threat rather than actual physical force, the crime could not be prosecuted.

One situation in which women may have been coerced into sexual relations by means other than violence is incest. Even more so than rape, this is a crime for which it is impossible to derive any statistics for the Middle Ages, so rarely would it have been reported. The many cases of incest found in court records are mainly concerned with people having sexual relations, even marriages, with people to whom they were related within the fourth degree, or to whom they were related by affinity (someone with whose relative, including relative by godparentage, one had already had sexual relations), rather than incest within the household. Because of high mortality rates many children grew up in step-families, a situation which in the modern world we know to be conducive to stepfather–stepdaughter sexual relations, but there is little evidence (even in stories) that this was the case in the Middle Ages. When we do have stories that discuss father–daughter incest, it is the biological father, not the stepfather.

Unlike medieval stories of mother–son incest, many of which involve hidden identities and the parties' lack of awareness, medieval stories that involved the theme of father–daughter incest were not based on mistaken identity. Both parties involved know perfectly well what is going on. The cause is attributed not to error, but to the father's cruelty or insanity, or to diabolical suggestion. In the story of Apollonius of Tyre, a tale from late antiquity that was frequently retold in the Middle Ages (and by Shakespeare), Antiochus of Antioch rapes his daughter.

> He struggled with madness, he fought against passion, but he was defeated by love . . . one day when he was awake at dawn he rushed into his daughter's room and ordered the servants to withdraw, as if he intended to have a private conversation with her. Spurred on by the frenzy of his lust, he took his daughter's virginity by force, in spite of her lengthy resistance.[44]

As Chaucer tells it,

> the cursed King Antiochus
> Bereft his daughter of her maidenhead

157

That is so horrible a tale to read,
When he threw her upon the floor.[45]

In one common story pattern, a man becomes so distraught over the death of his wife that he insists on marrying his daughter, who closely resembles her. (This happens as well in the story of *Yde and Olive* discussed above – her father's wish to marry her is what causes Yde to flee, dressed as a man.) The father is not presented as evil or predatory, but rather as driven insane by grief. The point of the story as presented is not, in fact, about the incest, but about patience and steadfastness under tribulation; this incident is only the beginning of the girl's hardships, but she perseveres, maintains her virginity, and receives a heavenly reward. The story may, however, have touched on a medieval anxiety: in a patriarchal society, where the father has the final say over many aspects of the child's life, including marriage, how can a daughter resist coercion from him? A daughter who does so cuts off her means of financial support. The story does not treat this sort of coercion to incest as a common problem, and there is very little evidence that it was, but from more recent times we know that it can go on without being discussed or reported, and we must at least hold open the possibility that this was the case in the Middle Ages.

Another story that circulated widely in the Middle Ages was *Gregorius*, in which a boy is tempted by the devil to have sex with his sister, who sleeps in the same room. She chooses not to bring dishonor on both of them by crying out. Their son, abandoned, grows up and marries his mother; when they find out the relationship, they repent and he becomes pope. The moral of the story is the importance of repentance: double incest, when followed by contrition, does not prevent Gregorius from becoming a good priest and pope. What emerges from the story is the passivity of the woman involved, who more or less falls into both relationships. It is Gregorius whose penance forms the focus, although it is his mother who has committed incest not once but twice. Sleeping in the same room as her brother, "Of course, the girl was blind/To love of sinful kind"; he assaults her while she sleeps, and though she wakes and complains, "at last against her will/The contest to the end he played." When she (unknowingly) meets her grown son, and is attracted to him, "The devil's schemes were to blame/Who also tempted Eve."[46] When she finally agrees to marry, it is at the advice of her counselors. The story also illustrates the danger of not marrying off daughters at a young age, leaving them to tempt the male members of their households.

The incest taboo as codified by the medieval church extended beyond the medieval family to more distant relatives. Robert Mannyng, the early-fourteenth-century English moralist and author of *Handling Sin*, gave the incest prohibition as a reason for men not to have sex with prostitutes: a customer does not know whether this particular woman may in the past have had sex with a relative of his. This reasoning was different from that of the early Christian Justin Martyr in Rome in the second century: he had argued that a man should not patronize prostitutes because he does not know if the woman may actually be his own daughter, abandoned at birth and picked up by slave traders to be used in the sex trade. By the high Middle Ages, Mannyng could assume that a man would know if the prostitute herself were his relative; the incest risk depended upon whether her customers were.

The most common way in which women were coerced into sex in the Middle Ages, however, was probably not incest and may not have been violent physical force either, but rather was slavery. When the women were slaves, rape in the legal sense was not in question, because the man had the right to do as he wished with his property. Slavery was known in Europe throughout the Middle Ages, more commonly in the earlier period, where we know less about it, and later on mainly in the south; the enslavement of one's co-religionists was frowned upon, so slavery tended to be more prevalent in regions where there was a pool of non-Christians or non-Muslims on which to draw. Under Muslim law, and Spanish Muslim practice, it was perfectly legitimate for a man to have sex with his slave women. A child born of such a relationship (if acknowledged) had all the rights of a child born in marriage, and a slave who bore a child to her master received special privileges including her freedom at her master's death.

In Christian western Europe the slave and her children for the most part had no such rights, although in the Kingdom of Valencia Pedro III ruled in 1283 that a man whose slave bears him a child must free her and the child. More typical was the situation cited in a letter about a pregnant slave who arrived in Genoa from Majorca: she claimed that her previous owner had gotten her pregnant, and the matter was investigated, but as the correspondent reported back,

> he says you may throw her into the sea, with what she has in her belly, for it is no creature of his. And we believe he is speaking the truth, for if she had been pregnant by him, he would not have sent her.[47]

The assumption here that a master would not send away his own child may not have been always justified. A slave child to rear was not an economic benefit, and many slave women were forced to abandon their children (who may or may not have been fathered by their owners) at foundling hospitals. There are, however, cases where the children were raised within the family, either as slaves or as free.

In Spain, where Muslims were enslaved by Christians, the gender balance among slaves may have been fairly even, but elsewhere, in Italy (especially

Venice and Genoa) and the south of France, the ratio was heavily weighted toward women, who composed about 80 percent of all slaves sold. This was likely a result of both supply and demand. Girls were more likely than boys to be sold or bartered into slavery by needy families, and women may also have been more vulnerable to capture than men; but slaves were in demand mainly for domestic labor (considered women's work) and for sexual use. Sally McKee has demonstrated that prices for slave women varied according to how attractive their ethnic group was deemed; this does not mean that they were purchased solely for sexual purposes (though some may have been), but that owners expected to have sexual access to the women they purchased for household work. Unmarried men, in particular, may have bought slaves to fulfill the various household functions that a wife would otherwise have performed, but married men could also prey upon the slave women in the household. So could other men: there are records of many court cases in which a man got another man's slave pregnant and had to pay damages to the owner for the loss of her labor. The woman's consent did not make a difference. For example, in Florence in 1453, one Francesco was punished for breaking into the house of Andrea della Stufa and raping his slave Caterina. The punishment was based on the amount of work that she missed.[48] It was considered a property offense against her owner, not a violent crime against the woman herself.

Not all such relations between slave women and free men were necessarily premised on physical violence. A slave's livelihood depended on her owner. She might have nowhere else to turn, and threats of violence, or economic coercion, could be just as effective. The same was true of servants, to a lesser degree; they might have more alternatives than slaves (such as relatives in the region who could protect them), but they had very little power in relation to their masters. Some of these women could even have initiated a relationship with their owner or another free man, in the hope of improving their economic situation, gaining protection for themselves and their children, and possibly seeing their children freed. Although the evidence does not tell us one way or the other, there could also have been real affection in the relationship. And yet given the power differential between slaves and their owners, we cannot say that the sex was without coercion even if the woman initiated it.

Although slavery was most common in the Mediterranean, slave women lived under some of the same kinds of coercion in the north. In the thirteenth-century Icelandic *Laxdaela Saga*, set in the tenth century, Höskuldr purchases a slave woman, Melkorka, specifically to serve as a concubine. He sets her up in a separate household because of the jealousy of his wife (which was not the rule in Icelandic sagas, where the wives often do not object to their husbands' concubines). Höskuldr especially loves Melkorka's son despite the fact that he has many sons by his wife, and he manages to trick his legitimate sons into consenting to their half-brother sharing in their inheritance. Again, while the trick with the inheritance is noteworthy, as is the royal Irish blood of this particular slave, the act of taking a concubine is not.

In eastern Europe laws provided that a slave woman who bore her master's child could go free, but these were not often observed. Clerics acknowledged the pressures put on slave women by their masters in not imposing penance on them for sexual relations, or imposing lighter penances than on free women. A slave woman even had the legal right to be freed if she were raped by her owner, although the standard of proof was high, requiring witnesses.

Women's sexuality as threat

Women's sexuality threatened medieval men in many ways: they might be temptresses and lure men into fornication or worse sins, they might behave in masculine ways with each other and so usurp male gender privilege, or they might use sexuality in other ways to control men. The use of magic was a fear that recurred repeatedly. Burchard of Worms, in the tenth century, allotted penances to women who drank their husbands' semen or gave their husbands a potion made with their own menstrual blood. These women were condemned more for their superstition than for their actual performance of magic. Women appeared in literature as sorceresses and enchantresses who seduced men, not necessarily an entirely negative portrayal; but outside the realm of fantasy the possibilities of erotic magic were taken all too seriously, in both Christian and Jewish traditions. A Hebrew compendium, the *Book of the Love of Women*, which contains both gynecological and magical material, addresses women's concerns, although it is not entirely clear that it was intended for a female audience. There are recipes by which both men and women could prevent their lovers' taking another partner. Men could "anoint [your privates] with the blood of a young pigeon," or "Dry a young cock's testicles, pound them well and soak the powder in vinegar," or "anoint your privates with the gall of a suckling lamb," or with "turtledove's blood at the time of intercourse." Women could "take some of his semen during intercourse and pour it on some wool; she must embrace her husband and put the cotton wool into a necklace while saying: 'may my husband be bound' "; or tie seven colored threads while saying a charm over the knots, and use the knots to tie up a frog; or give him a cake to eat made with her menstrual blood.[49] These kinds of recipes, medical or magical – or even these particular recipes – are not unique to Jewish culture, and since Jewish tradition did not disapprove of marital sexuality it is to be expected that medical treatises there as well as in Christian tradition would focus on cures for various reproductive problems. Nevertheless, the modern editor of this text also suggests that the instructions for performing magic reflect a tradition of women's practices.

Condemnations of witchcraft up until around 1100 continued to focus more on eradicating an erroneous belief in witchcraft than eradicating witchcraft itself. After this point, real witches rather than the belief in witches came to be seen as a major threat. Over the period of the central to later Middle Ages belief in witches moved from a belief in people who do magic to a belief in people who worship or are in league with the devil – from sorcery to diabolism. In the period 1300–1500 two-thirds of those condemned for witchcraft were women, with the fraction smaller earlier and larger later. The great persecutions of witches were not a medieval phenomenon, but rather began in the sixteenth century.

The fifteenth century, however, had begun to witness a growing belief in, and fear of, witches. The *Malleus Maleficarum* or *Hammer of Witches*, written by two German Dominican friars before 1487, situates its anti-witch polemic in a long tradition of misogyny, including women's sexual insatiability and threat to men. Women are more likely to be involved in witchcraft than men because:

> they are more credulous; and since the chief aim of the devil is to corrupt faith, therefore he rather attacks them . . . women are naturally more impressionable, and more ready to receive the influence of a disembodied spirit . . . they are feebler both in mind and body . . . she is more carnal than a man, as is clear from her many carnal abominations . . . we find that nearly all the kingdoms of the world have been overthrown by women . . . as she is a liar by nature, so in her speech she stings while she delights us. . . . All witchcraft comes from carnal lust, which is in women insatiable . . . these women satisfy their filthy lusts not only in themselves, but even in the mighty ones of the age, of whatever state and condition; causing by all sorts of witchcraft the death of their souls through the excessive infatuation of carnal love.[50]

The traditional misogynistic attacks on women and the authorities adduced for them are given new force here by the connection with witchcraft and the emphasis on sexuality.

Among the other ways in which witches harm men, according to the *Malleus*, is by putting a spell on them so that they believe that their penises have disappeared. The witches are not accused of actually removing them, but the effect is much the same: "it is no illusion in the opinion of the sufferer." In fact, the authors may protest too much that it is an illusion, all the while telling stories that imply it is real:

> And what, then, is to be thought of those witches who in this way sometimes collect male organs in great numbers together, and put them in a bird's nest, or shut them up in a box, where they move themselves like living members, and eat oats and corn, as has been seen by many

and is a matter of common report? It is to be said that it is all done by devil's work and illusion, for the senses of those who see them are deluded in the way we have said. For a certain man tells that, when he had lost his member, he approached a known witch to ask her to restore it to him. She told the afflicted man to climb a certain tree and that he might take which he liked out of a nest in which there were several members. And when he tried to take a big one, the witch said: You must not take that one; adding, because it belonged to a parish priest.[51]

This is both a humorous anecdote and an attempt to come to terms with how magic could make things appear other than they are, but in none of the stories of missing penises that the *Malleus* recounts do the men involved realize or discover that it is all an illusion. If the stories did not build on an existing fear of women as castrators, they may well have helped to create one.

Witches also harm women by encouraging them to fornicate:

> For when girls have been corrupted, and have been scorned by their lovers after they have immodestly copulated with them in the hope of promise of marriage with them, and have found themselves disappointed in all their hopes and everywhere despised, they turn to the help and protection of devils; either for the sake of vengeance by bewitching those lovers or the wives they have married, or for the sake of giving themselves up to every sort of lechery. Alas! Experience tells us that there is no number to such girls, and consequently the witches that spring from this class are innumerable.[52]

Witches have sexual intercourse with the devil or his assistants. The demon is visible to the witch but not to anyone else:

> But with regard to any bystanders, the witches themselves have often been seen lying on their backs in the fields or the woods, naked up to the very navel, and it has been apparent from the disposition of their limbs and members which pertain to the venereal act and orgasm, as also from the agitation of their legs and thighs, that, all invisibly to bystanders, they have been copulating with Incubus devils.[53]

Demons in female form (succubi) can also seduce human men; they do this in order to collect the men's semen, which they then use to impregnate human women.

> But the reason that devils turn themselves into Incubi or Succubi is not for the cause of pleasure, since a spirit has not flesh and blood; but chiefly it is with this intention, that through the vice of luxury

they may work a twofold harm against men, that is, in body and in soul, that so men may be more given to all vices. And there is no doubt that they know under which stars the semen is most vigorous, and that men so conceived will always be perverted by witchcraft.[54]

This text, which gives numerous stories and examples of female witches, exhibits both fear and loathing of women, whose power over men is deeply connected to their sexual nature. And this was not just the opinion of two obscure German friars: the book became extremely popular in early printed versions and had a great influence on the persecutions of the sixteenth century. The work may not have been written, or read, in order to demonize women; one recent interpreter has suggested that the authors were using an already existing misogyny in the service of their larger purpose, to prove the corporeal existence of demons and thus strengthen their own Christian faith. However, while misogyny is not the whole story, it is certainly present; witchcraft accusations built on an existing set of beliefs about women's sexuality. Demonic copulation may have been something the witch hunters desperately needed to prove, rather than something the society took for granted, but they were able to prove it because of what society did take for granted about women.

I do not want to end the chapter on a wholly negative note. Medieval women were in a situation where they could often be coerced, and when they did make choices for themselves they could often be condemned as sinful. And yet, they were not locked up inside their homes. They were told by the church that virtuous women did not engage in non-marital sex, but many people in the society did not take that very seriously. Medieval texts depict women as the passive partners, the ones something is done *to*, but in the sexual arena, as in other areas of medieval society, real women ignored the norms of their society and made decisions for themselves, within the substantial constraints under which they lived.

We need to keep in mind that most of the evidence for the way women's sexuality was understood in the Middle Ages comes from sources written by men – and in particular by churchmen, for whom women's sexual availability represented a threat to their own chastity. The teaching of the church did represent a powerful current in medieval thought, which profoundly affected women's and men's lives. But it was by no means the only current. Women lived within the constraints of the two acceptable models, virgin or wife. This does not mean, however, that any other relationship in which they engaged was always racked by guilt and self-loathing. As in any other society, subgroups made their own norms. That we do not have the evidence to study these alternative standards does not mean that they did not affect medieval people's lives.

Notes

1 *The Southern Passion*, ed. Beatrice Daw Brown, Early English Text Society Original Series 169 (London: Early English Text Society, 1927), 71.
2 Babylonian Talmud, Tractate Shabbat 56a.
3 Guido Ruggiero, *The Boundaries of Eros: Sex Crime and Sexuality in Renaissance Venice* (New York: Oxford University Press, 1985), 47.
4 Jean de Meun, *The Romance of the Rose*, trans. Harry W. Robbins (New York: E. P. Dutton, 1962), 172, 182.
5 *The Fables of Odo of Cheriton*, trans. John C. Jacobs (Syracuse: Syracuse University Press, 1985), 143.
6 *The Lais of Marie de France*, trans. Robert Hanning and Joan Ferrante (Durham, NC: Labyrinth, 1982), 138, ll. 45–50.
7 Bernart de Ventadorn, poem no. 21, in *Lyrics of the Troubadours and Trouvères*, ed. and trans. Frederick Goldin (Garden City, NY: Anchor Books, 1973), 127–30.
8 Comtessa de Dia, "Estat ai en gren cossirier," in *Songs of the Women Troubadours*, ed. and trans. Matilda Tomaryn Bruckner, Laurie Shepard and Sarah White (New York: Garland, 1995), 11.
9 Andreas Capellanus, *The Art of Courtly Love*, trans. John Jay Parry (New York: W. W. Norton, 1941), 2:7, p. 171.
10 Capellanus, 2:7, pp. 169–70.
11 Capellanus, 2:7, p. 175.
12 Samuel ha-Nagid, *Dīwān*, 302, trans. in Tova Rosen, *Unveiling Eve: Reading Gender in Medieval Hebrew Literature* (Philadelphia: University of Pennsylvania Press, 2003), 43.
13 "The Merchant's Tale," ll. 1851–4, in *The Riverside Chaucer*, ed. Larry D. Benson, 3rd edition (Boston: Houghton Mifflin, 1987), 161.
14 "The Miller's Tale," ll. 3846–54, *Riverside Chaucer*, 77.
15 Ruggiero, *The Boundaries of Eros*, 30. This work is the source for all the information I present about sexuality in Venice.
16 Paris, Archives Nationales, Z/1o/19, 285r. The first reference is to a separate slip of parchment, undated, that has been bound into the book; the second is an identical, dated entry. This suggests how the register may have been compiled: each case noted on a separate slip and then copied into the register.
17 "A Servant-Girl's Holiday," in *The Oxford Book of Medieval English Verse*, eds. Celia Sisam and Kenneth Sisam (Oxford: Clarendon Press, 1970), 452–4, my modernization.
18 "Reeve's Tale," ll. 4313–18, *Riverside Chaucer*, 84.
19 Cited in Ruggiero, *Boundaries of Eros*, 17.
20 Quoted in Carol Lansing, "Concubines, Lovers, Prostitutes: Infamy and Female Identity in Medieval Bologna," in *Beyond Florence: The Contours of Medieval and Early Modern Italy*, eds. Paula Findlen, Michelle Fontaine and Duane J. Osheim (Palo Alto: Stanford University Press, 2003), 85–100, here 93–4.
21 John of Bromyard, *Summa Praedicantium*, l.7.35 (Venice: Domenico Nicolino, 1586), 1:463v.
22 *Speculum Sacerdotale*, ed. Edward N. Weatherly (London: Oxford University Press, 1936), 89.
23 Jean Duvernoy, ed., *Le registre d'inquisition de Jacques Fournier* (Toulouse: Édouard Privat, 1965), 1:224–6, trans. in *Readings in Medieval History*, ed. Patrick J. Geary (Peterborough, ON: Broadview Press, 1998), 505–6.

24 *Abelard & Heloise: The Letters and Other Writings*, trans. William Levitan (Indianapolis: Hackett, 2007), 11–12.

25 Levitan, 15.

26 Heloise to Abelard, "Third Letter," in Levitan, 78.

27 *Fasciculus Morum: A Fourteenth-Century Preacher's Handbook*, ed. Siegfried Wenzel (University Park: Pennsylvania State University Press, 1989), 7:7, p. 69. I have substituted "whore" for "prostitute" as a translation for "meretrix" because I think it best conveys the broad range of meaning.

28 *The Early South-English Legendary or Lives of Saints*, ed. Carl Horstmann, Early English Text Society vol. 87 (London: N. Trübner, 1887), 261, lines 15–16.

29 Ptolemy of Lucca, *On the Government of Rulers: De Regimine Principium*, 4:14:6, trans. James M. Blythe (Philadelphia: University of Pennsylvania Press, 1997), 254. Ptolemy attributes the analogy to Augustine, but it is found in none of the latter's works.

30 Stadtarchiv München, Urkunden A Ia Nr. 24, cited in Peter Schuster, *Das Frauenhaus: Städtische Bordelle in Deutschland (1350–1600)* (Paderborn: Ferdinand Schöningh, 1992), 41.

31 Corporation of London Records Office, Repertory Book 3, fol. 40r (1515).

32 Quoted and translated in Rasma Lazda-Cazers, "Oral Sex in Oswald von Wolkenstein's 'Es Seusst dort her von orient' (Kl. 20)," in *Sexuality in the Middle Ages and Early Modern Times: New Approaches to a Fundamental Cultural-Historical and Literary-Anthropological Theme*, ed. Albrecht Classen (Berlin: Walter de Gruyter, 2008), 598.

33 *Medieval Handbooks of Penance*, trans. John T. McNeill and Helena M. Gamer (New York: Columbia University Press, 1938), 185.

34 Penitential of Bede, 3:14, 3:19, 3:23–4, in *Die Bussordnungen der abendländischen Kirche*, ed. W.H. Wasserschleben (Halle: Ch. Graeger, 1851), 222–3.

35 Heloise to Abelard, "Fifth Letter." I here use Lochrie's translation, from Karma Lochrie, *Heterosyncrasies: Female Sexuality When Normal Wasn't* (Minneapolis: University of Minnesota Press, 2005), 31, rather than that in Levitan, 108, because it better preserves the ambiguity in the Latin.

36 Translated in Robert L.A. Clark, "Jousting without a Lance," in *Same Sex Love and Desire among Women in the Middle Ages*, eds. Francesca Canadé Sautman and Pamela Sheingorn (New York: Palgrave, 2001), 166.

37 Stadtarchiv Speyer, 1A704/11, fols. 12r–14r, ed. and trans. Helmut Puff, "Female Sodomy: The Trial of Katherina Hetzeldorfer (1477)," *Journal of Medieval and Early Modern Studies* 30 (2000), 59–61.

38 Translated in Sahar Amer, *Crossing Borders: Love between Women in Medieval French and Arabic Literatures* (Philadelphia: University of Pennsylvania Press, 2008), 58.

39 Al-Mas'ūdī, *Murūj al-dhahab*, trans. in Everett Rowson, "Gender Irregularity as Entertainment: Institutionalized Transvestism at the Caliphal Court in Medieval Baghdad," in *Gender and Difference in the Middle Ages*, eds. Sharon Farmer and Carol Braun Pasternack (Minneapolis: University of Minnesota Press, 2003), 45–72, quotation at p. 47.

40 *Opera Arnaldi de Villanova* (Lyon: F. Fradin, 1504), fols. 190v–191r; trans. D. Jacquart and C. Thomasset, *Sexuality and Medicine in the Middle Ages*, trans. Matthew Adamson (Princeton: Princeton University Press, 1988), 153. This text, the *Breviarum Practice*, is wrongly attributed to Arnaud of Villanova; the actual author is not known.

41 Joanot Martorell and Marti Joan de Galba, *Tirant lo Blanc*, trans. David H. Rosenthal (New York: Warner Books, 1984), 426.

42 *The Saga of Grettir the Strong*, 75, trans. Bernard Scudder, *The Complete Sagas of Icelanders*, ed. Viðar Hreinsson (Reykjavík: Leifur Eiríksson, 1997), 2:166.

43 *Pleas before the King or His Justices 1198–1202, vol. 4*, ed. Doris Mary Stenton, Selden Society 84 (London, 1967), 114.

44 *Historia Apollonia Regis Tyri*, ch. 1, trans. in Elizabeth Archibald, *Incest and the Medieval Imagination* (Oxford: Oxford University Press, 2001), 96–7.

45 "Man of Law's Prologue," ll. 82–5, *Riverside Chaucer*, 88.

46 Hartmann von Aue, *Gregorius: A Medieval Oedipus Legend*, ll. 345–6, 394–5, 1960–1, trans. Edwin H. Zeydel (Chapel Hill: University of North Carolina Press, 1955), 27–8, 74.

47 Iris Origo, "The Domestic Enemy: The Eastern Slaves in Tuscany in the Fourteenth and Fifteenth Centuries," *Speculum* 30 (1955), 321–66.

48 Maria Serena Mazzi, *Prostitute e lenoni nella Firenze del Quattrocento* (Milan: Il Saggiatore, 1991), 119.

49 *The Book of Women's Love and Jewish Medieval Medical Literature on Women*, ed. and trans. by Carmen Caballero-Navas (London: Kegan Paul, 2004), 112–14.

50 Heinrich Krämer and Jakob Sprenger, *Malleus Maleficarum*, 1:6, trans. Montague Summers (New York: Dover, 1971), 43–8.

51 *Malleus Maleficarum*, 1:9, p. 58; 2:1:7, p. 121.

52 *Malleus Maleficarum*, 2:1:1, pp. 97–8.

53 *Malleus Maleficarum*, 2:1:4, p. 114.

54 *Malleus Maleficarum*, 1:3, p. 25.

5

MEN OUTSIDE OF MARRIAGE

Despite the teachings of churchmen that sexual behavior outside of marriage was sinful for both men and women, medieval society in general held to the double standard by which men's sexual transgressions were expected and disregarded or regarded far less seriously than those of women. While women's sexual behavior was monitored and critiqued, men's raised objections most often when it impinged on the rights of other men to the exclusive sexual services of their wives, or the virginity of their daughters. A man who had a mistress or patronized prostitutes might be seen as less than honorable, and might be urged to do penance for it, but did not come in for the same type of opprobrium as a transgressive woman. In both eastern and western Christian traditions a man who had sex with another man's wife, a nun, or a virgin was seen as having taken something of value that belonged to another, but a man who had sex with an unmarried woman who was not a virgin committed a much lesser sin. In the Muslim tradition the latter did not sin at all.

Because most of the sexual relationships in which medieval men engaged were with women, and women have been discussed in the previous chapter, some of the material presented here will sound familiar. In this chapter we are seeing the flip side – what it looked like from the man's point of view. A large portion of this chapter is devoted to the subject of sexual relations between men. This topic is especially prominent here because it has not been treated in previous chapters, and because such relations were especially problematic and therefore occasioned a great deal of comment (despite being considered "unmentionable"). It is important to remember, however, that the gender of one's partner was not the main way of categorizing sexual activity in the Middle Ages. Sex between two men was illicit, but so was much sex between men and women. Anything that was not potentially reproductive, no matter who the partners were, fell into the illicit category.

Masculine privilege and illicit sex

Technically, any sexual liaison outside of marriage, even if it were potentially or even actively reproductive, was illicit. Medieval people would have been aware of this. But they did not always take the prohibitions against it seriously, especially in the case of the men involved. Readers over a certain age, and indeed many younger readers, will not find too much difficulty in imagining an era in which social norms prohibit non-marital sex for both men and women, but in which there nevertheless exists a contrary cultural current suggesting that "boys will be boys" and it is only to be expected that young men will seek a sexual outlet – moreover, in which male sexual prowess is respected by some other men even though it contravenes accepted rules. Men were prosecuted for fornication and for adultery; they by no means always escaped scot-free. Yet their punishment was often lighter, and the reputational damage to men could be a good deal less than to women. From the early to the later Middle Ages, very privileged men, royalty and high nobility, could commit adultery (against their own marriages or those of their partners) not only without punishment, but even without condemnation by ecclesiastical chroniclers, as demonstrated by the Lombard writer Paul the Deacon's account of the eighth century. The same was true of the elites in non-Christian societies.

What sketchy data we have (mainly from the later Middle Ages) indicate that the age at marriage for men was relatively high in both northern and southern Europe. In England the average age might be the late twenties, in Italy even later. People did not expect all these young men to go all that time without sexual activity. Indeed, providing an outlet for these men's desires that did not threaten the wives and daughters of respectable men was one of the reasons given for the establishment of municipal brothels. This reasoning privileged the male sex drive as something unstoppable, which could only be channeled into more or less socially acceptable outlets.

Patronizing prostitutes was such an accepted activity that groups of young men often visited brothels together. This may have provided an opportunity for them to bond through sharing a sexual experience; but even in the absence of any homoerotic aspects, it could be seen as part of a typical evening's entertainment, along with drinking. This was true of elite young men in Venice and Florence in the later Middle Ages, when family marriage strategies prevented them from marrying; it was also true of men at all levels of the social scale who were unable to marry because they could not support a household. Apprenticeship contracts were often very concerned that these workers not visit prostitutes, perhaps because it was feared that the money to finance the visit would be stolen from their masters; but the fact that this was such a concern indicates that the activity was not at all uncommon. References in French court records to young men visiting brothels mentioned that they had done so "as unmarried young servant-journeymen are wont to do," or that "nature moves them." Jacques Rossiaud says that this activity was viewed as "a proof of social and physiological normality."[1]

Of course, far from all non-marital liaisons would have been with prostitutes. Fornication could be a part of courtship and a prelude to marriage.

Indeed, the line between different kinds of liaisons may not always have been entirely clear. In one fifteenth-century English case of a disputed marriage contract, the woman claimed that the man had given her gifts – a pair of gloves, a set of knives, and fifteen pence – that were indicative of a marriage, and that she had given him gifts in return. The man claimed that these were not given "with the intention of having her as his wife, but to please her so she would continue with him in sin."[2] Perhaps the two had misunderstood each other; more likely, one of them was lying, although it is impossible to know which. But the fact that the same items could have represented either a marriage gift or a prostitute's fee indicates that the categories were not always sharply delineated. For the man, one sort of premarital sex was not necessarily more acceptable than another. Legal materials would indicate that Muslim and Jewish societies were a good deal stricter in regulating men's access to marriageable daughters, but in practice this likely applied more to the elites.

Men were often, but not always, the ones seen as initiating sexual relationships. Medieval sources speak of prostitutes accosting men, pulling them into their houses or calling to them from an upper story to come up. This is not, however, the only situation in which women are depicted as the aggressors. The satirical fabliaux and the tales in the One Thousand and One Nights, discussed in previous chapters, include some in which women are depicted as sexually insatiable. Despite this motif, and despite the fact that medical texts considered women to be more lustful than men, most medieval evidence points to men as being the more aggressive in initiating sexual relationships. The woman may be a seductress, like Eve, but her seduction functions to arouse the man's desire, not actually to initiate the sexual contact. The frequency of rape motifs in literature, or the situations below (pp. 175–177) in which the line between rape and not-rape is hard to define because women's consent is seen as largely irrelevant, are examples of men as aggressors. So are the romance stories in which men are seen as attempting to earn their ladies' love and its physical solaces.

The idea that men were more aggressive and women more reluctant is logical enough given the potential consequences for the two. Women could get pregnant; even if they did not, their reputations could be ruined if they engaged in illicit intercourse, whereas men's would not be damaged nearly as much. Thus a belief in women's greater lust is not necessarily incompatible with a culture that depicts men as taking the initiative; women may desire more but have much greater incentive to control that desire, whereas in the Middle Ages men's desire, even if somewhat less, was privileged.

The consequences to men of overindulgence in sex, as medieval people understood them, were not negligible. They were the same regardless of whether they engaged in sex with other men or with women, except that women were mentioned as bearers of disease much more frequently than other men. Disease was but one possibility. It is not clear that any disease that existed in Europe before the later fifteenth century can be identified as syphilis (scientists do not agree on whether it was brought from the Americas to Europe after contact, whether a disease that was mild and possibly transmitted nonsexually in the Americas evolved rapidly in a new population, or some other possibility). There were other diseases, with no more specific name than "burning sickness," that were known to be sexually transmitted, and medieval people also believed that a man could get what they called leprosy (a name applied to various conditions, not necessarily only Hansen's disease) via sexual intercourse.

Overindulgence in sex could also bring with it an imbalance in the humors and make a man ill. Medical texts counseled moderation rather than chastity, but a man who indulged too often risked infertility or illness. The medical texts seem to be referring mainly to intercourse itself, and not masturbation. Unlike the Victorians, who worried about the debilitating effect of masturbation on boys, medieval writers, at least outside the monastery, do not seem to have been as concerned about it, although it was prohibited in Jewish as well as Christian law. The early medieval penitentials do provide penalties for masturbation, and also for nocturnal emissions, which created a ritual impurity. Nocturnal emissions continued to be a concern for moralists, not on the grounds of health but rather sin; the nocturnal emissions are not blameworthy if they arise from natural causes like illness, but are considered worse if one has consented to the sin by doing something to encourage it, like thinking lustful thoughts – giving in to pleasure as opposed to reason – before going to sleep. Indeed, even the fact of a nocturnal emission might be considered evidence that one had not sufficiently controlled one's desires, which reappeared in dreams. The Sefer Hasidim suggests that masturbation may be acceptable for a man in order to satisfy his desire and avoid committing a more serious sin, although the man had to do penance afterward. The kabbalistic text Zohar, however, considered masturbation to be akin to murder – killing one's own children – and nocturnal emission demonic.

In Christianity masturbation continued to be a concern within the monastery especially. Guibert of Nogent in the twelfth century describes a monk who wished to learn about black magic. A Jew of his acquaintance agreed to introduce him to the devil. The devil required that the monk offer him a libation of his semen: "When you have poured it out to me, you will taste it first, as it behooves the one offering the sacrifice."[3] Guibert does not say that all masturbation is a libation to the devil, but the implication is clear – as is the connection of Jews with the devil.

For the most part, a single Christian man outside the monastery risked little from engaging in non-marital sexual relations, as long as he did not overindulge and did not choose as his partner the wife, daughter, or son of a man of higher social standing. As long as he played the active role, people outside the church were willing to be very forgiving of his sexual behavior, aside from a few periods of concern over sodomy. Despite a wide variety of ecclesiastical texts that repeated that even simple fornication, between an unmarried man and an unmarried woman, was a mortal sin for both parties, the church's teaching on chastity for men never made it into the public mentality to the same extent as that of women (or, rather, the teaching of the church on women's sexuality supported and reinforced secular attitudes as that on men's did not).

The church imposed some shame punishments for fornication, such as a certain number of processions around a church carrying a candle. One wonders, though, how shameful the punishment really was. Given the way the society at large objected so little to men's sexual activity, how much ridicule would it have caused a man to be publicly displayed as a fornicator? It was not the stocks, and these were not Puritans. Medieval men might not have had quite the same sexual freedom as, say, those in ancient Rome – the church's teaching had at least the effect of making people aware that they had something to conceal and to confess – but it was not all that different. Medieval European Jews encouraged their children to marry young, at least the children of elites, and generally considered marriage the appropriate response to sexual temptation.

A disconnect between the views of unmarried men's sexual activity held by their peers and those held by their elders or social superiors should not be surprising; it can be found in many societies. When medieval authors criticized men for fornicating, it was often not because of the sinfulness of their acts or the temptation they offered to others (as was the case with women), but rather on the grounds of social disorder. Men who had sex with other men's daughters or wives disrupted the patriarchal system that assigned control over women to particular men. They could also subvert urban social hierarchies among men, in which a father or master was supposed to have control over a young man's behavior (including his choice of marriage partner) and a guild or clan over an older man's. In some cases, too, they could be seen as disrupting the divine order of things: when a man had sex with a nun or a woman with a priest, or a couple had intercourse in a church, or a Jew had sexual relations with a Christian, these could sometimes (as in fifteenth-century Venice) be seen as crimes against God. This particular type of accusation, however, was uncommon. For the most part men's fornication was at the same time illicit and quite ordinary.

Naming practices give some indication of the way in which male heterosexual activity was privileged, even outside the elites. The English lay subsidies of the late thirteenth and early fourteenth centuries record a great number of bynames, used to identify individuals before the use of surnames had become routine practice. The taxpayers in these surveys included everyone who owned more than a certain value of disposable chattels – not all the peasantry by any means, but certainly the wealthier ones. Names come from other sources as well, mainly court and taxation records. What is striking here is the number of names with sexual referents that had become recognized and official enough to be used in such records, not just in casual conversation. Bynames include Balloc (testicle), Daubedame (seduce-woman), Levelaunce (raise spear, the French equivalent of Wagstaff or Shakespeare), Grantamur (great love), Coyldeor (golden testicles), Clawcunte (meaning just what it sounds like), Coltepyntel (colt's penis), Wytepintell (white penis), Silvirpintil (silver penis), Assbollock (donkey's testicles), Plukkerose (pluck a rose, a metaphor for sexual intercourse), Pryketayl (penetrate-vagina), Swetabedde (sweet in bed), Luvelady (love ladies), Strekelevedy (stroke lady). Some of these names may have been given derisively and happened to stick, but they were probably not all derisive, many may have been given with a nudge or in backhanded admiration. The church might exhibit a fear and censure of sexual behavior, but the laity tended to accept it as usual and not shocking for men.

Dominance and sexual opportunity

Masculine sexual privilege meant that single men were less condemned for fornication than their female partners. It also meant that both single and married men often entered into sexual relationships characterized by asymmetries of class and power. Aristocratic men had sexual access to women of other social groups, sometimes for brief encounters but sometimes for long-term relationships. One example is Robert, Duke of Normandy, the father of William the Conqueror (also known as William the Bastard because his parents were not married). The daughter of a palace official (or possibly, as William's enemies alleged, a tanner) bore him two children, a son and a daughter, whom he acknowledged; the son became his heir. The fact that a son born out of wedlock was able to inherit was due to the peculiarities of Norman custom. Marriage *more danico* (in the Danish manner), non-Christian, non-binding, and possibly plural, was not far in the past. The Normans had brought the custom with them from Scandinavia a century and a half before, and while these relationships were no longer recognized as marriages, the children that resulted were allowed to inherit in the absence of legitimate heirs, although they sometimes had to fight hard for the right. In Muslim law the sons of a man's slave concubines had the same inheritance rights as any son.

Usually they could not be their fathers' heirs, but throughout the Christian Middle Ages illegitimate children of aristocrats were given lands and titles (if boys) and/or married to other aristocrats slightly lower in status. The existence of such children was not a blot upon the reputation of their fathers, and medieval sources never refer to the revelation of extramarital sexual activity as a reason for not acknowledging them. Henry I of England (1069–1135), whose legitimate son died young (thus occasioning a civil war upon Henry's death between his daughter Matilda and his nephew Stephen), had six known concubines and more than twenty known illegitimate children, but was still considered a good Christian and supporter of the church. William of Malmesbury even wrote of him that:

> all his life he was completely free of fleshly lusts, indulging in the embraces of the female sex (as I have heard from those who know) from love of begetting children and not to gratify his passions; for he thought it beneath his dignity to comply with extraneous gratification, unless the royal seed could fulfill its natural purpose.[4]

It is doubtful whether this was truly the motivation, as Henry was only following the pattern usual among aristocratic men of his day.

Ecclesiastical chroniclers might make excuses for a king, as William did for Henry, or for other members of the nobility. Georges Duby famously argued that Lambert of Ardres' *History of the Counts of Guines and Lords of Ardres*, written in Flanders in the early thirteenth century, tolerated and even praised men's sexual license. Duby takes Lambert's writing as reflective of aristocratic attitudes, presenting the image his patrons wished to project. And it is true that Lambert takes the fathering of illegitimate children before a nobleman's marriage as more or less routine. But even Lambert is a bit apologetic, as William of Malmesbury was about Henry I. Lambert wrote, he claimed, for Baldwin II of Guines and his son. But he does not brag about Baldwin's sexual activities. On the contrary, he places his description of Baldwin's sexual exploits in the mouths of Baldwin's enemies:

> He was, in fact, so ardent, as they say, toward young girls and especially virgins, that neither David nor his son Solomon is believed to be his equal in the corruption of so many young women, nor even Jupiter, so long as his sophistical flatteries fell upon girls.[5]

Lambert calls these enemies liars, although he never explicitly denies the accusation. The text reads more as though Lambert were trying to explain away Baldwin's reputation than to glorify it. But even if sexual indulgence and the fathering of illegitimate children was seen as excusable rather than glorified, it was mainly for the aristocracy that it was so.

Not only aristocrats fathered children with subordinate women. The fifteenth-century Florentine merchant Gregorio Dati, for example, recorded in his diary his twenty-five children by three of his four wives, and also his son by his Tartar slave Margherita. The slave was not part of his Florentine household but rather lived in Valencia, where Dati had spent two years. When he lists his children, he notes, "I was single when my first son, Maso, was born," instead of labeling him illegitimate. When he first recorded Maso's birth, however, he did note that he was born to a slave.[6] However, he brought Maso to Florence and had him raised in his household, where his wife treated him as one of her own children. The pieties Dati expresses in his diary do not include any regret over his extramarital relationship. Everyone treated it as normal and expected masculine behavior.

Because of the power differential inherent in sexual relations between an aristocratic man and a servant woman, coercion, expressed or implied, was always present. It is therefore not possible to draw a sharp line between consensual relations and rape. Where a relationship lasted for a period of years and the couple had several children, we may assume that the woman consented on some level, but we do not know what kinds of pressure were brought to bear, nor how the relationship began initially. Prosecutions for rape are rare enough in the Middle Ages, but prosecutions of a man for the rape of his own servant are practically non-existent. The last chapter discussed rape from the point of view of the woman; here we focus on the man.

The pastourelle, a genre of medieval French literature, eroticizes the idea of rape across class lines. In this type of poem, a knight meets a shepherdess and tries to seduce her. In some, she consents; in others, he attempts to rape her but a shepherd defends her; and in 38 of the 160 extant pastourelles, he rapes her. The same sorts of language are used for the rape and the seduction. Because the woman is simply a shepherdess, her consent does not matter that much. In one poem, for example, the speaker says,

> When I saw that neither by my pleas nor my promises of jewels could I please her, whatever my whims, I threw her down on the grass; she did not imagine she was to have great pleasure, but sighed, clenched her fists, tore her hair, and tried to escape.

Nevertheless she ends up enjoying it: "As I was leaving she said to me, 'Sire, come back this way often.' "[7] The pastourelles project class conflict on to the body of the peasant woman: the lords screw the peasants, and the peasants don't mind. Similarly, in his twelfth-century *Art of Love*, Andreas Capellanus provides advice to men on how to woo women of different classes, but when it comes to peasant women, he urges his implicitly aristocratic reader simply: "when you find a convenient place, do not hesitate to take what you seek and to embrace them by force," since peasants cannot be persuaded by words.[8] This passage may be intended highly ironically, but it finds many later echoes.

Romance, too, normalizes rape. The twelfth-century French author Chrétien de Troyes, in his *Lancelot*, explains the customs of the (fictional) kingdom of Logres:

> At that period the customs and rights decreed that a knight, finding a damsel or girl alone, if he wished to keep his good reputation, would no more treat her with less than total honour than he would cut his own throat; and should he rape her, he would be disgraced for ever in all courts. But if she had an escort, then another person

wishing to fight a combat with him for her and win her by force of arms would be able to have his will of her without incurring any shame or reproach.[9]

This, of course, is not an actual law of any European jurisdiction. It does, however, indicate that what counts in the romance world is not the woman's desires but male etiquette. One cannot rape a lone woman, but if one defeats her defender in a fair fight, then one may.

Rape was not only a literary phenomenon, it was a part of men's and women's lived experience. Statistical study of rape prosecutions in Venice reveals that context was everything in terms of determining how it was treated under the law. Rape of a child was punished very severely. Rape of a married woman was worse than that of a widow. However, rape of marriageable women was prosecuted quite lightly, being considered little more than a stage of courtship or a step toward marriage, and rape of a single woman of lower social status than the rapist was rarely punished. Elsewhere in Italy, too, certain women were treated as incapable of giving consent, because their sexuality was under the control of someone else, and other women were of ill fame and therefore rape against them was rarely treated as serious; the fine could be the same as for sex with a consenting woman. A case from Bologna from 1435 accused two Jewish merchants from France of raping an eleven-year-old Jewish girl and a Jewish boy "whose name it is better not to mention at the moment." The archives of Bologna from 1400 to 1465 contain twenty-five cases of rape of women, and sixty-seven of children or adolescents, including thirty-four of boys and thirty-three of girls, but the language used is quite different; for girls and women, the sex was "violently and against her will" but for the boys it was simply "sodomitically."[10] In Italian towns it was quite common for young girls (aged between seven and twelve) to be placed in the houses of wealthier families as something between a servant or slave and a family member: they were to serve for a period of years and then be given a dowry. A 1420 case from Venice in which a householder raped such a girl and was punished severely stresses that in this particular instance the girl had been well dressed and treated as a member of the family, but this unusually high penalty only reveals the contrast with the more normal situation in which servant women or girls were sexually available to the head and other men of the household. As discussed in Chapter 4, this was especially true of slaves.

Even when they were not enslaved, women of a subordinate group were often available sexually to men of a dominant group. In Muslim Spain, for example, Muslims and Jews not uncommonly had Christian concubines, while in Christian Spain Christians and Jews had Muslim concubines. The authorities were mainly concerned about protecting "their" women from sex with men of other groups, and were less concerned with what their own men did. They might condemn inter-ethnic or inter-religious liaisons involving their own men and other women, but they did not commonly punish them. The Fourth Lateran Council of 1215 ordered that Jews and "Saracens" (Muslims) throughout Christendom should wear distinguishing clothing so that neither Christian men nor Christian women would mistakenly have sex with members of the other groups.

From the point of view of masculine identity and the ways in which sexuality supported it, there was not much difference between fornication and rape, unless the rape was of a woman in a somewhat protected category. This was a matter of class privilege as much as of gender privilege. There are certainly instances, such as the epidemic of gang rapes in Dijon in the fifteenth century, in which rape was an assertion of the gender order: women were not supposed to transgress outside marriage, servant women were not supposed to sleep with their masters, and wives were not supposed to be left alone for a few days by their husbands. The women could be punished with rape for any transgression. The rape may have been directed against the husband or other male guardian of the victim, even though she was the one who suffered physically; it had symbolic meaning in terms of power relationships among men. But in many of the cases, particularly in those where it is clear to us that what is going on is rape but people in the Middle Ages did not classify it as such, it was an expression of power not just over women but over a subordinate social class, both men and women.

Rape was not only a sexual act, an act of class privilege, and an act of violence against women (as discussed in Chapter 4), it was also an act against the woman's family and its honor. In this context, too, the woman's consent may be irrelevant: the lack of the family's consent becomes central. One example comes in accounts of the Muslim invasion of Spain in 711. According to this story, the last Christian Visigothic king, Rodrigo, not only usurped the throne from the sons of the previous king, but he also raped the daughter of a powerful lord, who took his revenge by inviting the Arab conquerors in. The historical accuracy of this story is unverifiable and unlikely. What is important here, however, is that it was seen as plausible, retold by different chroniclers because it provided an explanation of why someone might betray his king and his religion. But these texts do not discuss the issue of the daughter's consent, nor the use of violence against her. What they emphasize, on the contrary, is the taking of a daughter against a father's will, and her social disparagement: "King Rodrigo hotly snatched her away, not as his wife, but because she seemed to him beautiful as a concubine."[11] The rape becomes one example of the moral failings of the last Visigothic king, punished by God by means of the Muslims.

The medieval gender system allowed men privileges of sexual indulgence that it did not allow women, and it also pressured men continually to prove their masculinity. Sexual activity and violence were not the only ways in which they proved it; self-control and honesty were also masculine values, as was providing for a household. But the latter required sexual activity in

177

order to generate the children who would be provided for. Sex and violence remained important ways of demonstrating masculine identity in the Middle Ages, and the opportunity to combine them was all too common.

Gender roles and male sexuality

In many medieval texts, whether concerning rape or other issues, the woman's consent was largely irrelevant because in any case she was the passive partner, having something done to her, "suffering" it. Indeed, in some instances, the fact that the man was the active partner, the penetrator, made not only the consent of his partner but even the gender of his partner irrelevant. Medieval Europe did not exactly follow the ancient Greek pattern where as long as a man was the active partner, whether he penetrated a woman or a boy (or young man) was not a moral question but simply one of preference. However, there were echoes or elements of such a pattern in medieval culture.

It was possible for some medieval people to take the attitude that an active man was an active man, regardless of the gender of the passive partner, because there was no concept of a "homosexual identity" based on object choice. That is, men were not defined by the gender of the person they preferred, but rather by the role they played. Today we tend to label men who prefer to have sex with other men as "gay," regardless of the active/passive distinction. The Middle Ages did not have such a category. Just as a man and a woman who had sex together were not understood as committing the same act, the same was true of two men who had sex together. For example, when the accused heretic Arnold of Verniolles confessed to the Inquisition, he described his sexual relations with other men carefully to indicate that both acted: "Each of them once committed sodomy," or "He committed sodomy with Guillaume Ros and Guillaume with him."[12]

The classical scholar David Halperin has described four categories of "male sex and gender deviance" found in historical societies that did not have a concept of homosexuality. The first is effeminacy. As Halperin points out, however, effeminacy is not always connected with male same-sex relations; in the ancient world and occasionally in the medieval world the effeminate man was a womanizer who spent too much time in the company of women rather than that of men. The second category, pederasty or active sodomy, we certainly do find in the Middle Ages, but the active sodomite was not seen as unmasculine or as having an exclusive preference for men. The third category, male friendship and love, was especially common in the monastic context, but found elsewhere too. The men who felt and expressed love for each other may indeed sometimes have been the same ones who committed sodomy together, but medieval sources do not assume this; the phenomena may overlap but are still distinct. Finally, Halperin's fourth category is gender inversion, men who play the passive role. This is different from effeminate behavior, although again there may be a good deal of over-lap. Halperin suggests that this is the only one of the four categories that can be said to constitute a sexual orientation. And this category was very prominent in the way medieval Europeans understood men's sexual behavior. A man who played the passive role did not have a sexual preference for men, he had a preference for being a woman.

An example of how these different types of male sex and gender deviance may be distinct comes from the writings of the ninth-century Arabic writer al-Jāḥiz at the court of Baghdad. He comments of eunuchs:

> What is astonishing is that, despite their transferral from the realm of male characteristics to that of females, they are not susceptible to effeminacy (*takhnīth*). . . . And what is yet more astonishing about them in this connection is how common passive homosexual-ity (*hulāq*) is among them, despite the rarity of effeminacy.[13]

This author expected that lack of masculine genitalia, effeminacy, and sexual passivity would normally go together, but he was open-minded enough to observe that in this instance they did not. A century later, under the Abbasids, *mukannathūn*, male entertainers who cross-dressed, who in the previous Ummayad period had been forbidden to enter the women's quarters and who had sometimes been married, were assumed and expected to be passive partners for other men. Al-Jāḥiz quotes extensively from a genre of Arabic and Persian poetry from the ninth century that includes both love poetry to boys and crude sexual poetry:

> I have no need for cunt
> I think fucking is revolting
> No one screws the cunt
> Except those who were poor and needy.
> So if you screw, screw
> A beardless youth, pale as a piece of ivory.[14]

Here, as with Christian society, there was a difference between religious teaching and courtly attitudes, and we do not really know to what extent more popular practices reflected one or the other. It seems that preference for young men over young women did not make a man effeminate or make him the same thing as a modern "homosexual," although Hugh Kennedy argues that the preference was seen as involuntary, permanent, and defining.

"Male homosexual behavior," then, was not a single category any more than was "sodomy." We can, however, draw some conclusions about how the average person – not the theologian – understood the different types of sexual relations in which men might engage, or the different categories for men who engaged in them, by looking at the kinds of insults people leveled

179

against each other. We know about these insults primarily from defamation cases in which one person sued another for the insult. Reputation was very important in the Middle Ages – one's economic livelihood could depend on it (as indicated in the semantic shift in the word "credit" from "belief" to "reputation" to "worthiness to be loaned money"). Thus an insult might be not just fighting words but actually quite harmful. These cases were heard in the church courts rather than secular courts.

For England in the later Middle Ages, where a number of such cases survive, what is striking is the lack of sexual insults directed against men – at least, the lack of sexual insults that people complained about in court. If women were defamed by their neighbors, it was most often by impugning their sexual behavior, calling them whores or adulteresses. Men, however, were most often insulted on grounds of their honesty, by calling them thieves or otherwise untrustworthy. The sexual insults directed against men found in the London records mainly concern the sexual behavior of the women in their lives: "cuckold" or "whoremonger," for example. It may be that men were most eager to complain in court about insults that directly challenged their livelihoods, which were those referring to their integrity in business, and that sexual defamations were dealt with in other ways, but there is little evidence for this. Women brought issues about sexual defamation into court, seeking a public declaration that their honor was in fact untainted, and the fact that men did not would seem to indicate that in London men were either not frequently taunted with accusations of having sex with other men, or not seriously bothered by it. In London church courts, out of over five thousand defamation cases in the late fifteenth century, only one had to do with male homosexual behavior, and only one case of actual sodomy (as opposed to an insult of sodomy) appeared in these records.

From Iceland, however, where our evidence comes from narrative literature rather than court records, it appears that insults involving a man's sexual activity with another man were among the most damaging. However, these insults were all of a particular sort. It was no insult to allege that someone was the active partner; it was to behave like a woman or to be used as a woman that was problematic. The term *argr*, which meant a man who was passive in sex with another man, also meant "coward," which in Viking Age civilization was the worst thing a man could be.

Icelandic and Norwegian law provided that comparing a man to a female animal was one of the insults that demanded full outlawry as a punishment. One Norwegian law held:

> These are the insulting remarks that call for full atonement. The first is when a man says of another that he has given birth to a child. The second is when he says that the man has been used as a woman. The third is when he likens him to a mare or calls him

a slut or a whore or likens him to any kind of a female beast. For these he shall pay the man a full atonement; but the man may also seek satisfaction in blood and outlawry for the sayings that I have now enumerated.[15]

Icelandic law limited the right to kill over insults to three words, all denoting being the passive partner (two meaning having been sexually used by a man, the third meaning a tendency to cowardice, effeminacy, and sexual passivity).

In the sagas themselves, the most common insults are either of cowardice or of passivity. The latter include: "If you are the sweetheart of the troll at Svinafell, as it is said, he uses you as a woman every ninth night," a gratuitous insult that causes a complex settlement of a feud to collapse; an accusation that a stallion had mounted a mare that a man was riding and may have mounted the man himself; and in response to a threat of an ambush in a mountain pass, "It would be a serious mistake on your part if you close Ljosavatn pass to me so that I may not travel there with my companions, yet you couldn't keep the little 'pass' between your own buttocks decently closed."[16]

In another Icelandic story, a man admires an engraved axe belonging to the king of Norway.

> The king noticed that at once and asked Halli if he liked the axe.
> Halli said he liked it very much.
> "Have you seen a better axe?"
> "I don't think so," said Halli.
> "Will you allow yourself to be fucked for the axe?" said the king.
> "I will not," said Halli, "but it seems understandable that you should want to sell the axe for the same price you paid for it." "So it shall be, Halli," said the king. "Take it and use it for the best – it was given to me and so shall I give it to you."[17]

The humor of this story derives from the man's ability to return the king's insult without being explicit about it. In none of these stories, however, is the insult a defamation in the sense that the speaker is really trying to get people to believe it literally. No one believed that another man was anally penetrated by a troll. Rather, these insults were in a sense self-fulfilling accusations of cowardice. If a man did not respond with physical violence, then the meaning, if not the literal details, of the insult was true: he was a coward. The insults were prohibited in the law because they were destructive of peace. In Iceland the passive role in intercourse was connected not with sin but with lack of manliness. It was not an insult to suggest that a man had sex with other men if he was the active partner.

Sodomy and otherness

Homosexual behavior between men could be used as an insult, although often only against a man playing the passive role. It could also be used as a social critique of a society that medieval Europeans wished to depict as "other." This could be almost any society: for example, after the Norman conquest of England, Gerald of Wales, part Norman himself, directed it against Normans whom he felt were too French:

> That unspeakable and horribly outrageous crime of the Normans, which they took from the French but made especially their own, was so strong in this particular Norman that he acted like the standard-bearer of all the rest in that abuse.[18]

Other English writers during the twelfth century also used sodomy as part of their critique of all things French, but it was not contrasted with a desire for women. Rather, all sorts of sexual excess were part of a luxurious and effeminate style of life that was criticized and cast as alien as part of moral campaigns.

Another group particularly connected with sodomy were heretics, perhaps because of the accusations against the Cathars involving non-reproductive and therefore "unnatural" sex practices. In late medieval Germany, the word *Ketzer* (heretic) was commonly used for a sodomite, and "to commit heresy with one another" was a euphemism for male same-sex intercourse, as in a 1456 Regensburg case where a man was accused of "heresy with several men and boys."[19] The prevalence of this term may reflect the fact that sodomy was not just seen as a secular offense but was deeply connected with sin and was considered, at least by the authorities, to be an act against God.

The use of sodomy as a sign of otherness, though, was particularly connected in Christian writings with Islam. There was a long tradition of Christian Europeans connecting Muslims with sodomy; one of the earliest texts is *Pelagius*, by Hrotsvitha of Gandersheim, about a Christian youth who prefers to be martyred rather than give in to the sexual advances of the Emir of Cordoba. A letter purporting to come from the Byzantine emperor Alexius Comnenus before 1098, urging western Europeans to carry out a crusade against the Muslims in the Holy Land, listed among their abuses:

> They have degraded by sodomizing them men of every age and rank – boys, adolescents, young men, old men, nobles, servants, and, what is worse and more wicked, clerics and monks, and even, alas and for shame! something which from the beginning of time has never been spoken of or heard of, bishops! They have already killed one bishop with this nefarious sin.[20]

This was not the Muslims' only sexual crime, according to Alexius: their rape of mothers and daughters precedes their sodomy in the list, which is more an attempt to attribute to the enemy the worst crimes possible than an attempt accurately to catalog their activity. Somewhat surprisingly, in light both of the common use of same-sex practices as a means to critique Muslim societies and of harsh denunciations of sodomy in East Asian cultures in the early modern period, medieval discussions and travelers' accounts of Mongolia, China, Burma, India, and southeast Asia do not refer prominently to these practices.

Those among western European Christians who had the most contact with Muslims – Spanish Christians – at least in the earlier part of the Middle Ages did not single out sodomy as a particularly Muslim sin. Many Muslim writers, too, condemned same-sex relations in much the same way that Christians did. Some authors in Muslim Spain discuss same-sex relations in great detail, but always with the understanding that it is transgressive. Ahmad al-Tifashi, a thirteenth-century North African Muslim writer, begins his chapters on same-sex relations by noting:

> It should be borne in mind that a great many of the literati, as well as the majority of the members of the upper crust of society, belong to the ranks of homosexuals. We have accordingly thought it wiser not to spell out their names, so as not to tarnish their popularity.

The behavior is widespread but not entirely acceptable. In the course of bawdy anecdotes about male–male relations, his work refers repeatedly to the fact that sex with wives or slave women is licit but that sex with men is not.[21]

Even though homosexual behavior was no more officially acceptable under Islam than under Christianity, the letter from pseudo-Alexius falls in a tradition about sodomitical Muslims that continued through the Middle Ages. William of Adam in the fourteenth century criticized Christians who sold boys as slaves to Muslims for sexual purposes:

> And when they are able to find some boy, Christian or Tartar, suitable in body, as he is dispatched for sale, no supplication is too dear for the sake of those whom, more apt to total sinfulness of this sort, they seek. After they buy them, like a statue, they are dressed in silk and covered in gold, their bodies and faces are washed often in baths and other washings. And they are fed sumptuous meals and delicate beverages to make them plumper, pinker, and more voluptuous, and thus they appear more alluring and apt to satisfy the full lust of the Saracens. And when the libidinous, vile, and abominable men, the Saracens, corrupters of human nature, see the boys, they

immediately burn with lust for them and, like mad dogs, race to buy the boys for themselves so that they can have their evil way with them.[22]

Attributing sodomitical desire to the "Saracens" – particularly sodomy involving the rape of Christian boys – allowed the demonization of Muslims. More recent scholars also employed the connection of Muslims with homosexual acts to present Islamic civilization not as abominably sinful but rather as decadent, thereby explaining the Christian reconquest of Spain.

Not only Muslims were cast as "others" by suspicion of sodomy. The Talmud cautioned against allowing one's children to be educated by idolaters, that is, non-Jews; the northern French author Rashi (1040–1105), one of the most important medieval commentators, explained that this was because of the possibility of the (male) teacher attempting to have sexual intercourse with them. The references to "idolaters" and to the practices of "the nations" may have been an oblique way of referring to Christians without directly accusing them. Muslims as well as Christians were suspect: a thirteenth-century Iberian Jewish author wrote that the "Ishmaelites" (Arabs or Muslims) practiced ritual male prostitution. Elsewhere the Talmud explicitly stated that "Israel is not suspected of male–male intercourse or bestiality" – that is, passages that might suggest that Jews would commit this offense, such as a prohibition on an unmarried man teaching children, should be interpreted as addressing a different problem, such as the teacher's encounter with the students' mothers.

Christians sexually demonized Jewish men in a different way; they were thought to pose a threat to Christian women, rather than to Christian men. When the Fourth Lateran Council in 1215 required all Jews to wear an identifying badge, the reason given was so that Christian women would not unknowingly have sex with Jewish men. The study of Jewish communities in medieval Umbria shows that this concern was not unfounded: many Jewish men did have sexual relations, even love relationships, with Christian women, although they married Jewish women in arranged marriages. The punishment on the books for such relationships could be death, but in practice they were punishable by fines. The fear of such sexual relations was one of the issues that, at least ostensibly, prompted the forced conversion of Spanish Jews and the expulsion of the remainder from Spain. Access to the bodies of Christian women, as discussed in Chapter 4, formed an important boundary between in-group and out-group in Spain in the later Middle Ages. In the early fifteenth century it was used by preachers like Vincent Ferrer as a justification for the total segregation of Jews and Muslims from Christians. Even earlier and elsewhere in Europe, general distrust of Jews could be expressed in sexual terms; for example, when Guibert of Nogent described the evil Count Jean of Soissons who "could spurn his young and lovely wife to cavort with a wrinkled old hag," this cavorting took place in the house of a Jew.[23] Jews were not, however, widely connected with same-sex relations.

Sodomy and sin

Most of what we know about men having sex with other men in the Middle Ages comes from the writings of those who were concerned with the morality of Christian society. The "sin against nature" did not always mean sodomy but was often used synonymously with it. But sodomy did not only refer to sex between two men. It was against nature because it was sterile, and it could refer to any sort of non-procreative intercourse. Some Slavic authors considered the female superior position to be sodomy; on the other hand, they considered intercrural (between the thighs) intercourse between two men akin to masturbation, not as serious as anal sex or indeed heterosexual adultery. In western Europe, William Peraldus (quoted above, p. 111), in his widely cited treatise, classified the sin against nature into two types, heterosexual vaginal intercourse in an unusual position or the ejaculation of semen other than in the vagina. Even if we disregard the first type, which was not widely picked up by those who used Peraldus, it is still clear that anal intercourse (or indeed oral, although that seems to have been less common or at least less discussed) would be included regardless of the sex of the participants. What was objectionable about this sin was the fact that it was sex without reproduction, contrary to the church's view that the two should be inextricably linked. If it involved two men, it upset the gender order by placing a man in the feminine role, but it need not always have involved two men.

It would be disingenuous to argue that sodomy was always used in such a general way that we don't know exactly what it meant in any given circumstance. Much of the time people seem to have used it to refer to anal sex between two men, even though it did not lose its more general meaning. When a particular group of men, like the Templars, were accused of having sex with each other as part of their heretical practice, contemporaries labeled it "sodomy." Even though the formal accusations used terms like "carnaliter commiscere" (mingle carnally), chronicles equated this with sodomy. Accusations like those against the Templars were a conventional part of heresy prosecutions and cannot be taken as evidence of their practices, but they can be evidence of what medieval people understood by the category of sodomy.

There were a variety of anti-sodomy penitentials and laws in the early Middle Ages, but these did not go into detail about the sin itself; rather, they gave specific penances for anal and interfemoral intercourse and various ages of partner. The penalties were comparable to penalties for other sexual activities like adultery. The Christian critique of sodomy really began, however, with Peter Damian in the eleventh century. Damian's vehement polemic was especially critical of the clergy who engaged in this vice. Indeed, sodomy in the sense of sex between men was associated with the clergy throughout the Middle Ages, possibly because their unmarried status made them suspect, possibly because the monastery encouraged and provided an opportunity for particularly close relationships between men. The depictions of Ganymede on capitals in medieval cloisters suggest that abbots found this problematic. Priests and monks throughout the Middle Ages were satirized for their heterosexual adventures, but also for their love of boys. Walter Map quotes a Cistercian abbot telling of St. Bernard attempting to perform a miracle by reviving a dead boy: he lay down on top of him on the bed and prayed, but to no avail. Walter then remarked: "He was surely the most unlucky of monks; for never have I heard of a monk lying down upon a boy without the boy arising immediately after the monk."[24] By the fifteenth century, the supposed sodomy of the clergy was one of the arguments used by the English Lollards (a heretical group) to criticize the church and in particular its rule of celibacy: "the law of continence annexed to priesthood, that was first ordained in prejudice of women, induces sodomy in all Holy Church."[25]

The Byzantine church, which did not require clerical celibacy, was concerned with same-sex relations mainly within the monastery. That does not mean that homosexual behavior was acceptable among the laity: there were certainly church canons against it. Medieval commentaries on these canons, however, are not as detailed or rich with examples as commentaries on other subjects. Authorities seem to have been less concerned with the issue after the fifth century, perhaps because the behavior was tolerated as long as it did not become publicly notorious. Byzantine society also knew of a rite of *adelphopoiia*, which some scholars have taken as brotherhood and others as a same-sex union akin to marriage. Frowned on by the church, its main purpose does not seem to have been sexual, but it could create a bond in which sexual relations often did take place.

In the west, Thomas Aquinas provided an influential discussion of the sin against nature, arguing that certain activities were not natural because they were not "for the benefit of the species."[26] Other writers in the university setting, however, were not so opposed. "Natural philosophers" (roughly the medieval equivalent of scientists), addressed a question attributed to Aristotle about why some men "with whom intercourse is had" (again, sex as something done to someone else) experience pleasure. Some considered passive sodomy to be "natural" for some men who had biological peculiarities that caused them to receive pleasure from penetration or anal friction. Peter of Abano, for example, writing about 1310, suggested that in some men the passages by which sperm accumulates in the penis are blocked, causing it to accumulate instead around the anus, and causing the men to experience pleasure from anal penetration. Although in some men this may be "natural" – these men are born that way – this tendency is still unnatural in that it is a deformation of nature. Peter compares it to blindness. In other men, however, the desire for anal stimulation arises from habit. For the active man, it was the discharge of seed that was necessary (in moderation) for good health, not necessarily the discharge in a particular receptacle.

Dante makes sodomy prominent in his *Inferno*, although the prime example – his former mentor Brunetto Latini, whom he meets on a burning plain in the seventh circle of Hell – is not called a sodomite specifically. However, Virgil describes this subcircle to Dante with reference to Sodom:

> One can use force against the Deity by denying it and cursing it in one's heart or by scorning Nature and its goodness; and therefore the smallest subcircle [of the seventh circle] stamps with its seal Sodom and Cahors and whoever speaks with scorn of God in his heart.[27]

Murderers and suicides are found in the first two rings of the seventh circle; sodomites and usurers (the town of Cahors was associated with finance) are in the third. This is where Dante finds Brunetto, along with a crowd of other sinners, some of them identified in the text of Cantos 15–16. The question of whether the reference to Sodom from Canto 11 applies to them, and whether they are meant to be understood as men who engaged in sexual relations with other men, has been bitterly disputed. Scholars from widely varying perspectives have questioned this identification, because they wish to deny that Dante focused so strongly on sexuality at all, or because they wish to stress the "queerness" and lack of specific referentiality of the term "sodomy" and its incommensurability with contemporary homosexuality. Michael Camille argues that artistic representations of Brunetto Latini, particularly in a manuscript in the Château de Chantilly (Figure 5.1), make clear reference to sodomy as it was understood in the fourteenth century.

Latini, then, is clearly located in Hell for this crime, although there are also sodomites in Purgatory (Canto 26), whose sin is excessive love rather than violence against nature. The difference between the sodomites in Hell and in Purgatory may be that the former corrupted others, but the fact that a sinner in Purgatory says "our sin was hermaphrodite" indicates that these men may perhaps have been seen as acting according to their nature rather than against it. Clearly Dante is not in agreement with theologians that sodomy is the worst of all sins, since those in Purgatory can someday enter Paradise. The fiery plain of the Inferno suggests sterility, which in the medieval view was what made sodomy unnatural and reprehensible, while those punished in Purgatory, along with male lovers of women, suffer for their extreme desires, which are not considered unnatural, rather than their actions.

Sodomy was not only frowned on by the church, it was actively outlawed from the twelfth century on. The Third Lateran Council in 1179 prescribed that clerics who committed "that incontinence, which is against nature,

Figure 5.1 Dante, *Inferno*, punishment of Brunetto Latini. Bibliothèque du Château de Chantilly, Ms 597, fols. 113v–114r

© Bibliothèque et archives du château de Chantilly

because of which 'God's wrath came upon the sons of disobedience' [Ephesians 5:6] and consumed five cities with fire," should be expelled from the clergy or do penance in a monastery, and lay people should be excommunicated.[28] Local church councils followed suit, and canon law picked up the provision. A number of secular jurisdictions – Castile, Portugal, several Italian towns and French counties – came over the course of the thirteenth century to prescribe the death penalty for male same-sex relations, although we do not have court records to indicate from this early a date whether this punishment was ever carried out (we know that it was in the fourteenth and fifteenth centuries). Although the church actively condemned sodomy as sin, the church courts pursued sodomy much less than the courts of the various urban jurisdictions. It may be that the church courts were concerned not to make too public the incidence of sodomy among the clergy.

Some scholars have held that although sodomy was an illicit act regulated by law, the Middle Ages had no sense of the sodomite as a species or type of person. A look at the medieval evidence reveals that this is not entirely the case. Sodomy was an act that could be committed by anyone, and not just with another man. Yet there were some men who had a distinct preference, whether for sodomy as an act or for men as partners. Edward II of England, for example, was married and fathered children (whose paternity is not questioned by any medieval source), and had an illegitimate son as well, yet had notorious relationships with at least two male lovers. The contemporary chronicles hesitated to call Edward's relationship with Piers Gaveston "sodomy," and Pierre Chaplais writes that "nowhere in the *Vita* [*Edwardi Secundi*, one of the most detailed contemporary chronicles] is there any suggestion that anything improper of a physical nature ever took place between Edward and Gaveston,"[29] but they did cite his immoderate love for Gaveston. The implication of Edward's manner of death, reportedly by means of a red-hot poker inserted in his anus, is that people did understand him as a participant in anal sex, which they surely would have considered something "improper of a physical nature." To call him a "homosexual" or "bisexual" would be inappropriate, but his penchant for sex with men clearly affected his identity, at least in the eyes of chroniclers.

Such a preference for sex with other men was often not exclusive, however, as revealed in some court cases. Arnold of Verniolles, who had posed as a priest although only a subdeacon, was one of those interrogated for heresy in the thirteenth century by the Inquisition in the south of France. He confessed to sodomy with several young men. One of the witnesses against him, the Carmelite friar Pierre Recort, testified that:

> When Pierre asked why he had carried on in this way with youths when he could have had enough women, Arnold told him that during the period that they were burning lepers, he was in Toulouse and had sex with a prostitute. After perpetrating that sin, his face swelled up and as a result he was afraid of becoming a leper. He therefore swore from then on not to know women carnally; and, in order to keep that oath, he carried on in the above manner with those youths.[30]

For him, at least so the witness said he claimed, his sexual partners were fungible. To the modern ear he may seem to protest too much, insisting that boys were just a substitute for women in order to prevent his labeling as homosexual. However, the reasons for his choice of male partners did not mitigate his offense, nor would he have expected them to; and, more to the point, the witness found the fungibility argument plausible. The English transvestite prostitute John/Eleanor Rykener, when arrested, described his sexual exploits as a woman with a variety of men, but also with women (see p. 197 below for a more detailed discussion). He, too, was not someone who can be clearly identified as having homosexual preferences.

To the extent that sodomy was an act, or a set of acts, that a man could commit, rather than an orientation, it was not seen as limited to a minority group but was a more generalized threat. Manuals for confessors envisioned it as a sin that anyone could commit: they held that a confessor should be careful about asking people about it, because simply raising the question might give them ideas. Robert of Flamborough told confessors to ask men: "Have you ever been polluted with lust? Ever against nature? Ever with men? With clerics or with laymen?" but was careful not to get too specific: "I will never mention to him anything from which he could obtain an occasion of sin, but only general things which everyone knows to be sins."[31] Constant references from across Europe to "the unmentionable sin" also indicate that a danger, perhaps of temptation, was perceived even in naming the offense.

This is a very revealing attitude. Sodomy might be the worst possible sin, the sin that could not be named, but it was at the same time a very attractive sin, one that could tempt any and all, in contrast to the modern view that people have inclinations one way or the other (although certainly contemporary discourse also contains elements of fear that if homosexuality is tolerated, more people will choose to become homosexuals). The fifteenth-century medical writer Jacques Despars issued a similar warning:

> It would be possible . . . to relate several types of sodomite coitus, which men and women abusively indulge in . . . but I judge it better to keep silence, so that human nature, inclined towards evil and towards the exercise of new lusts, may not attempt, on hearing them, to put them into practice, and thus prejudice one's honor and one's soul.[32]

This attitude reveals, perhaps, as much about medieval views on human nature as about medieval views on sex: the more horrible the sin, the more people are inclined toward it. But it also tells us that the confessors believed sodomy could be pleasurable for anyone, not just for a few, even though in practice it might be a few who were particularly active in committing it.

Although sodomy might be a sin attractive to many, not just a few with a particular orientation, under some circumstances there were men who developed something quite close to what one might call a sexual identity as a sodomite. Late medieval Italian representations of punishments for sodomites, including spit-roasting with its reference to anal penetration, seem to refer specifically to men who have sex with other men. Late medieval Florence is the place from which we have the most information about same-sex relations in the Middle Ages. This is not merely a result of chance survival of more records; Florence was notorious at the time for sodomitical behavior, so much so that "florentzen" became common slang for "to have homosexual intercourse" in fifteenth-century Germany (another example of the attribution of sodomy to the Other).

We know about Florence in part from the fiery sermons of Bernardino of Siena (1380–1444). Bernardino found much to criticize in the sexual and other behavior of all Florentine men and women, not just those men who participated in sodomy. His comments on the latter, though, were among the most vehement; he considered the "sin against nature" as the worst of all sins, as opposed to, for example, Aquinas who thought the spiritual sins were worse. Bernardino asserted that sodomy was so common as to be an epidemic. As he described it, sodomy involved an older man as active partner and a teenage boy as passive partner. He accused boys of inviting sodomy by wearing effeminate and elaborate clothing, and families (particularly mothers) of encouraging it by letting their sons dress up in order to gain the attentions of a wealthy lover. Sodomites were killers of their own children because they engaged in non-procreative sex. The sin was so horrible that "a horrible stench fills my soul at the mere thought." He praised Venice for burning sodomites at the stake.[33]

Both Florence and Venice changed their administrative and judicial structures for dealing with sodomy over the course of the fifteenth century, and began to treat the offense more seriously. In both cases this seems to have been due not to changes in the practice of sodomy but rather to changes in the moral climate. In Venice the existence of a sodomitical subculture seems to have caused alarm, and prosecution focused on sodomy "rings" or groups; in Florence the preaching of Savonarola and other reformers changed attitudes.

Medieval Jewish or Muslim culture never developed the same sort of moral panic over same-sex relations that Christian culture did. Like Christians, they distinguished between the active and the passive role; both could be considered culpable, and yet there are few examples of the brutal repression sometimes imposed by Christian governments. Hebrew and Arabic love poetry addressed to young men or boys, whether or not it is in all cases an authentic expression of the author's feeling, is an indication that such love was imaginable within literary culture.

Patterns of same-sex practice

Bernardino was not the only person in Florence who worried about sodomy, although much of the concern among other people may have been stirred up by his preaching. The concern may have been in part due to what was seen as a dangerously low birth rate. The age of marriage for Florentine men was in fact quite late, and the municipal authorities blamed this at least in part on sodomy. In 1403 they established the Office of Honesty to regulate public morality. The legislation gave as its purpose the extirpation of the "sodomitical vice," but the method used was to establish an officially regulated brothel to make female prostitutes available.

A concern about non-reproductive sex can only have been the real reason for the critique of sodomy if the sodomites were not also having sex with women. For Florence, unlike other places, there are plenty of data, unearthed by Michael Rocke, with which to determine whether that is in fact the case. In 1432, in part spurred on by Bernardino's sermons, the city established an "Office of the Night." This body set up boxes in which people could deposit anonymous accusations of sodomy. Those accused would be interrogated and invited to implicate others. The penalty was remitted if a man denounced himself and named his partners, and about forty men on average did so every year, presumably because they had word that they had been accused or that a prosecution was coming.

Because the records of the Office of the Night survive, we are able to know a great deal about the patterns of accusation. This is not necessarily the same thing as knowing about the patterns of the practice of sodomy itself, and yet it is a lot closer than we can get in most places. According to the data from the Office of the Night, passive sodomy was mainly an offense of teenagers (again, in modern terms, mainly boys too young to have consented and thus, by definition, rape victims). Passive partners tended to be aged from twelve to eighteen or twenty (84 percent between thirteen and eighteen, 92 percent between thirteen and twenty); only 3 percent were over twenty. Of active partners, 82.5 percent were nineteen or older. In the fourteenth century, the partners were distinguished as "whatever person committed the said crime with any other person" and "a person who might have willingly suffered the said crime to be inflicted upon him"; in the fifteenth-century denunciations the two parties were distinguished grammatically.[34]

The first of these norms – that passive partners were young – was violated far less often than the second – that active partners were mature. It was considered especially degrading for someone to remain a passive sodomite once he was a grown man. An inveterate sodomite, Salvi Panuzzi, was condemned to death in 1496 at the age of 63, but the sentence was commuted to a fine and life on bread and water because the publicity of an execution might embarrass the city by revealing the existence of old men in the passive role. For a boy, who was not yet a real man, behaving in the manner of a woman was much less of a slur on the character; boys of the same age sometimes had sex together too.

The shift from passive to active came sometime in the late teenage years. It is not only that passive partners are younger than a certain age and active partners are older, it is also that a number of the same names turn up; the same boys are involved as passives earlier and actives later. Usually sodomitical activity as reflected in these sources began to taper off in the late twenties or thirties. This was approaching the time at which a Florentine man usually married, and indeed when Rocke can trace the careers of particular individuals, he finds that their names cease appearing in the accusations around the time of their marriage. This might suggest either that sex with boys was a temporary expedient – that these men had no special inclination to sex with other men or boys, but found it convenient until they had a licit marital relationship – or else that it was considered unseemly for a married man to consort with boys as it was not for a younger, unmarried man. Some men, however, did not cease with marriage but continued to be accused of sex with boys into maturity and old age. Others never married. These men might be laughed at as dirty old men, but they did not come in for anything like the kind of opprobrium directed at older men who played the passive role.

The dichotomy between active and passive is complicated in the case of oral sex. In anal, interfemoral, or for that matter vaginal sex, the active partner was understood as the penetrator. As the Romans understood the active/passive dichotomy, the penetrator in oral sex was also the active partner, while the fellator was the passive partner; the conceptual distinction was based on penetration. In Florence, however, the distinction was based on who actually did the work, not on who penetrated and ejaculated, and the fellator was considered the active partner. Thus it was permissible for an older man to fellate a boy, but not to be anally penetrated by him. In general, however, fellatio is mentioned far less in medieval sources about same-sex contact than anal sex.

Although in one sense the passive partner transgressed more than the active one because he assumed the woman's role and thereby abdicated his gender, in Florence, Venice, and other places the passive partner was treated more leniently as long as he was a boy, although he was still not considered a victim as he would be today. A particularly striking example took place in Avignon in 1320. According to an account by Cardinal Jacobo Caetani degli Stefaneschi, a couple were caught committing sodomy; the passive partner was thirteen years old. Both were condemned to be burnt, but although the man died as condemned, the boy was saved by the miraculous appearance of the Virgin Mary, who released him just as the pyre was about to be lit. The Pope subsequently had a chapel built in honor of this miracle. An illustration from the late 1330s (Figure 5.2) depicts the boy being saved from the flames as a young child.

Perhaps a boy was considered less permanently corrupted than a man engaged in the vice, or perhaps it was not as perverse for him to be the passive partner because he was not yet fully a man. By contrast, in northern Europe both the dichotomy between active and passive and the strict age hierarchy were far less important.

The fact that the active partner was often punished more seriously than the passive, even though he was transgressing gender roles to a lesser degree, could also be related to notions of responsibility. The passive partner, who had something done to him, could more easily claim the position of victim (of persuasion, seduction, or even rape, although this claim is rare in the Middle Ages) than could the active partner. However, as we have seen with the blame placed on adulterous women, passivity in the sexual act itself did not necessarily correlate with lack of blame in initiating the relationship. The age structure of relationships must be seen as the more important factor in determining differential treatment of the two partners.

Figure 5.2 Boy saved from burning by the Virgin Mary. Drawing by Simone Martini, in Jacobo Caetani degli Stefaneschi, *Historia de miraculo Mariae facto Avinione*, Paris, Bibliothèque Nationale, MS Lat 5931 fol. 99r, detail

The age pattern of same-sex relations in Florence (and Venice as well) was similar to that in ancient Greece: active mature man, passive youth. Indeed, some scholars have suggested that this was the pattern that held across Europe until modernity brought with it a rupture, although others see the invocation of this pattern in the Middle Ages as reflecting a widespread pattern of abuse on the part of the church, which went unremarked because of the church's concern about creating scandal. For Florence itself the distinctive pattern can most usefully be related not to patterns of same-sex relations elsewhere, but to patterns of heterosexual relations in Florence itself. The marriage pattern for Italy was different from that in northwestern Europe: women tended to marry in their early to middle teens, men in their late twenties to early thirties. This need not mean that same-sex relations were following a heterosexual pattern, or vice versa. It could mean that in this case social conventions about age trumped those about gender, and that in areas where those age conventions were different for heterosexual relations, they may have been so for homosexual relations as well.

The extreme age asymmetry in marriage in Florence meant both that men, even those who would eventually marry, spent many years unattached to a woman and in someone else's household, and that married couples would have little in common, not only because of the age gap but also because marriages of this sort are likely to be arranged rather than freely chosen by the couple. For both of these reasons Florentine men developed a homosocial life. Couples did not go out together, men went out by themselves, to taverns frequented mainly by other men. They worked together with other men in their workshops. A man whose sexual relations, too, were with men could end up living in a woman-free world. This was more the case in Florence than in other places where men and women married closer to the same age – early twenties for women, mid-twenties for men. In those areas, France and England, the marriages were more likely to have been chosen by the parties, who would have opportunities to meet potential partners on their own and were more likely to be companionate. Women who married at a later age were also more likely to be involved in the job market, which meant that the workplace became a less exclusively homosocial environment.

Even under less homosocial circumstances, however, taverns were often primarily masculine gathering places. In Regensburg, Germany, in the fifteenth century, several taverns were named in court records as locations for sexual encounters between men. Both there and in other German towns public latrines also provided an opportunity for men to encounter and have sex with each other (in Regensburg the latrines of the Augustinian monastery in particular).

We do not have the same kind of information for anywhere else in Europe as we do for Florence, although Venice provides a number of cases and documents. There, as in Florence, city authorities tried a variety of approaches to root out what they saw as a serious crime (including burning a number of sodomites, and beheading one man in 1481 for "frequent sodomy with his own wife").[35] As for Florence, however, most of the evidence from across Europe that we do have for same-sex relationships comes from criminal records. These cannot be trusted as to the prevalence of the behavior in question. More cases crop up at some times than at others, probably not because of an increase in the activity but rather because of an increase in prosecution. Periodic "homosexual panics" (a modern term, not a medieval one) led to spates of prosecution, then nothing would happen for a while. This was the case in Florence also: the preaching of Savonarola in the late fifteenth century, for example, led to a period of intensified persecution. But there are also isolated cases, such as those of a man burned at the stake by the Holy Roman Emperor in 1277 and another in 1369. In the latter case, Emperor Charles IV had himself allegedly observed the man having sex with a ten-year-old boy, apparently in public, as they could be seen from his window. German and Swiss towns in the late Middle Ages saw a scattering of prosecutions; 5 out of 388 death sentences in Zurich during the fifteenth century, for example, were for sodomy. Prosecutions were less frequent in the north than in Italy, but punishments also tended to be more serious, particularly for anal intercourse (intercrural intercourse and mutual masturbation were considered lesser offenses).

The distinguishing feature of many sodomy accusations was their political nature. The accusation was a handy one with which to blacken the name of an enemy. This became apparent in the prosecution of the Templars in France, but also in other outbreaks of prosecution elsewhere, for example in Bruges in the later Middle Ages under the Burgundians. Perhaps the accused did engage in homosexual behavior and perhaps they did not, but the fact that they were prosecuted for it at a particular time had more to do with the political circumstances than the fact that they engaged in it on that occasion.

England, strangely enough, did not experience any such panics, despite the fact that Edward II (r. 1307–1327) was widely rumored to be a sodomite and met his death in such an ignominious manner. In England, of course, another accusation was widely available to toss around against one's political adversaries, that of Lollardy. Although accusations of sodomy had accompanied those of heresy on other occasions (as with the French Cathars or Albigensians), in the case of Lollardy they did not, perhaps because the Lollards themselves were leveling the charge of sodomy against a celibate clergy who did not want to bring the issue any farther out into the open than they had to.

This discussion of sodomy, because it relies on court records, has focused much more on acts than on feelings. We do not know whether these sexual relationships were merely temporary encounters or whether they were long-term love affairs. On rare occasions there is evidence for the latter. Some of the cases from Florence speak of a man keeping a boy as a wife (*come sua donna*, but also *per moglie*, which more specifically means "wife").[36]

Most of the men whose voices we hear in the court records, however, were engaged in short-term encounters. A disproportionate number, indeed, were prostitutes, because the authorities were more interested in interrogating men with a long history of many encounters than those who were only casually involved. Rolandino/Rolandina Ronchaia, arrested in 1354 in Venice, was possibly intersex, or at least quite feminine in appearance. Although he was married to a woman, he claimed that he

> never knew her or any other woman carnally, because he never had any carnal appetite, and his virile member could never become erect . . . and since he was feminine in face, voice, and behavior, even though he did not have a female orifice and had the member and testicles of a

man, many people thought him to be a woman because of his external features.

He also had "breasts like a woman." He therefore dressed as a woman and became a prostitute. When he had sex with men he "hid his member," which never became erect.[37] In modern terms Rolandino/Rolandina might be considered intersex or transgender rather than homosexual. He saw himself more as playing a woman's role than as being attracted sexually to men.

The case of John/Eleanor Rykener, from London in 1394, is similar. Rykener, dressed in women's clothing, was arrested "committing that detestable, unmentionable, and ignominious vice" in the street with one John Britby. Rykener named the woman who "first taught him to practice this detestable vice in the manner of a woman" and the one who "first dressed him in women's clothing" and found customers for him. He listed other men who had had sex with him as a woman: he had worked as an embroidress in Oxford and had sex with several students, none of whom knew that he was a man, and as a tapster in Burford, where he had sex with many clerics who paid him well. He also "had sex as a man with many women married and otherwise," but not apparently for pay.[38]

Neither Rykener nor Ronchaia is typical of accused sodomites, most of whom did not wear women's clothing. The testimony preserved in the court records, in Latin (which neither man likely spoke), may not represent their actual words. It can tell us little about sexual identities in the Middle Ages. It can, however, tell us of the powerful connection between the passive sexual role and femininity. The cases that struck medieval authorities enough to interrogate and record were those in which the men did not just behave in an effeminate way but went so far as to change their gender. But these were prostitutes and their activity revealed little of their own desires. Rykener said that his sexual preference was for priests, but only because they paid more than other people. His emotions are absent from his story.

Love between men

There are other instances where we do not have a court case or any evidence for a sexual relationship but where there was a powerful emotional bond between two men, and these instances are as much a part of the history of same-sex relations as are sodomy prosecutions. Some of these instances come from a monastic context. Aelred of Rievaulx, a twelfth-century English Cistercian abbot, wrote eloquently about the deep friendships he developed with other monks, including one who was his peer when he first entered the cloister and another who was a youth when he was an old man.

He spoke of them in terms that, were they used today, would be considered unquestionably erotic:

> to the fold of whose dear friendship, whose loving breast you can approach, safe from all the temptations of the world, and if you unite yourself to him without delay in all the meditations of your heart, by whose spiritual kisses, like healing balm, you will discharge the weariness of your stressful concerns.[39]

We are in a twelfth-century context here, and Aelred probably did not think of this love as carnal, but the language resembles that which secular lovers might use. In lamenting the death of his friend Simon, he even admitted that other people thought his love for him was too carnal. Yet he insisted it was not: he claimed that God, to whom he addressed his account, would judge him blameless. "But some may judge by my tears that my love was too carnal. Let them interpret them as they want; you, however, Lord, see them and consider them."[40] A man in his position would not likely have made this claim if he had in fact been engaged in a sexual relationship. On the other hand, in a letter to his sister he described a monk he knew who was afflicted by lust and had to strive to overcome it with cold baths and by rubbing nettles on his skin. This monk is likely to have been Aelred himself, and although he did not say which sex the monk lusted after, his deep and loving relationships with men make it likely that it is to them he was attracted. His biographer comments that unlike some strict abbots who do not allow their monks to form friendships with each other, Aelred permitted those in his flock to hold hands.[41] Clearly this was a man for whom same-sex erotic relationships, even if chaste, were important.

These relationships could also be important at the highest level of the aristocracy. Scholars have debated the nature of the friendship between Richard I (the Lionhearted) of England and Philip Augustus of France. Chroniclers report that "at night their beds did not separate them. And the King of France loved him as his own soul."[42] Sleeping in the same bed did not mean the same thing in the Middle Ages as it would automatically mean today, as people often shared beds with others, especially when traveling, sometimes even with strangers. A prince, of course, would not have to share a bed if he did not want to, but to do so would not have been unusual. Nevertheless, it is entirely possible that there was more to the relationship than friendship. Richard married very late, largely ignored his wife once he had married her, and did not leave an heir. This cannot be taken as evidence for the exclusivity of his sexual inclinations, since he is known to have fathered an illegitimate child. Sexual preferences in the Middle Ages were often not exclusive, so this does not mean that he and Philip were not lovers also, but it does mean that we cannot put too much weight on his not having children with his wife.

The real problem here is that not only can we not know what Philip and Richard actually did with each other, it is also very difficult even to ascertain what people at the time thought they did. Sodomy was condemned by the church, and it is possible that if chroniclers and others thought that the princes were committing sodomy with each other they would have commented negatively on it. It may be, though, that there was a certain level of tolerance, and people did not necessarily connect two men having a loving and physical relationship with sodomy, which was a rejection of God. And accounts that stress Richard and Philip's love do not imply that either one was effeminate.

Another friendship among knights, from two centuries after Philip and Richard, conjures up a range of possibilities, although again we cannot know the answer. The tomb slab of two English knights who died at Constantinople in 1391 states that they had been constant companions for thirteen years. When one of them died, the other refused food and died a few days later. In addition to this romantic story, the carving on the slab shows the two knights each bearing the same shield, which showed the arms of their two families impaled with each other (each coat of arms takes up half the shield). This is very unusual. Impaling of arms was done by married couples and by bishops who impaled their family arms with those of their see. It is rare indeed to find this done with two men, and certainly indicates a special sort of relationship, even if we cannot say exactly what.

Indeed, the most striking feature of male same-sex relationships during the Middle Ages seems to have been that medieval society celebrated a type of deep, passionate friendship between men that modern society does not. Men today who expressed their feelings for each other in the same way medieval men did would be universally believed to be sexually involved with each other. Medieval people either did not believe that they were, or did not think it noteworthy if they were, because there is no comment about it.

But these close and loving relations between men, while they were a good deal more accepted than similarly expressed feelings would be today, nevertheless did not always go unquestioned. People were well aware of the social system in which young men, chosen for their military prowess (which required strong, well-built bodies) and good looks, would be fostered and given privileges at court. In an early twelfth-century romance, *Amis and Amiloun*, the two men:

> both pledged their faith to each other. . . . They made their way together to the court of Charles the king, where he perceived them to be modest, wise, and very handsome young men. . . . Amicus was made the king's treasurer and Amelius his cup-bearer.[43]

This position given to a beautiful young man would certainly have reminded an educated public of the story of Jupiter and his cupbearer Ganymede, from whose name the word "catamite" (passive male partner) was derived. The story was well known in the Middle Ages, appearing frequently in art, such as on a capital from the twelfth-century church at Vézelay in France (Figure 5.3). This sculpture presents Jupiter as violently preying on the lad and may be an allusion to one possible fate of young oblates in monasteries.

But it was not only monks, under a vow of chastity, for whom Ganymede could serve as a warning story, but also lay people. Indeed, the mid-twelfth century archbishop of Tours, Hildebert of Lavardin, reminded them:

> A boy is not at all a safe thing; do not devote yourself to any of them. Many a house is reported to have many Joves. But you should not hope for heaven through Ganymede's sin: no one comes to the stars through this type of military service. A better law consecrates heavenly castles to Junos alone: a male wife has the underworld.[44]

The love between kings and their knights – Arthur and Lancelot; Mark and Tristan; or Marie de France's unnamed king who rejoices when Bisclavret is

Figure 5.3 Jupiter and Ganymede. Vezelay, abbey church of Ste.-Marie-Madeleine

returned from wolf to human form, "hugging and kissing him more than a hundred times"[45] when he returns to the court – is not explicitly depicted as sexual, but it is nonetheless deep and emotional, and we may be justified in calling it erotic. Deep bonds between lords and men go back to Germanic literature, as for example *Beowulf*; there they do not seem so erotic, but neither are descriptions of love between men and women, further signaling how dangerous it can be to assume that the relationship between depth of feeling and enthusiastic textual expression of that feeling is the same in all societies.

Warriors could engage in male bonding, but they were not supposed to ignore women. Marie de France has Guinevere complain to a man who rejects her advances (because in fact he loves another woman): "People have often said as much, that you have no liking for women. You like handsome young men and it's with them that you take your pleasure."[46] This sort of behavior was unacceptable if it drew men away from women and hence reproduction. Orderic Vitalis, writing before 1140, criticized sodomy at the court of the English king William Rufus: "At that time effeminates set the fashion in many parts of the world: foul catamites, doomed to eternal fire, unrestrainedly pursued their revels and shamelessly gave themselves up to the filth of sodomy." Effeminacy did not necessarily mean that the men did not have sex with women: "Our wanton youth is sunk in effeminacy, and courtiers, fawning, seek the favours of women with every kind of lewdness."[47] William Rufus, however, never married, and this refusal to associate with women threatened the succession to the throne.

One of the most famous cases of male-male love, celebrated in both Christian and Jewish texts in the Middle Ages, was that of David and Jonathan; here again this was understood as a courtly and aristocratic friendship, and also an ennobling one, which paralleled marriage without replacing it or excluding it. The sexual nature of the love of David and Jonathan, often evoked by contemporary Christians and Jews as a precedent for gay rights, is much disputed by Biblical scholars. In its medieval incarnations, either within Christianity or Judaism, it was not discussed in such a way as to invoke a sexual nature: it was a pure and selfless love (see Figure 5.4, from a late-thirteenth-century manuscript of the moral compendium *Somme le Roi*). Its hierarchical nature, too, is ambiguous: Jonathan is the king's son and an experienced fighter when David is a boy with a slingshot, and he grants David arms and armor. In the Latin Vulgate bible used in the Middle Ages, however, David clearly describes himself on Jonathan's death as the lover and Jonathan as the beloved, and de-eroticizes the statement by comparing his love to that of a mother for her child.

Although in many cases sodomy was connected with gender inversion, and passivity and femininity went together, this was not always the case. The body of courtly chivalric literature, while it did not reflect medieval social behavior, was extraordinarily popular among influential people and

Figure 5.4 Embrace of David and Jonathan from the thirteenth-century *Somme le Roi*, illustrating the virtue of friendship

for centuries has provided the source material for scholarly discussions of medieval love. Recent scholars looking at it "queerly" have shown that medieval literature does not quite present the picture of dominant hetero-sexuality that has been previously assumed. While it is true that the love of ladies appears as a main motivator for knights, we may wonder how deep that love runs. Knights performed for the sake of renown before other men; they acquired the love of women to demonstrate to other men that they could. Women were a means by which a knight measured his manhood, but it was manhood, not love, that was the goal. Even in the greatest stories of heterosexual love, like those of Chrétien de Troyes, the knight's closest ties are often to his lord or his fellow knights. Loving women is something a knight is supposed to do – Marie de France's Guigemar, for example, is unusual because he never showed any interest in love. There was not a lady or a maiden under heaven, no matter how noble or beautiful, who would not have taken him as a lover, if he had sought her love. Many women often sought his love, but he felt no such desire.[48] Over the course of his *lai* he is cursed and can only be cured by the love of a woman.

Twelfth-century French literature clearly envisioned some knights whose erotic preference was for men rather than women, without that making them less masculine. Indeed, for the queen of Latium, trying to dissuade her daughter from marriage, the hero Aeneas is one of these men, as witnessed by his treatment of Dido:

> What have you said, you crazy madwoman? Do you know who you've given yourself to? That lustful tormentor is one of those, the type who has little interest in women. He prefers those who trade in flexible rods: he won't eat hens, but really loves the flesh of a cock. He would rather embrace a boy than you or any other woman. He doesn't know how to play with women, and you wouldn't find him hanging around the hole in the gate; but he really goes for the crack of a young man. Haven't you heard how he mistreated Dido? No woman has ever got anything good from him, and neither will you, if you ask me, not from a traitor and a sodomite. He will always be ready to leave you. If he finds a pretty boy, it will seem perfectly fair to him that you should let him go off to do his courting. And if he can attract the boy by means of you, he won't think it strange at all to make an exchange: in return for letting the boy have his pleasure from you, he gets to do him.[49]

In the context of the story, the accusation against Aeneas turns out to be untrue, but the terms in which the queen makes it are nevertheless impor-tant. The preference for boys does not make Aeneas a coward or effeminate. Indeed, it does not make the boy effeminate either, since she suggests that a young man could be bribed into passivity with an older man by the promise of activity with the latter's young wife. Sodomy here refers to a male–male sexual practice, but the queen's words assume that it is a preference that is compatible with knighthood. Richard I (the Lionhearted) may be another example of a man whose sexual interest in other men did not compromise his knighthood or his masculinity.

Most of the knights in courtly or chivalric literature do not engage in sodomy, and most do love women. This love is not a result of their orientation or innate desire, but, as the literature depicts it, the effect of beautiful bodies and courtly behavior. The lover is attracted to the woman not because she is a woman but because she is a beautiful and noble one; indeed, sometimes he falls in love based on reputation without having met the woman. The ideal is class-bound: knights in medieval literature must behave in a chivalric manner toward ladies but not toward women of lower status, and the behavior of medieval armies in reality bears this out. But it is not as gender-bound as it might be, because the qualities of beauty and courtly behavior are found in men as well as women, and the love between two men sometimes competes with the love for women. Love literature does not give us explicit sex scenes either between a man and a woman or between two men, but passionate love can exist in both places (less so, in this body of literature, between two women).

A man who pleads for any sort of love would seem to place himself in a submissive position and therefore make himself less masculine. This, of course, is a literary conceit. It is perhaps more obviously so when the man submits himself to a woman: this is so obvious a role inversion that its effect is a flourish, a dramatic move in a game, rather than a permanent demeaning of the man. As James Schultz argues, "love service, in both narrative and lyric, is a stylization of male behavior that is accomplished by men for men." It demonstrates masculine self-control.[50] But the authors were not recommending this as a way for men to behave in real life. For a man to submit (emotionally) to another man, even in literature, might be more demeaning, but this effect would depend on their relative social status. In a hierarchical society, it was less shameful to serve and be subordinate to one's social superior, just as it was not shameful to be submissive to the highest in rank of all, God. Not all subordination was emasculating, or even queer.

The friends Amis and Amiloun, whose story was repeatedly retold both in Latin and in the vernaculars, provide a good example of the deep bond between two men that competes in medieval literature with the bond between a woman and a man. The two friends swear an oath to each other that comes to take precedence over the marriage vow. Whether their love is sexual is not really even the question: the reader is probably not meant to understand them as engaging in genital contact, but the story is as much a love story as any other romance.

The criticism of men's taking "Ganymedes" and thus rejecting women did not prevent the ideal of male love and friendship from continuing throughout the Middle Ages. This was because, as much as churchmen might criticize sodomitical behavior, medieval people did not understand it as exclusive. If the main problem with male friendships and loves was that they led men to ignore their marital duties, then as long as men carried out those marital duties properly there was nothing wrong with their relations with men. And even though criticism of sodomy continued, so did male love, and the two were not always juxtaposed. They tended to be treated as two different categories of activity.

Loving relations between men appear in a large body of poetry from Muslim Spain, written by both Muslims and Jews. Both these religions condemned sodomy in terms not dissimilar to those used in Christianity, but among the elites the prohibitions seem to have had little effect, again similar to the situation in Christian culture.

A 1994 book by John Boswell, *Same-Sex Unions in Premodern Europe*, excited great controversy as scholars debated whether the ceremony he discussed really amounted to marriage or whether it was a ceremony of some sort of brotherhood (this is the ceremony of *adelphopoiia*, mentioned above, p. 186). The real historical importance of the type of relationship this ceremony sanctified was not that it represented an antecedent to today's gay marriage. Marriage in the Middle Ages was not an affirmation and official recognition of love between two people as much as it was the establishment of a legal unit that legitimized children and facilitated the transfer of property from one family to another and one generation to another. Same-sex unions were clearly not this. This ceremony represents a type of relationship that has no formal legitimation in modern society, what we could call passionate or erotic friendship. This is not marriage, but neither are these men "just good friends." They were committed and pair-bonded to each other in a way that contemporary culture does not recognize.

Contemporary cultural theory uses the term "queer" for that which upsets or subverts the heterosexual order. The passionate friendships between men that the medieval sources reveal to us were distinctly queer. They did not prevent men from marrying (if they were not vowed celibates) and fathering children, nor did they preclude men from having casual sexual liaisons with women. But many men in the Middle Ages whose only sexual relations were with women would have expected to have their most fulfilling and rewarding non-physical relationships with men (and women with women as well). Those fulfilling, rewarding, even passionate relationships must not infrequently have been combined with sexual involvement.

What distinguishes these love relationships – or at least some of them – from the sexual encounters found in the court records is that they were not necessarily hierarchical by age. The activity the courts treated as criminal seems generally to have involved a man and a "youth," or at least to be framed that way, whatever the actual ages of the individuals involved. We don't know the relative ages of men who wrote lovingly to or about each other, and sometimes these writings do speak of boys or youths, but often they do not. It may be that speaking of youth is a literary convention anyhow, as people tended then, as now, to associate youth with beauty.

The limits of the sources often mean that we cannot say whether sexual intercourse took place between two particular individuals. As historians, we must beware of applying different standards of evidence to same-sex and opposite-sex relationships. If we do not want to assume that a man who writes love poetry to another man is sexually involved with him, we should make the same demands for proof in the case of a man who writes love poetry to a woman. This problem of evidence becomes particularly acute when we are dealing not with consummated relationships but with desires. In one sense we can say that it doesn't matter whether two particular individuals were actually having sex or not. What matters historically are the kinds of relationships and emotions that were considered appropriate or inappropriate, and how society understood the individuals who were or were not involved in a relationship. But these emotions and desires are even more difficult than actions to document from medieval sources.

The use of language in the Middle Ages was different from the use of language today, even if we set aside the obvious difference that people then were writing in Latin or in an archaic form of the languages we use today. Some phrases or ways of speaking that might seem highly freighted with emotion today might have been merely conventions or allusions then. When we address someone as "Dear" in a letter, or end with "Very truly yours," we do not mean that they are dear to us, or that we belong to them; they may be total strangers. This is simply formulaic language, and historians in the future would be wrong to take it as reflecting anything in particular in our collective or individual psyche. Similarly, in reading medieval texts we must beware of taking particular phrases out of context and assuming that they are evidence for erotic desire.

Even with language that is clearly addressing the occasion at hand, rather than merely conventional, however, it is still problematic to know whether we should classify it as erotic. To say that we can recognize sexual desire in the language of someone in a different culture is to say that desire is universal, part of human nature that will always express itself in similar ways even in different societies. This is a claim made, for example, by followers of psychoanalysis, who argue that the human mind works a certain way, that there are certain developmental stages, and so forth.

A historian is trapped in a dilemma here. On the one hand, many historians are rightly reluctant to accept explanations that are based on an idea of a universal human nature, because this would lead them to ignore the ways in which past cultures (or other contemporary cultures for that matter) are profoundly different from ours. On the other hand, if we do not believe that we can draw conclusions about the state of a person's mind or heart from the things he or she wrote, this places severe limits on our ability to interpret the evidence. We have to attempt to find a balance between assuming that medieval people experienced sexual desire in much the same ways and in the same kinds of circumstances as modern people do, and assuming that they were so radically different that we cannot know anything about them. I suggest that when we have writings in which one person expresses profound desire for the presence and physical touch of another, we can consider this desire to be erotic, even if the person involved would not have recognized it as such. This does not mean that all such erotic desires, whether heterosexual or homosexual, were put into action, or that medieval people wished to put them into action. But it does mean that the history of such desires belongs as part of the history of sexuality.

Notes

1 Jacques Rossiaud, *Medieval Prostitution*, trans. Lydia G. Cochrane (Oxford: Basil Blackwell, 1988), 39; the quotations from court records are as cited by Rossiaud.
2 Greater London Record Office, Consistory Court Instance Act Book, DL/C/1, fol. 55v.
3 Guibert, *A Monk's Confession: The Memoirs of Guibert of Nogent*, trans. Paul J. Archambault (University Park: Pennsylvania State University Press, 1995), 1:26, p. 89.
4 William of Malmesbury, *Gesta regum anglorum*, 5:412, ed. and trans. R.A.B. Mynors, R.M. Thomson and M. Winterbottom (Oxford: Oxford University Press, 1998), 1:744–5.
5 Lambert of Ardres, *The History of the Counts of Guines and Lords of Ardres*, 89, trans. Leah Shopkow (Philadelphia: University of Pennsylvania Press, 2001), 122.
6 *Two Memoirs of Renaissance Florence*, ed. Gene Brucker, trans. Julia Martines (New York: Harper Torchbooks, 1967), 112, 134.
7 Karl Bartsch, *Romances et Pastourelles françaises des XIIe et XIIIe siècles* (Darmstadt: Wissenschaftliche Buchgesellschaft, 1870, reprinted 1967), 2:17, trans. in Kathryn Gravdal, *Ravishing Maidens: Writing Rape in Medieval French Literature and Law* (Philadelphia: University of Pennsylvania Press, 1991), 110–11.
8 Andreas Capellanus, *The Art of Courtly Love*, trans. J.J. Parry (New York: W. W. Norton, 1941), 1:11, p. 150.
9 *Lancelot (The Knight of the Cart)*, in Chrétien de Troyes, *Arthurian Romances*, trans. D.D.R. Owen (London: J. M. Dent, 1987), 202.
10 Didier Lett, "Genre, enfance et violence sexualle dans les archives judiciaires de Bologne au xve siècle," *Clio: Femmes, genre, histoire* 14 (2015), 203–5.
11 *Historia Silense*, eds. Justo Pérez de Urbel and Altilano González Ruiz-Zorilla (Madrid: Consejo Superior de Investigaciones Científicas, 1959), 127.
12 *Le registre d'inquisition de Jacques Fournier, vol. 3*, ed. Jean Duvernoy (Toulouse: Edouard Privat, 1965), 41.
13 Al-Jāḥiẓ, *Kitāb al-ayawān*, trans. in Everett Rowson, "Gender Irregularity as Entertainment: Institutionalized Transvestism at the Caliphal Court in Medieval Baghdad," in *Gender and Difference in the Middle Ages*, eds. Sharon Farmer and Carol Braun Pasternack (Minneapolis: University of Minnesota Press, 2003), 55.
14 Translated in Hugh Kennedy, "Al-Jāḥiẓ and the Construction of Sexuality at the Abbasid Court," in *Medieval Sexuality: A Casebook*, eds. April Harper and Caroline Proctor (New York: Routledge, 2008), 175–88, quote on 181.

15 Gulathing Law, 196, in *The Earliest Norwegian Laws*, ed. Laurence M. Larson (New York: Columbia University Press, 1937), 143.
16 *Njal's Saga*, 123, trans. Robert Cook, *Complete Sagas of Icelanders*, ed. Viðar Hreinsson (Reykjavík: Leifur Eiríksson, 1997), 3:148; *Olkofri's Saga*, 3–4, trans. John Tucker, *Complete Sagas of Icelanders*, 5:236–7.
17 "The Tale of Sarcastic Halli," trans. George Clark, *Complete Sagas of Icelanders*, 1:356.
18 Gerald of Wales, *Opera*, 4:423–4, trans. in Hugh M. Thomas, *The English and the Normans: Ethnic Hostility, Assimilation, and Identity 1066–c. 1220* (Oxford: Oxford University Press, 2003), 329.
19 Christine Reinle, "Zur Rechtspraxis gegenüber Homosexuellen: Eine Fallstudie aus dem Regensburg des 15: Jahrhunderts," *Zeitschrift für Geschichtswissenschaft* 44 (1996), 323.
20 Trans. in John Boswell, *Christianity, Social Tolerance, and Homosexuality: Gay People in Western Europe from the Beginning of the Christian Era to the Fourteenth Century* (Chicago: University of Chicago Press, 1980), 368.
21 Ahmad al-Tifashi, *The Delight of Hearts, or What You Will Not Find in Any Book*, ed. Winston Leyland, trans. Edward A. Lacey (San Francisco: Gay Sunshine Press, 1988), 55. I do not know what Arabic word is here translated as "homosexual," but this term is as problematic in a medieval Muslim context as in a Christian one.
22 Guilielmus Adae, *De modo Sarracenos extirpandi*, trans. Michael Uebel in "Re-Orienting Desire: Writing on Gender Trouble in Fourteenth-Century Egypt," in *Gender and Difference*, eds. Farmer and Pasternack, 244.
23 Guibert, *A Monk's Confession*, 3:16, p. 194.
24 Walter Map, *De Nugis Curialium*, 24, trans. Frederick Tupper and Marbury Bladen Ogle (London: Chatto and Windus, 1924), 49.
25 "Twelve Conclusions of the Lollards," in *Selections from English Wycliffite Writings*, ed. Anne Hudson, Medieval Academy Reprints for Teaching 38 (Toronto: University of Toronto Press, 1997), 25.
26 Thomas Aquinas, *Summa Theologica I*, 2a2ae.154.11 (New York: McGraw-Hill, 1964), 43:245.
27 Dante Alighieri, *The Divine Comedy, vol. 1, Inferno*, Canto 11, 46–51, ed. and trans. Robert M. Durling (New York: Oxford University Press, 1996), 172–3.
28 "Concilio Laternanense III," ch. 11, in *Conciliorum Oecumenicorum Decreta*, eds. Giuseppe Alberigo, Perikle-P. Joannou, Claudio Leonardi and Paulo Prodi, 3rd edition (Bologna: Ediziani Dehoniane, 1991), 217–18. Although the term "sodomy" is not used, the reference to the destruction of the cities of the plain (which is in the council's decree, not in the biblical quotation) is a clear reference to Sodom and Gomorrah.
29 Pierre Chaplais, *Piers Gaveston: Edward II's Adoptive Brother* (Oxford: Clarendon Press, 1994), 8.
30 *Le registre d'inquisition de Jacques Fournier*, ed. Jean Duvernoy (Toulouse: Edouard Privat, 1965), 3:31, translated in Michael Goodich, *The Unmentionable Vice: Homosexuality in the Later Medieval Period* (Santa Barbara, CA: ABC-Clio, 1979), 105–6.
31 Robert of Flamborough, *Liber Poenitentialis*, 4:8:223–4, trans. J. J. Francis Firth (Toronto: Pontifical Institute of Medieval Studies, 1971), 195–6.
32 Jacques Despars, *Expositiones in librum tertium canonis Avicennae*, fen 20, tr. 1, ch. 6, translated in Danielle Jacquart and Claude Thomasset, *Sexuality and Medicine in the Middle Ages*, trans. Matthew Adamson (Princeton: Princeton University Press, 1988), 159.

33 Bernardino of Siena, *Opera Omnia, 9 vols.* (Quaracchi: Collegio San Bonaventura 1950–65), 3:267, translated in Franco Mormando, *The Preacher's Demons: Bernardino of Siena and the Social Underworld of Early Renaissance Italy* (Chicago: University of Chicago Press, 1999), 150.

34 Michael Rocke, *Forbidden Friendships: Homosexuality and Male Culture in Renaissance Florence* (Oxford: Oxford University Press, 1996), 89–90. All the rest of the material here on Florence is also taken from Rocke.

35 Venetian State Archives, Dieci, *Miste*, Reg. 20, fl. 117v, quoted in Guido Ruggiero, *The Boundaries of Eros: Sex Crime and Sexuality in Renaissance Venice* (Oxford: Oxford University Press, 1985), 135.

36 Rocke, 108.

37 Archivio di Stato, Venice, Signori di Notte al Criminal, R.6, f.64. I am grateful to Alan Stahl for transcribing this document.

38 David Lorenzo Boyd and Ruth Mazo Karras, "The Interrogation of a Male Transvestite Prostitute in Fourteenth-Century London," *GLQ: A Journal of Lesbian and Gay Studies* 1 (1995), 482–3.

39 Aelred of Rievaulx, *Speculum Caritatis*, 3.109, in *Opera Omnia, vol. 1*, ed. Anselm Hoste, Corpus Christianorum Continuatio Medievalis 1 (Turnhout: Brepols, 1971), 159. The rest of the passage is quoted above, p. 19.

40 Aelred, *Speculum Caritatis*, 1:112, p. 63.

41 Walter Daniel, *Vita Aelredi Abbatis Rievall'*, ed. M. Powicke (Oxford: Oxford University Press, 1978), 40.

42 Roger of Hoveden (Benedict of Peterborough), *Gesta Regis Henrici II*, 7, ed. William Stubbs, Rolls Series 49:2, trans. in C. Stephen Jaeger, *Ennobling Love: In Search of a Lost Sensibility* (Philadelphia: University of Pennsylvania Press, 1999), 11.

43 "Life of the Dear Friends Amicus and Amelius," in *Medieval Hagiography: An Anthology*, ed. Thomas Head, trans. Matthew S. Kuefler (New York: Garland, 2000), 448.

44 Hildebert of Lavardin, "Ad S. nepotem," trans. in Matthew S. Kuefler, "Male Friendship and the Suspicion of Sodomy in Twelfth-Century France," in *Gender and Difference*, eds. Farmer and Pasternack, 155.

45 Marie de France, "Bisclavret," in *The Lays of Marie de France*, trans. Edward J. Gallagher (Indianapolis: Hackett, 2010), 33.

46 Marie de France, "Lanval," *Lays*, 37.

47 Orderic Vitalis, *The Ecclesiastical History*, 8:325, ed. and trans. Marjorie Chibnall (Oxford: Clarendon Press, 1973), 4:189.

48 Marie de France, "Guigemar," *Lays*, 4.

49 *Roman d'Eneas*, trans. in William E. Burgwinkle, *Sodomy, Masculinity, and Law in Medieval Literature: France and England, 1050–1230* (Cambridge: Cambridge University Press, 2004), xi–xii; see Noah D. Guynn, *Allegory and Sexual Ethics in the High Middle Ages* (New York: Palgrave Macmillan, 2007), 81–6, for another translation and interpretation.

50 James Schultz, *Courtly Love, the Love of Courtliness, and the History of Sexuality* (Chicago: University of Chicago Press, 2006), 164.

AFTERWORD
Medieval and modern sexuality

The discussion of medieval sex and sexuality presented in the foregoing chapters raises larger questions: how important is the study of sexuality to an understanding of the Middle Ages, and how important is the study of the Middle Ages to an understanding of sexuality? It may seem a bit strange to raise these questions in the conclusion of the book; if you didn't find the topic important you probably would not have read this far. But at this point, with a basic understanding of how medieval people understood the sexual, it is possible for us to draw out some of the broader implications.

In an era without photography, video, and the internet, medieval people could not spend time contemplating naked human bodies in all their permutations as can we moderns. Without mass media and advertising, the attempt to use sexual desire to stimulate the desire for goods would have been pointless in the Middle Ages. Sex permeates contemporary Western, indeed global, culture such that it is impossible to avert the eyes from all its representations. New communications media (notably video and the internet) grow rapidly, largely because they make it easier to distribute pornography; consumer capitalism sexualizes children by marketing to them clothing and music originally designed to be used seductively by adults; frank sex advice appears in a wide variety of public media; sexual behavior by public figures, or the sexual humiliation of prisoners, appears on the front page of the newspaper.

Medieval people, on the other hand, did not see suggestive or explicit images glaring out at them from newsstands, billboards, and computer screens, although occasionally they may have seen them carved on churches. Sex undoubtedly stood in a different relation to other human needs and concerns in medieval society than it does today, and this fact might call into question both the centrality of sexuality in medieval culture and the significance of the Middle Ages in the history of sexuality. I will turn first to the place of sexuality in understanding the Middle Ages and then to the place of the Middle Ages in understanding sexuality.

210

This book became possible to write only because of the spate of fine scholarship on a wide range of topics in medieval sexuality that has been published over the last forty years. Some medievalists, however, have deplored this trend in the scholarship, arguing that a focus on sexuality reflects modern concerns rather than medieval ones, that it distorts medieval culture, that it panders to the sensationalist tastes of the general public, and that it represents an obsession with the bizarre and marginal. By focusing on sex, we create a Middle Ages in our own image. In essence, they are arguing that sexuality is not or should not be central to our understanding of the European Middle Ages. Some of this criticism is simply cranky, or concerned with defending an idealized Middle Ages where everyone lived piously under the wise leadership of the church. Some criticisms of scholarly emphasis on sexuality, however, come from authors of the most important work in medieval history in recent decades, sensitive and thoughtful inter-preters of medieval texts who are concerned to represent faithfully the ways medieval people differed from our contemporaries, not in order to idealize them but in order to reveal the richness of the past.

Depictions of a Middle Ages concerned only with spiritual issues as opposed to material, a culture whose people were so radically different from us that their bodies became irrelevant, have been superseded by recent scholarship. Some of this scholarship has moved away from the spiritual entirely, focusing on the material conditions of everyday life and downplay-ing implicitly or explicitly the centrality of religious belief to the average medieval European. But one need not deny the importance of the spiritual to admit that of the material. It is now abundantly clear that the spiritual and the material were deeply intertwined (as expressed in the incarnation of Christ, whose very material and bloody death became a focus of devotion in the later Middle Ages), and that body was in no way irrelevant to soul. The body was, rather, a fundamental reality that all medieval people, including those who had taken up a religious life withdrawn from the world, had to deal with, whether they did so in terms of its physical needs and their rela-tion to the path to salvation, or in terms of its role in God's creation. The question becomes: which aspects of the material body were most important to medieval people's understanding of themselves and their relation to the world and to God?

Caroline Bynum, the most innovative and influential historian of the medieval body, has suggested that while we may think today of bodies primarily in sexual terms, for medieval people other concerns were para-mount. She has raised two topics in particular – food and the status of the body after death – that served as focal points for society's obsessions. We – middle-class westerners – are able to focus on pleasure because our basic bodily needs are, for the most part, taken care of. As Bynum's famous work *Holy Feast and Holy Fast: The Religious Significance of Food to Medieval Women* has taught us, this was not the case for medieval people, for whom food could have a far greater symbolic significance than it does for us precisely because its availability was not always assured and its acquisition and preparation required major effort. Far more significant to medieval people than erotic desire was the desire for nourishment, and more significant than sexual renunciation was fasting, which particularly for monks represented the truest control of the body. The central Christian ritual involved a sharing in the body of God, not through a sexual merging but through ingestion. Codes of ritual purity in Judaism and Islam had a great deal to do with what could and could not be eaten.

Besides hunger, another force also haunted the medieval body: death and decay. In the battle between Eros and Thanatos in the Middle Ages, some argue, Thanatos wins every time. Medieval people saw sick and dying bodies every day, and if they temporarily forgot the ubiquity of death, Christians were reminded on church walls and in sermons. If people thought of "the body," they were as likely to think of rotting flesh and skeletons as they were of nubile wenches and virile hunks. They were vitally concerned about the status of their bodies after death: could a decayed, worm-eaten body be resurrected? Would their bodies remain incorrupt like those of saints? These questions about the physical aspects of death accompanied the concern with the spiritual aspects – what happens to the soul after death? – which would have been uppermost in the minds of a great many medieval people of all religions.

Against these central themes of food and of death, how significant could sex be to medieval life? Food constituted a more basic need than sex, and Bynum has elevated it to its appropriate status in our understanding of the medieval body. And yet, it is medieval attitudes toward sex – the particular forms and circumstances under which sexual activity is legitimate – that have come down to the contemporary world, rather than attitudes toward food. And, while food carried with it great religious symbolism, sermons, exempla, and moral exhortation to the laity in general, on a concrete rather than symbolic level, focused on sexual more than on alimentary desire, at least within Christianity.

Indeed, the two desires remained closely linked. Advice on how to remedy sexual desire involved fasting, and overindulgence in food often appeared as one of the factors likely to cause or promote sexual temptation. Food permitted the existence of the flesh – a flesh that was not in itself evil, but that always carried within it the risk of carnal, notably sexual, sin. Jesus's assumption of human flesh emphasized that the flesh was part of God's good creation, but few medieval people could hope to be as firmly in control of their fleshly desires as Jesus was.

Women's role as feeders and nurturers of their family was also related to their role as mothers, and in the age before effective contraception their fertility and their sexuality were inextricably linked. The female breast depicted in medieval art may not have had the same sexual meanings as the breast does

212

today, since it was used mainly to represent nurturing (of Christ by Mary, most commonly), but motherhood in terms of the nurturing of children was inseparable from the bearing of those children, which was inseparable from the process of their conception. In all cases except the Virgin Mary, that process involved sexual intercourse. Engels's formulation of household work (usually performed by women) as "reproductive labor," as opposed to the productive labor in industry or agriculture usually performed by men, refers to social reproduction (work that keeps the labor force fed, clothed, and housed) rather than physical reproduction (the process of conception and birth). Nevertheless, social reproduction presumes physical reproduction. Without food sex is not possible, but without sex there is no need for food.

The relation between sex and death (even if we forgo psychoanalytic explanations) is even more complex but equally ubiquitous. Late medieval art cautioned people to keep death constantly in mind; holding this thought would enable them to live a good life and be prepared for its inevitable end. Yet the symbols that are used in art to represent life, and to contrast with those for death, are often connected with sexuality: youth and physical beauty, for example, and fertility in the natural world of plants and animals. Birth and growth were the opposite of death, and sex was inseparable from birth.

By no means did all representations of death in the Middle Ages involve the complementary process of birth. The ubiquitous representations of the Crucifixion in the Christian world, for example, emphasized either the triumph or the suffering of Christ, but either way the focus was firmly on death rather than birth, as was also the case with the martyrdoms of the saints. However, the nativity of Christ was also a common subject for artistic representation, and the Madonna and child even more common. These latter scenes (whether viewed, or imagined as a result of reading or preaching) would have brought to people's minds the notion of the purity of the Virgin Mary, which implied the relative impurity of all other human reproduction. It is perhaps a bit of a stretch to argue that the Crucifixion implies the Madonna and Child, which implies conception without sin, which implies other conceptions achieved by means of sex and sin. But the Crucifixion certainly implies the incarnation – its emphasis, especially in the later Middle Ages, is firmly on the humanity of Christ – which would have called to people's minds the question of divine versus human fatherhood, conception without intercourse versus conception with it. Indeed, it has been suggested (though disputed) that scenes both of the Madonna and Child and of the Crucifixion place an emphasis on Christ's genitalia. Even if the emphasis on his penis is intended to emphasize his circumcision (as a symbol of the Crucifixion), circumcision still marks him as male and pertains to the organ connected with male sexuality and fertility.

The comparison with food and death questions the centrality of sex in medieval discourse. It is true that it is far less prominent in medieval discourse than in modern; simply for technological reasons, if nothing else, medieval people could not have had access to such a variety of explicit images and texts, even had the elites wanted them to. But sex can be ubiquitous even without mass media. Medieval people would be much less likely to see representations of sex acts, but they would be much more likely than modern ones to witness the actual performance of those acts. The vast majority of medieval people, after all, were rural dwellers who would be familiar with the behavior of barnyard animals, if only roosters and hens. Sleeping arrangements, among the aristocracy as well as the peasantry, did not provide much privacy. Weddings could include the couple being placed in bed together, naked, in front of witnesses. A medieval child would probably have a great deal more sexual knowledge by the time she or he reached puberty than a modern one who has been exposed to billboards and film trailers from an early age. That sexual knowledge would probably be much less titillating and much more matter-of-fact than that of a contemporary child.

The whole idea of the innocence of youth, indeed, worked out quite differently in the Middle Ages. American parents purchase filtering software for their children's computer use – and mandate its purchase by public libraries – that interdicts any page using the word "breast" (including pages on cancer, lactation, and chicken recipes) or "bitch" (including dog shows). Before digital photography people were arrested because photo developing shops turned them in as pornographers for taking photographs of their children in the bath. The female breast, so common in medieval art (although often in a nurturing rather than an erotic context), cannot be displayed in many American jurisdictions. Modern American children's innocence is preserved by teaching them that body parts are shameful and to be hidden.

Medieval children, on the other hand, could marry (and among the aristocracy not uncommonly did) at age 12 for girls, 14 for boys. Contemporary reaction to sexual activity among children of this age universally deplores it (and criminalizes any adult who participates). A medieval person of that age, on the other hand, was no longer a child, though in some ways not yet fully an adult, and was nubile. Medieval court records are full of examples of the rape of girls (and sometimes boys) under that age. This is not because medieval society was disproportionately full of pedophiles, but because the line between childhood and sexual maturity was placed earlier. One reason pedophiles find children attractive is their presumed innocence, an innocence that would not have been presumed in the same way in the Middle Ages, when young teenagers and pre-teenagers were working for a living and preparing to take on the management of a household. Sex was an acknowledged, not hidden, part of the adulthood for which they were preparing themselves. Of course, sexual activity outside of marriage was roundly condemned. But as Foucault argued, in his discussion of the "repressive hypothesis" (see Chapter 1), a more permissive society is not

214

necessarily the one that talks about sexuality the most. Discussing why sex is sinful is still discussing it, and keeps it at the forefront of people's minds.

Abstinence from food was also a denial of bodily temptation, but there were no medieval schemes for the division of society into groups that involved, say, vegetarians versus meat-eaters. The denial of sexual activity was a fundamental part of the identity of priests and members of religious orders (and a good number of the laity as well); this did not make sexuality insignificant to them but rather kept it constantly at the forefront of their minds and of the way that others saw them.

Besides an awareness of who was or was not, should or should not be, sexually active, medieval people would also have been aware of another manifestation of the erotic in medieval culture: it was used in all three religions to express humans' relation to the divine. Chapter 2 discussed the question of the metaphorical nature of erotic language in this context. Whether or not it was metaphorical, the language of desire, of merging with another in a height of pleasure, of penetration and possession, would have been familiar to medieval people from sermons, if not from their own reading. In this sense we can say that sexuality was central to medieval culture, its language often being used for the central mysteries of the faith that dominated the society. Along with food, death, and other aspects of medieval culture, an understanding of medieval attitudes toward sexuality is necessary fully to understand the way medieval people approached God.

Sexuality, then, is important to the study of the Middle Ages; the Middle Ages are also important to the study of sexuality, both because this period saw the origin of many of the laws and norms governing sexual behavior today and because, despite a shared cultural tradition, the ways in which medieval people constructed sexual identities are quite different from those of the modern and post-modern world. It is precisely this quality of being similar and at the same time different that makes medieval Europe worth studying. To suggest that sexual identities, attitudes, and practices in Papua New Guinea are different from those in modern North America and Europe is not surprising. To suggest that sexual identities, attitudes, and practices in the culture that gave us our legal systems and religious traditions were different teaches us that the way things are, or the way we imagine them to be, is not the "natural" way but historically contingent.

Non-medievalists have tended to think of the Middle Ages as so different from the modern era as to invalidate any comparisons or any relevance. The Middle Ages become the Before (the chronological equivalent of the Other). Everything that is historically interesting begins with the rise of capitalism or of the state, whether one situates these developments in the sixteenth, seventeenth, eighteenth, or nineteenth century. It has been suggested that sexuality as a field of discourse in general, and homosexuality as an identity in particular, cannot have existed before the regulatory apparatus of the state was brought to bear upon people's sexual behavior. This book has established, however, that there was indeed a field of discourse that could be called "sexuality" in the Middle Ages. It is not the same thing as modern "sexuality" but is antecedent to it, and the changes it has undergone tell us a great deal about the evolution of modern western society.

Non-medievalists have not been the only ones to wish to make the Middle Ages totally Other. Medieval scholarship for a long time ignored the material bases of medieval culture in favor of the spiritual, assuming that the Middle Ages were an Age of Faith where everyone, in whatever religion, focused on God, not on the social world around them. But religious leaders were concerned not only with souls but with the bodies those souls inhabited and how the behavior of those bodies should be regulated. The great achievements of medieval thought included not only abstract theology but also law, political theory, science, and economic theory, all of which had concrete temporal consequences of which the thinkers were well aware. Sexuality is only one of the realms of discourse in which medieval thought is commensurable with, if far from identical to, the modern.

The idea that sex is bad because the body must be denied, or because it is in some way impure, does not have its origins in the Middle Ages; as discussed in Chapter 2, it developed during the Middle Ages out of more or less prominent strands of thought in the ancient Mediterranean. It was in the Middle Ages, however, that it came to shape a whole body of law: not canon law (the law of the church) alone but also that of governmental jurisdictions at various levels. Placing the government in the bedroom is a medieval development, although it was the modern period that brought it to a fine art.

The medieval period is also when western Christian (and to some extent Jewish and Muslim) culture came to define the limits of what sexual activity was and was not permissible. The idea that marriage is monogamous and indissoluble was elaborated in this period. The notion of what constituted legal marriage – a relationship in which sexual intercourse could give rise to children who could inherit property – was hammered out through the course of the medieval era. The question of whether a sex act had to be procreative or at least potentially open to procreation in order to be licit was also debated at this time.

Within the medieval period we see the roots of the modern debate over whether sex is a gift from God, connected with love and intended to enhance human existence, or a necessary evil for the procreation of the species, accompanied by a sort of madness, leading humans to disregard everything but immediate pleasure, which is a consequence of sin. Medieval theologians took, and bequeathed to the early modern world, a variety of positions on this question. The split continues within Christianity today, within its Catholic, Orthodox, and Protestant branches: is sex something to be tolerated within marriage but minimized, or is it something to be celebrated as an expression of love? The anti-sex views of some medieval monks seem

216

closer to the puritanism of some modern Protestant denominations than to the teachings of the modern Roman Catholic Church, at least with regard to the married laity.

A number of the changes that have been suggested as central to the emergence of the modern world and modern sexualities have their roots in the Middle Ages. It is true that the Protestant Reformation brought with it a valorization of marriage and reproduction that served as part of its condemnation of monasticism and clerical celibacy. But as we have seen, many medieval authors praised marriage, including its sexual aspects, as well; the reformers' innovation was to make it universal rather than to exclude one privileged group from it. The Reformation did lead, not immediately but ultimately, to a secularization of society in the Enlightenment and after. But the religious roots of attitudes toward sexuality developed during the Middle Ages have proven remarkably persistent even in a secular world, even among non-believers. From figures like Mae West, who refer to themselves as "bad" when they don't think they're bad at all, to contemporary T-shirts with which people can self-identify as "bad girls," even those who do not accept medieval standards of appropriate feminine sexual behavior acknowledge that the wider society accepts them.

Both church and state came to play a greater role in the policing of marriage after the Reformation. The Council of Trent in 1563 required for the first time that a Roman Catholic marriage be performed by a priest in order to be valid, and various Protestant jurisdictions enacted a variety of legislation about the performance and validity of marriage. Those who violated the bonds of marriage through adultery or even premarital sex could be pursued in secular as well as ecclesiastical courts. And yet, as we have seen throughout this book, while in some places marriages may have received increased scrutiny, the involvement of the government in assessing their propriety and validity was not new. Urban governments regulated the sexual behavior of town residents during the Middle Ages too – not only prostitution, which was widely considered a public nuisance, but often adultery and fornication as well. This regulation may not have been especially effective, but the change in the modern era was in the ability to carry out its regulatory goals, not in the nature of those goals themselves.

Alongside various other early modern developments – the Reformation, bourgeois capitalism, the Enlightenment – scholars have identified the rise of individualism and the decline of communitarianism. This led, among other things, to a focus on the nuclear family as opposed to the larger kin group, and to a focus on the household as a place of privacy opposed to the public sphere. This shift is obviously important in the history of sexuality, as modern ideas about sex often make it something very individual and private. But, as the discussions of increasing governmental intervention in regulating, or indeed creating, "sexuality" indicate, it was not the case that the early modern period saw a shift from sex as something to be regulated by the community to something best left to the individual's conscience. And the literature of the Middle Ages shows us that conceptions of a highly individualistic romantic love permeated the culture, even if they may not have drastically affected everyday behavior. Not all marriages during the Middle Ages were made by families and unconnected with individuals' love and desire, and not all marriages made after the Middle Ages were made by individuals on the basis of love and desire, unconnected to families' economic and social needs.

Nor do we see a major shift in the modern era in scientific understandings of the body. Thomas Laqueur argues that an Aristotelian "one-seed" theory dominated in Europe from ancient times until the eighteenth century, when it was dislodged by the discovery of the ovum. However, as we have seen in Chapter 3, Aristotle's view was far from universally accepted in the Middle Ages, and many did believe that women contributed seed in reproduction (although neither the sperm nor ovum were known). Laqueur shows how early modern views of the female body as homologous to the male were shaped by understandings of the nature of reproduction – society shaping the body, rather than the other way around. This, of course, is still the case. Medical school textbooks in gynecology show side-view cutouts of the "female reproductive system" that do not show the clitoris, presumably on the basis that it has nothing to do with "reproduction" as the textbook constructs it. In the Middle Ages just about everything about the female body had something to do with reproduction, and female sexual pleasure was quite relevant.

The argument about whether homosexuality was a sexual identity in the pre-modern period was discussed at some length in Chapter 5, and I will not repeat it here. Suffice it to reiterate that the drastic discontinuities between medieval and modern that some scholars have proposed have been questioned in this area as well. And yet there are differences worth seriously considering, notably the difference between sex as something two (usually) people do together as opposed to something someone does to someone else. This shift (although the transitive or subject–object version still survives in contemporary culture) is closely related to the development of ideologies of gender and a move away from the equating of femininity with passivity. The history of sexuality and the history of gender are inextricably entwined, and we can see this when we draw comparisons between the European Middle Ages and the contemporary world.

The Middle Ages, then, constitute not just a "before" period distinguished from modernity by a major paradigm shift in the history of sexuality. Rather, it was a period whose attitudes were as diverse and as changeable (if perhaps not as rapidly changing) as those found in the modern era. And yet its attitudes were different enough from those of educated westerners in the twenty-first century – notably in sex being something that one person does to another rather than something that two people do together, and in one's "sexuality" being primarily a matter of object choice rather than a matter of gender role – that they become very useful to think with.

Many people hold what they believe to be traditional views about various sexual practices, but the yearning for tradition is often based on a dream of an unrecoverable idealized past, rather than a knowledge of what the attitudes and mores of the past were. Medieval Europe provides us with an example of a society similar to that of the modern west because it is antecedent to it in its laws and attitudes, and yet it constructed genders and sexualities in strikingly different ways. It is my hope that this book uses the medieval world to help us understand the contemporary one by revealing medieval attitudes in all their variety and complexity.

The European Middle Ages, in the area of sexuality or in any other, can be reduced neither to a Golden Age in which everyone faithfully followed the teachings of the church, nor to a counter-Golden Age in which both women and men were free to enjoy and indulge, one big earth festival. Neither model is useful to any project beyond a false nostalgia for better days. What is useful is the example of how a society in many ways like and in many ways unlike our own can interpret human behavior and desire in ways that are at the same time so similar and so different.

FURTHER READING

Each of the following bibliographical essays will indicate some works that may be of interest to the reader who wants to follow up on the topic generally, and then discuss the specific works on which the chapter has drawn. As with all scholarship, this work builds on the ideas, research, and interpretations of many other scholars, and I am grateful to the authors whose work I have attempted to synthesize here.

1 Sex and the Middle Ages

There is no recent book-length study of medieval sexuality in general (which, of course, is why I have written this one). There are, however, collections of essays that attempt to cover most aspects of the topic, with many of the articles written by major scholars in their fields. The more recent one is *A Cultural History of Sexuality in the Middle Ages*, ed. Ruth Evans, vol. 2 of *A Cultural History of Sexuality* (Oxford: Berg, 2011). Pathbreaking but now a bit dated is *Handbook of Medieval Sexuality*, eds. Vern L. Bullough and James A. Brundage (New York: Garland, 1996). There are also a great many other collections of essays that do not make the same effort to be comprehensive, but that nevertheless cover a wide range of topics. Some of these include: *Sexual Practices and the Medieval Church*, eds. Vern L. Bullough and James Brundage (Buffalo: Prometheus Books, 1982); *Constructing Medieval Sexuality*, eds. Karma Lochrie, Peggy McCracken and James A. Schultz (Minneapolis: University of Minnesota Press, 1997); *Desire and Discipline: Sex and Sexuality in the Pre-Modern West*, eds. Jacqueline Murray and Konrad Eisenbichler (Toronto: University of Toronto Press, 1996); *Sexuality in the Middle Ages and Early Modern Times: New Approaches to a Fundamental Cultural-Historical and Literary-Anthropological Theme*, ed. Albrecht Classen (Berlin: Walter de Gruyter, 2008).

There are a great many other works that cover one aspect or another of medieval sexuality, and these will be mentioned here and in the other chapters. Several works give a comprehensive view based on one particular kind of source. For canon law, the indispensable reference is James A. Brundage, *Law, Sex, and Christian Society in Medieval Europe* (Chicago: University of Chicago Press, 1987). For later medieval theology, Pierre J. Payer, *The Bridling of Desire: Views of Sex in the Later Middle Ages* (Toronto: University of Toronto Press, 1993) is less comprehensive but generally useful. John W. Baldwin, *The Language of Sex: Five Voices from Northern France around 1200* (Chicago: University of Chicago Press, 1994) focuses on a particular time and geographical region and the differing views of writers across a variety of genres. For representations of sexual themes in medieval art see many of the works of Michael Camille, especially *The Medieval Art of Love: Objects and Subjects of Desire* (New York: Abrams, 1998), and Diane Wolfthal, *In and Out of the Marital Bed: Seeing Sex in Renaissance Europe* (New Haven: Yale University Press, 2010). On *Game of Thrones* see Carolyne Larrington, *Winter Is Coming: The Medieval World of Game of Thrones* (London: I.B. Tauris, 2015). On child molestation and the clergy see Dyan Elliott, "Sexual Scandal and the Clergy: A Medieval Blueprint for Disaster," in *Why the Middle Ages Matter: Medieval Light on Modern Injustice*, eds. Celia Chazelle, Simon Doubleday, Felice Lifshitz and Amy G. Remensnyder (London: Routledge, 2012), 90–105.

On the *Dante's Inferno* video game, see the introduction by the Executive Producer and Creative Director of Electronic Arts to the reissue of the Henry Wadsworth Longfellow translation of Dante's work: Jonathan Knight, "Is Dante Alighieri Laughing, or Rolling, in His Grave?," in Dante Alighieri, *Inferno*, trans. Henry Wadsworth Longfellow (New York: Ballantine Books/Del Rey, 2010), ix–xxiv, and Lorenzo Servitje, "Digital Mortification of Literary Flesh: Computational Logistics and Violences of Remediation in Visceral Games' Dante's Inferno," *Games and Culture* 9 (2014), 368–88. Among the substantial scholarship on Alain of Lille, the works by Jan Ziolkowski, *Alain of Lille's Grammar of Sex: The Meaning of Grammar to a Twelfth-Century Intellectual* (Cambridge, MA: Medieval Academy of America, 1985) and Elizabeth B. Keiser, *Courtly Desire and Medieval Homophobia: The Legitimation of Sexual Pleasure in Cleanness and Its Contexts* (New Haven: Yale University Press, 1997) are two of the most useful.

The original exponent of the view that in Aristotelian biology there was only one sex, rather than a binary system, is Thomas Laqueur, *Making Sex: Body and Gender from the Greeks to Freud* (Cambridge, MA: Harvard University Press, 1990). On the idea that medieval society included more than two genders, see R.N. Swanson, "Angels Incarnate: Clergy and Masculinity from Gregorian Reform to Reformation," in *Masculinity in Medieval Europe*, ed. Dawn M. Hadley (New York: Longman, 1999), 160–77, a number of the articles in *Gender and Difference in the Middle Ages*, eds. Sharon Farmer and Carol Braun Pasternack (Minneapolis: University of Minnesota Press, 2003), and Jacqueline Murray, "One Flesh, Two Sexes, Three Genders?" in *Gender and Christianity in Medieval Europe: New Perspectives*, eds. Lisa M. Bitel and Felice Lifshitz (Philadelphia: University of Pennsylvania Press, 2008), 34–51. Most of the scholarly discussion on the fluidity of gender appears in studies of women in religion; for the historiography on this topic see Dyan Elliott, "The Three Ages of Joan Scott," *American Historical Review* 113 (2008): 1390–1403.

Work in the history of sexuality generally, outside the Middle Ages, has proliferated tremendously in the last decade. The foundational theoretical text in the history of sexuality is Michel Foucault, *The History of Sexuality, vol. 1, an Introduction*, trans. Robert Hurley (New York: Vintage, 1990). The most important historical interpreter of Foucault is David M. Halperin; see for example his "Forgetting Foucault: Acts, Identities, and the History of Sexuality," *Representations* 63

(1998), 93–120, reprinted along with other articles in his *How to Do the History of Homosexuality* (Chicago: University of Chicago Press, 2002), in which he explains how Foucault's acts/identities distinction has been misinterpreted, as well as his earlier *One Hundred Years of Homosexuality, and Other Essays on Greek Love* (New York: Routledge, 1990). The essentialist/constructionist debate, in which Halperin represents the constructionist side, is now largely over, but for those interested in its historical development see *Forms of Desire: Sexual Orientation and the Social Construction Controversy*, ed. Edward Stein (New York: Garland, 1990). Anna Clark, *Desire: A History of European Sexuality* (New York and London: Routledge, 2008) is a general history that covers the Middle Ages and makes very judicious use of Foucault and the insights of other theorists. James Schultz, *Courtly Love, the Love of Courtliness, and the History of Sexuality* (Chicago: University of Chicago Press, 2006), ch. 4, critiques scholars who persist in using the term "heterosexuality" even while recognizing "homosexuality" is anachronistic. Karma Lochrie, *Heterosyncrasies: Female Sexuality When Normal Wasn't* (Minneapolis: University of Minnesota Press, 2005) uses the neologism "heterosyncrasy" to make the point that it is impossible to talk about "heteronormativity" in the Middle Ages, before the sociological idea of the "norm" had emerged.

The now standard statement of queer theory in medieval studies is Karma Lochrie, "Mystical Acts, Queer Tendencies," in *Constructing Medieval Sexuality*, eds. Karma Lochrie, Peggy McCracken and James A. Schultz (Minneapolis: University of Minnesota Press, 1997), 180–200; see also *Queering the Middle Ages*, eds. Glenn Burger and Steven F. Kruger (Minneapolis: University of Minnesota Press, 2001). Besides the articles included in the latter volume, scholars who have written about the concept of the "queer" in the Middle Ages include Tison Pugh, *Sexuality and Its Queer Discontents in Middle English Literature* (New York: Palgrave Macmillan, 2008). David Clark, *Between Medieval Men: Male Friendship and Desire in Early Medieval English Literature* (Oxford: Oxford University Press, 2009) discusses *The Wife's Lament* and other Anglo-Saxon poetry where scholars have assumed a male–female relationship.

The scholarship on sexuality in the ancient Greek and Roman world has been well ahead of that on medieval Europe in the development of new conceptual frameworks. Examples include Eva C. Keuls, *The Reign of the Phallus: Sexual Politics in Ancient Athens, an Illustrated History* (New York: Harper and Row, 1985); *Before Sexuality: The Construction of Erotic Experience in the Ancient Greek World*, eds. David M. Halperin, John J. Winkler and Froma I. Zeitlin (Princeton: Princeton University Press, 1990); Eva Cantarella, *Bisexuality in the Ancient World*, trans. Cormac Ó Cuilleanáin (New Haven: Yale University Press, 1992); Amy Richlin, "Not before Homosexuality: The Materiality of the Cinaedus and the Roman Law against Love between 'Men'," *Journal of the History of Sexuality* 3 (1993), 523–73; *Roman Sexualities*, eds. Judith Hallett and Marilyn B. Skinner (Princeton: Princeton University Press, 1997); James N. Davidson, *Courtesans and Fishcakes: The Consuming Passions of Classical Athens* (New York: St. Martin's, 1998); Craig A. Williams, *Roman Homosexuality: Ideologies of Masculinity in Classical Antiquity* (New York: Oxford University Press, 1999).

On the fabliaux as a genre, and in particular their sexual attitudes, see R. Howard Bloch, *The Scandal of the Fabliaux* (Chicago: University of Chicago Press, 1986);

Marie-Thérèse Lorcin, *Façons de sentir et de penser: les fabliaux français* (Paris: Honoré Champion, 1979); and several of the articles in *Obscenity: Social Control and Artistic Creation in the European Middle Ages*, ed. Jan Ziolkowski (Leiden: E.J. Brill, 1998). On the Bayeux Tapestry, see Karen Rose Mathews, "Nudity on the Margins: The Bayeux Tapestry and Its Relationship to Marginal Architectural Sculpture," in *Naked before God: Uncovering the Body in Anglo-Saxon England*, eds. Benjamin C. Withers and Jonathan Wilcox (Morgantown: West Virginia University Press, 2003), 138–61; for manuscript margins, Michael Camille, *Image on the Edge: The Margins of Medieval Art* (London: Reaktion Books, 1992); for stone carvings, Anthony Weir and James Jarman, *Images of Lust: Sexual Carvings on Medieval Churches* (London: B.T. Batsford, 1986).

On medieval uses of the Song of Songs, see E. Ann Matter, *The Voice of My Beloved: The Song of Songs in Western Medieval Christianity* (Philadelphia: University of Pennsylvania Press, 1990).

On Aelred of Rievaulx and friendship, several works of Brian Patrick McGuire are useful, particularly *Brother and Lover: Aelred of Rievaulx* (New York: Crossroad, 1994). A very important work on the nature of friendship and love in the central Middle Ages, and their relation to eroticism, is C. Stephen Jaeger, *Ennobling Love: In Search of a Lost Sensibility* (Philadelphia: University of Pennsylvania Press, 1999).

Peraldus and his discussion of the sin against nature are helpfully discussed in Karma Lochrie, *Covert Operations: The Medieval Uses of Secrecy* (Philadelphia: University of Pennsylvania Press, 1999), 179–205. The most useful discussion of Aquinas in this context comes in Mark D. Jordan, *The Invention of Sodomy in Christian Theology* (Chicago: University of Chicago Press, 1997). For the idea of nature in medieval Islam, see F. Jamil Ragep, "Islamic Culture and the Natural Sciences," in *The Cambridge History of Science, vol. 2, Medieval Science*, eds. David C. Lindberg and Michael H. Shank (Cambridge: Cambridge University Press, 2013), 1–26. Jordan's is also the key work for the medieval understanding of "sodomy." Susan Schibanoff, "Sodomy's Mark: Alan of Lille, Jean de Meun, and the Medieval Theory of Authorship," in Burger and Kruger, *Queering the Middle Ages*, 28–56, suggests that medieval writing and indeed all Aristotelian causality is "heterosexualized" because it is understood as an active masculine principle shaping a passive feminine matter – an important insight couched in an anachronistic term. The discussion of masochism is indebted to Robert Mills, *Suspended Animation: Pain, Pleasure, and Punishment in Medieval Culture* (London: Reaktion Books, 2005).

On the emotion of love in the Middle Ages see William Reddy, *The Making of Romantic Love: Longing and Sexuality in Europe, South Asia and Japan, 900–1200 CE* (Chicago: University of Chicago Press, 2012).

For modern comparisons see: on butch/femme organization of lesbian communities, Elizabeth Lapovsky Kennedy and Madeline Davis, *Boots of Leather, Slippers of Gold: The History of a Lesbian Community* (New York: Penguin, 1994); on the gay male world in New York; George Chauncey, *Gay New York: Gender, Urban Culture, and the Making of the Gay Male World, 1890–1940* (New York: Basic Books, 1994).

For sexuality in medieval Jewish society generally see David Biale, *Eros and the Jews: From Biblical Israel to Contemporary America* (New York: Basic Books, 1992);

specific aspects are discussed in subsequent chapters. The regulation of sexuality in Savoy is discussed by Prisca Lehmann, *La repression des délits sexuels dans les États Savoyards: Châtellenies des dioceses d'Aoste, Sion et Turin, fin XIIIe–XVe siècle* (Lausanne: Cahiers Lausannois d'histoire médiévale, 2006).

2 The sexuality of chastity

Ideas about chastity are so pervasive in medieval religious writing that it is discussed in all works on gender, sexuality, and the religious life, but there are few single works devoted to it. The study of virginity, however, has been a very active area. Key works include Jocelyn Wogan-Browne, *Saints' Lives and Women's Literary Culture c.1150–1300: Virginity and Its Authorizations* (Oxford: Oxford University Press, 2001), focusing in particular on Anglo-Norman literature (written in French in England in the twelfth and thirteenth centuries); Sarah Salih, *Versions of Virginity in Late Medieval England* (Woodbridge, Suffolk: D.S. Brewer, 2001); Kathleen Coyne Kelly, *Performing Virginity and Testing Chastity in the Middle Ages* (London: Routledge, 2000); Karen A. Winstead, *Virgin Martyrs: Legends of Sainthood in Late Medieval England* (Ithaca, NY: Cornell University Press, 1997). All of these works are by literary scholars and focus on texts about female virgins. Slightly more wide-ranging are the articles in several essay collections, *Menacing Virgins: Representing Virginity in the Middle Ages and Renaissance*, eds. Marina Leslie and Kathleen Coyne Kelly (Newark, DE: University of Delaware Press, 1999); *Constructions of Widowhood and Virginity in the Middle Ages*, eds. Cindy L. Carlson and Angela Jane Weisl (New York: St. Martin's, 1999); *Medieval Virginities*, eds. Anke Bernau, Ruth Evans and Sarah Salih (Toronto: University of Toronto Press, 2003). John Bugge, *Virginitas: An Essay in the History of a Medieval Ideal* (The Hague: Martinus Nijhoff, 1975) is less focused on literature than these other works, but also, because older, cannot take into account the huge amount of feminist scholarship on the subject. On chastity in romance see Peggy McCracken, "Chaste Subjects: Gender, Heroism, and Desire in the Grail Quest," in *Queering the Middle Ages*, eds. Steven Kruger and Glenn Burger (Minneapolis: University of Minnesota Press, 2001), 123–42.

On the early Christian church and its attitudes toward sexuality and chastity in general, the best work remains Peter R.L. Brown, *The Body and Society: Men, Women, and Sexual Renunciation in Early Christianity* (New York: Columbia University Press, 1988). More recent, and dealing with a slightly earlier period, is William Loader, "Marriage and Sexual Relations in the New Testament World," in *Oxford Handbook of Theology, Sexuality, and Gender*, ed. Adrian Thatcher (Oxford: Oxford University Press, 2014), 189–205. On women in particular, see Jo Ann McNamara, *A New Song: Celibate Women in the First Three Christian Centuries* (New York: Haworth Press, 1983). Many works by Elizabeth A. Clark also bear on the question of the early church and chastity, notably *Reading Renunciation: Asceticism and Scripture in Early Christianity* (Princeton, NJ: Princeton University Press, 1999).

On attitudes toward sexuality in Judaism generally, see David Biale, *Eros and the Jews: From Biblical Israel to Contemporary America* (New York: Basic Books, 1992). Daniel Boyarin, *Carnal Israel: Reading Sex in Talmudic Culture* (Berkeley:

University of California Press, 1993) makes a more complex argument rather than a chronological narrative. On menstruation see Sharon Faye Koren, *Forsaken: The Menstruant in Medieval Jewish Mysticism* (Waltham, MA: Brandeis University Press, 2011).

On women in early Christianity choosing virginity for themselves, see McNamara, *A New Song*. On saints Perpetua and Felicity, see Joyce E. Salisbury, *Perpetua's Passion: The Death and Memory of a Young Roman Woman* (London: Routledge, 1997). On the Virgin Mary, a highly readable if somewhat tendentious account is Marina Warner, *Alone of All Her Sex: The Myth and the Cult of the Virgin Mary* (New York: Vintage Books, 1983); see also Miri Rubin, *Mother of God: A History of the Virgin Mary* (Harmondsworth: Penguin, 2010).

The Church Fathers' views on sexuality are discussed in Brown, *Body and Society*, and much of my account relies on this work. For more background on Augustine, see also Peter Brown, *Augustine of Hippo: A Biography*, second edition (Berkeley: University of California Press, 2000) and for other patristic authors, Elizabeth A. Clark, *Ascetic Piety and Women's Faith: Essays on Late Ancient Christianity* (Lewiston, NY: Edwin Mellen Press, 1986). On sexuality in pagan Rome see *Roman Sexualities*, eds. Judith P. Hallett and Marilyn B. Skinner (Princeton, NJ: Princeton University Press, 1997). Excerpts from the work of St. Augustine on marriage and sexuality are also available in *Gender and Sexuality in the Middle Ages: A Medieval Source Documents Reader*, ed. Martha A. Brożyna (Jefferson, NC: McFarland, 2005). Kyle Harper, *From Shame to Sin: The Christian Transformation of Sexual Morality* (Cambridge, MA: Harvard University Press, 2013) argues that Christianity fundamentally changed sexual mores through its demand of chastity or fidelity from men as well as women.

The literature on monasticism is vast, and most of it does not focus specifically on chastity, which was a given. Most studies deal with learning and spirituality or else with property ownership and institutional structure. One very useful synthetic study is Jo Ann McNamara, *Sisters in Arms: Catholic Nuns through Two Millennia* (Cambridge, MA: Harvard University Press, 1996). On the origins of monasticism, see Albrecht Diem, "The Gender of the Religious: Wo/Men and the Invention of Monasticism," in *Oxford Handbook of Women and Gender in Medieval Europe*, eds. Judith M. Bennett and Ruth Mazo Karras (Oxford: Oxford University Press, 2013), 432–46, suggesting that female monasticism was central. On fasting and sexual desire in early monasticism, as well as other issues, see Joyce E. Salisbury, "When Sex Stopped Being a Social Disease: Sex and the Desert Fathers and Mothers," in *Medieval Sexuality: A Casebook*, eds. April Harper and Caroline Proctor (New York: Routledge, 2008), 47–58.

On the absence of desire as a goal, see Mary B. Cunningham, "'Shutting the Gates of the Soul': Spiritual Treatises on Resisting the Passions," in *Desire and Denial in Byzantium*, ed. Liz James (Aldershot: Ashgate, 1997), 23–32.

On eunuchs (and on many other issues involving sexuality in late antiquity) see Matthew Kuefler, *The Manly Eunuch: Masculinity, Gender Ambiguity, and Christian Ideology in Late Antiquity* (Chicago: University of Chicago Press, 2001). See also Kathryn M. Ringrose, "Living in the Shadows: Eunuchs and Gender in Byzantium," in *Third Sex, Third Gender: Beyond Sexual Dimorphism in Culture and History*, ed. Gilbert Herdt (New York: Zone Books, 1994), 85–110, and her more thorough account, *The Perfect Servant: Eunuchs and the Social Construction of Gender in Byzantium* (Chicago: University of Chicago Press, 2003).

On widowhood as compared to virginity in Christian thought, see Bernhard Jussen, *Der Name der Witwe: Erkundungen zur Semantik der mittelalterlichen Busskultur* (Göttingen: Vandenhoeck & Ruprecht, 2000).

For saintly women as well as other aspects of women's lives in the early Middle Ages, see Suzanne F. Wemple, *Women in Frankish Society: Marriage and the Cloister, 500 to 900* (Philadelphia: University of Pennsylvania Press, 1981), and Lisa M. Bitel, *Women in Early Medieval Europe 400–1100* (Cambridge: Cambridge University Press, 2002). On hagiography generally see Jane Tibbetts Schulenberg, *Forgetful of Their Sex: Female Sanctity and Society, ca. 500–1100* (Chicago: University of Chicago Press, 1998).

On penitentials and early monasticism, see Pierre J. Payer, *Sex and the Penitentials: The Development of a Sexual Code, 550–1150* (Toronto: University of Toronto Press, 1984), as well as discussion in James Brundage, *Law, Sex, and Christian Society in Medieval Europe* (Chicago: University of Chicago Press, 1987). Some excerpts from penitentials are included in Brożyna, *Gender and Sexuality*.

The suggestion that monks were in some way a third gender, not men, comes from R.N. Swanson, "Angels Incarnate: Clergy and Masculinity from Gregorian Reform to Reformation," in *Masculinity in Medieval Europe*, ed. Dawn M. Hadley (New York: Longman, 1999), 160–77; a slightly different version of this suggestion was made by Jo Ann McNamara, "Canossa and the Ungendering of the Public Man," in *Render unto Caesar: The Religious Sphere in World Politics*, eds. Sabrina Petra Ramet and Donald W. Treadgold (Washington, DC: American University Press, 1995), 131–50. For consideration of this possibility cross-culturally, including the examples of the *berdache* and the *hijra*, see the articles in *Third Sex, Third Gender: Beyond Sexual Dimorphism in Culture and History*, ed. Gilbert Herdt (New York: Zone Books, 1993).

A fine overview of clerical celibacy is Helen Parish, *Clerical Celibacy in the West: c. 1100–1700* (Farnham, Surrey: Ashgate, 2010), which covers the early church and the early medieval period in addition to the period claimed in the title. The changes brought on by the movement for clerical celibacy in the eleventh and twelfth centuries are discussed by Jo Ann McNamara, "The 'Herrenfrage': The Restructuring of the Gender System, 1050–1150," in *Medieval Masculinities: Regarding Men in the Middle Ages*, eds. Clare A. Lees with Thelma Fenster and Jo Ann McNamara (Minneapolis: University of Minnesota Press, 1994), 3–29; Megan McLaughlin, *Sex, Gender, and Episcopal Authority in an Age of Reform, 1000–1122* (Cambridge: Cambridge University Press, 2010), 31–35, discusses the implications of clerical celibacy for the laity; at 51–91 she discusses the image of bishop as bridegroom of the church. The misogynistic literature that the reform movement led to is discussed in Katharina M. Wilson and Elizabeth M. Makowski, *Wykked Wyves and the Woes of Marriage: Misogamous Literature from Juvenal to Chaucer* (Albany: State University of New York Press, 1990).

On Guibert of Nogent and the chastity of the soul, see Jay Rubenstein, *Guibert of Nogent: Portrait of a Medieval Mind* (London: Routledge, 2002). On sexual activity as polluting see Dyan Elliott, *Fallen Bodies: Pollution, Sexuality, and Demonology in the Middle Ages* (Philadelphia: University of Pennsylvania Press, 1999).

On the sexual activities of the clergy, see Jennifer D. Thibodeaux, "The Sexual Lives of Medieval Norman Clerics: A New Perspective on Clerical Sexuality," in Classen,

Sexuality, 471–83; Michelle Armstrong-Partida, "Priestly Marriage: The Tradition of Clerical Concubinage in the Spanish Church," *Viator* 40 (2009), 221–53; Daniel Bornstein, "Parish Priests in Late Medieval Cortona: The Urban and Rural Clergy," *Quaderni di Storia Religiosa* 4 (1997), 165–93. On priests' children see Ludwig Schmugge, *Kirche, Kinder, Karrieren: Päpstliche Dispense von der unehelichen Geburt im Spätmittelalter* (Zürich: Artemis & Winkler, 1995); Laura Wertheimer, "Children of Disorder: Clerical Parentage, Illegitimacy, and Reform in the Middle Ages," *Journal of the History of Sexuality* 15 (2006), 382–407.

On priests and marriage in the eastern Orthodox churches see Eve Levin, *Sex and Society in the World of the Orthodox Slavs, 900–1700* (Ithaca, NY: Cornell University Press, 1989). Nearly all the information and interpretations I present on eastern European belief and practice are taken from Levin's work. See also several articles in *Desire and Denial in Byzantium*, ed. Liz James (Aldershot: Ashgate, 1997).

Medieval schemes of classification of persons are discussed by Giles Constable, *Three Studies in Medieval Religious and Social Thought* (Cambridge: Cambridge University Press, 1995).

Christina of Markyate has been the subject of much interest lately, notably *Christina of Markyate*, eds. Samuel Fanous and Henrietta Leyser (London: Routledge, 2004). On Goscelin and Eve see H.M. Canatella, "Long-Distance Love: The Ideology of Male–Female Spiritual Friendship in Goscelin of Saint Bertin's 'Liber Confortatorius'," in *Desire and Eroticism in Medieval Europe, Eleventh to Fifteenth Centuries: Sex without Sex*, eds. Sally N. Vaughn and Christina Christoforatou, special issue *of Journal of the History of Sexuality* 19 (2010), 35–53, and Dyan Elliott, "Alternative Intimacies: Men, Women, and Spiritual Direction in the Twelfth Century," in Fanous and Leyser, *Christina of Markyate*, 160–83; for another such couple, a century later in France, see Jennifer N. Brown, "The Chaste Erotics of Marie d'Oignies and Jacques de Vitry," in Vaughn and Christoforatou, 74–93.

On the attribution of sexual depravity to heretics see Peter Dinzelbacher, "Gruppensex im Untergrund: Chaotische Ketzer und kirchliche Keuschheit im Mittelalter," in Classen, *Sexuality*, 405–27.

The holy women of late medieval Italy are discussed in a number of the articles in *Gendered Voices: Medieval Saints and Their Interpreters*, ed. Catherine M. Mooney (Philadelphia: University of Pennsylvania Press, 1999); *Women and Religion in Medieval and Renaissance Italy*, eds. Daniel Bornstein and Roberto Rusconi, trans. Margery J. Schneider (Chicago: University of Chicago Press, 1996); and controversially by Rudolph M. Bell, *Holy Anorexia* (Chicago: University of Chicago Press, 1985). For the historical veracity of the story of Thomas Aquinas, see James A. Weisheipl, *Friar Thomas d'Aquino: His Life, Thought, and Work* (Garden City, NY: Doubleday, 1974).

On women who remained chaste within marriage, see Dyan Elliott, *Spiritual Marriage: Sexual Abstinence in Medieval Wedlock* (Princeton, NJ: Princeton University Press, 1993). The work by John Arnold in which he draws a distinction between chastity and virginity for men is "The Labour of Continence: Masculinity and Clerical Virginity," in Bernau, Evans, and Salih, *Medieval Virginities*, 102–18.

The material presented here on medieval medicine relies heavily on Joan Cadden, *The Meanings of Sex Difference in the Middle Ages: Medicine, Science, and*

Culture (Cambridge: Cambridge University Press, 1993), Monica Green, *Making Women's Medicine Masculine: The Rise of Male Authority in Pre-Modern Gynaecology* (Oxford: Oxford University Press, 2008), and Katharine Park, "Medicine and Natural Philosophy: Naturalistic Traditions," in Bennett and Karras, *Oxford Handbook of Women and Gender in Medieval Europe*, 84–100. These are indispensable works in this area. Also of use is Danielle Jacquart and Claude Thomasset, *Sexuality and Medicine in the Middle Ages*, trans. Matthew Adamson (Princeton, NJ: Princeton University Press, 1988). On nocturnal emissions see Elliott, *Fallen Bodies*, and several articles in *Obscenity: Social Control and Artistic Creation in the European Middle Ages*, ed. Jan Ziolkowski (Leiden: Brill, 1998).

Clarissa Atkinson, " 'Precious Balsam in a Fragile Glass': The Ideology of Virginity in the Later Middle Ages," *Journal of Family History* 8 (1983), 131–43, makes the argument that by the late Middle Ages virginity was a spiritual rather than a physical state.

On women attracted to other women, who may still have been seen as chaste, see Judith M. Bennett, " 'Lesbian-Like' and the Social History of Lesbianisms," *Journal of the History of Sexuality* 9 (2000), 1–24; E. Ann Matter, "My Sister, My Spouse: Woman-Identified Women in Medieval Christianity," *Journal of Feminist Studies in Religion* 2 (1986), 81–93.

Medieval eroticism is discussed in Cory J. Rushton and Amanda Hopkins, "Introduction: The Revel, the Melodye and the Bisynesse of Solas," in *The Erotic in the Literature of Medieval Britain*, eds. Amanda Hopkins and Cory James Rushton (Woodbridge, Suffolk: D.S. Brewer, 2007), 1–17. On the use of love language for friendship, and the question of whether it is erotic, see C. Stephen Jaeger, *Ennobling Love: In Search of a Lost Sensibility* (Philadelphia: University of Pennsylvania Press, 1999). See also Sarah Salih, "When Is a Bosom Not a Bosom? Problems with 'Erotic Mysticism'," in Bernau, Evans, and Salih, *Medieval Virginities*, 14–32. For Christina of Markyate, see articles in *Christina of Markyate*, eds. Fanous and Leyser. On the torture of virgin martyrs and the question of whether it is erotic see Mills, *Suspended Animation*; see also Martha Easton, " 'Was It Good For You, Too?' Medieval Erotic Art and Its Audiences," *Different Visions: A Journal of New Perspectives on Medieval Art* 1 (2008), <http://www.differentvisions. org/issue1PDFs/Easton.pdf>, accessed November 24, 2010.

On imagery of the wound of Christ, see Lochrie, "Mystical Acts, Queer Tendencies"; Albrecht Classen, "The Cultural Significance of Sexuality in the Middle Ages, the Renaissance, and beyond: A Secret Continuous Undercurrent or a Dominant Phenomenon of the Premodern World? Or: the Irrepressibility of Sex Yesterday and Today," in Classen, *Sexuality*, 1–141.

On Rupert of Deutz see John Van Engen, *Rupert of Deutz* (Berkeley: University of California Press, 1983), and Garrett P.J. Epp, "Ecce Homo," in Burger and Kruger, *Queering the Middle Ages*, 236–51; on Margery Kempe see Clarissa Atkinson, *Mystic and Pilgrim: The Book and the World of Margery Kempe* (Ithaca, NY: Cornell University Press, 1985), and Karma Lochrie, *Margery Kempe and the Translations of the Flesh* (Philadelphia: University of Pennsylvania Press, 1991). For Jean Gerson see Dyan Elliott, "Seeing Double: John Gerson, the Discernment of Spirits, and Joan of Arc," *American Historical Review* 107 (2002), 26–54.

3 Sex and marriage

There is no one comprehensive book on medieval marriage. Christopher Brooke, *The Medieval Idea of Marriage* (Oxford: Oxford University Press, 1994), is a series of related essays, focusing on the church. Georges Duby, *The Knight, the Lady, and the Priest: The Making of Modern Marriage in Medieval France*, trans. Barbara Bray (New York: Pantheon, 1983), concentrates on the twelfth century and is untouched by the newer work in women's history. This book is an expansion of Duby's earlier *Medieval Marriage: Two Models from Twelfth-Century France*, trans. Elborg Forster (Baltimore: Johns Hopkins University Press, 1978). Dyan Elliott, *Spiritual Marriage: Sexual Abstinence in Medieval Wedlock* (Princeton, NJ: Princeton University Press, 1993), although it focuses on an unusual sort of marriage, is perhaps the best effort to think through the meaning of marriage overall. A collection of primary sources can be found in *Love, Marriage, and Family in the Middle Ages: A Reader*, ed. Jacqueline Murray (Peterborough, ON: Broadview Press, 2001).

The statistic of 15 percent who never marry in the "Northwest European Marriage Pattern" goes back to an essay by John Hajnal, "European Marriage Patterns in Perspective," in *Population in History*, eds. D.V. Glass and D.E.C. Eversley (Chicago: Aldine, 1965), 101–43. For an up-to-date summary of the views of demographers on marriage rates in the Middle Ages, see Maryanne Kowaleski, "Singlewomen in Medieval and Early Modern Europe: The Demographic Perspective," in *Singlewomen in the European Past, 1250–1800*, eds. Judith M. Bennett and Amy M. Froide (Philadelphia: University of Pennsylvania Press, 1999), 38–81. Tison Pugh, *Sexuality and Its Queer Discontents in Middle English Literature* (New York: Palgrave Macmillan, 2008), argues that marital sexual activity in the Middle Ages was "queer." Arguing that there is a conceptual space for single women is Cordelia Beattie, *Medieval Single Women: The Politics of Social Classification in Late Medieval England* (Oxford: Oxford University Press, 2007).

On marriage sermons see David D'Avray, *Medieval Marriage: Symbolism and Society* (Oxford: Oxford University Press, 2004); on the "bride of Christ" metaphor see Dyan Elliott, *The Bride of Christ Goes to Hell: Metaphor and Embodiment in the Lives of Religious Women, ca. 200–1461* (Philadelphia: University of Pennsylvania Press, 2011). For an overview of marriage and law in the Biblical and Classical periods see Ruth Mazo Karras, *Unmarriages: Women, Men, and Sexual Unions in Medieval Europe* (Philadelphia: University of Pennsylvania Press, 2012), 10–18; for Islam see Jonathan P. Berkey, "Women in Medieval Islamic Society," in *Women in Medieval Westsern European Culture*, ed. Linda E. Mitchell (New York: Garland, 1999), 95–111.

On concubinage and the Frankish kings, see Suzanne F. Wemple, *Women in Frankish Society: Marriage and the Cloister, 500 to 900* (Philadelphia: University of Pennsylvania Press, 1981), and Lisa M. Bitel, *Women in Early Medieval Europe 400–1100* (Cambridge: Cambridge University Press, 2002). On forms of Germanic marriage and concubinage, see Rolf Köstler, "Raub-, Kauf-, und Friedelehe bei den Germanen," *Zeitschrift der Savigny-Stiftung für Rechtsgeschichte, Germanistische Abteilung* 63 (1943), 92–136; Margaret Clunies Ross, "Concubinage in Anglo-Saxon England," *Past and Present* 108 (1985), 3–34; Ruth Mazo Karras,

"The History of Marriage and the Myth of Friedelehe," *Early Medieval Europe* 14 (2006), 114–51; Sylvie Joye, *La femme ravie: Le marriage par rapt dans les sociétés occidentales du haut Moyen Age* (Turnhout: Brepols, 2012).

On the church's assumption of control over marriage, see Duby, *The Knight, the Lady, and the Priest* (especially on the issue of indissolubility), and Jack Goody, *The Development of the Family and Marriage in Europe* (Cambridge: Cambridge University Press, 1983). The latter argues that the restriction of inheritance to the children of a formally married wife was a deliberate effort to minimize the number of heirs and thereby increase bequests to the church. Legal aspects of the church's views on marriage are discussed in James Brundage, *Law, Sex, and Christian Society in Medieval Europe* (Chicago: University of Chicago Press, 1987). Examples of the canon law of marriage in practice are found in David D'Avray, *Papacy, Monarchy and Marriage, 860–1600* (Cambridge: Cambridge University Press, 2015), which deals with a great deal beyond the canon law as well; Charles Donahue Jr., *Law, Marriage, and Society in the Later Middle Ages* (New York: Cambridge University Press, 2007); Ruth Mazo Karras, "The Regulation of Sexuality in the Late Middle Ages: England and France," *Speculum* 86 (2011), 1010–39; Shannon McSheffrey, *Marriage, Sex, and Civic Culture in Late Medieval London* (Philadelphia: University of Pennsylvania Press, 2006); *Matrimonio in dubbio: Unioni controverse e nozze clandestine in Italia dal XIV al XVIII secolo*, eds. Silvana Seidel Menchi and Diego Quaglioni, Annali dell'Istituto storico italo-germanico in Trento, Quaderno 57 (Bologna: Il Mulino, 2001); Sara McDougall, "Bigamy: A Male Crime in Medieval Europe?," *Gender & History* 22 (2010), 430–46, and *Bigamy and Identity in Late Medieval Champagne* (Philadelphia: University of Pennsylvania Press, 2012); Christina Deutsch, *Ehegerichtsbarkeit im Bistum Regensburg (1480–1538)* (Cologne: Böhlau Verlag, 2005), 296–9; R. H. Helmholz, *Marriage Litigation in Medieval England* (Cambridge: Cambridge University Press, 1974), and Michael Sheehan, *Marriage, Family, and Law in Medieval Europe*, ed. James K. Farge (Toronto: University of Toronto Press, 1996).

Avraham Grossman, *Pious and Rebellious: Jewish Women in Medieval Europe*, trans. Jonathan Chipman (Waltham, MA: Brandeis University Press, 2004), is the standard book on the subject and contains much material on Jewish marriage as well on other issues involving sexuality. For earlier Jewish marriage, see Michael Satlow, *Jewish Marriage in Antiquity* (Princeton: Princeton University Press, 2001). On plural marriage and medieval Jews, the discussion of the Geniza documents draws on S.D. Goitein, *A Mediterranean Society: The Jewish Communities of the Arab World as Portrayed in the Documents of the Cairo Geniza, vol. 3, the Family* (Berkeley: University of California Press, 1978). The situation in western Europe is discussed in Avraham Grossman, "The Historical Background to the Ordinances on Family Affairs Attributed to Rabbenu Gershom Me'or ha-Golah ('The Light of the Exile')," in *Jewish History: Essays in Honor of Chimen Abramsky*, eds. Ada Rapoport-Albert and Steven J. Zipperstein (London: Peter Halban, 1988), 3–23. On Muslim law and practice, see Basim Musallam, *Sex and Society in Islam: Birth Control before the Nineteenth Century* (Cambridge: Cambridge University Press, 1983); Shirley Guthrie, *Arab Women in the Middle Ages: Private Lives and Public Roles* (London: Saqi Books, 2001); Yossef Rapoport, *Marriage, Money and Divorce in Medieval Islamic Society* (Cambridge: Cambridge University Press, 2007), 38–44 on divorced or widowed women; Avner Giladi, *Muslim*

Midwives: The Craft of Birthing in the Premodern Middle East (Cambridge: Cambridge University Press, 2014). See *Gender and Sexuality in the Middle Ages: A Medieval Source Documents Reader*, ed. Martha A. Brożyna (Jefferson, NC: McFarland, 2005), for excerpts from texts regulating marital and other sexual behavior in Judaism and Islam.

Women's property-holding is discussed in most works on medieval women's history. Particularly useful are *Aristocratic Women in Medieval France*, ed. Theodore Evergates (Philadelphia: University of Pennsylvania Press, 1999); Martha Howell, *The Marriage Exchange: Property, Social Place, and Gender in Cities of the Low Countries 1300–1550* (Chicago: University of Chicago Press, 1998); Janet S. Loengard, "Legal History and the Medieval Englishwoman Revisited: Some New Directions," in *Medieval Women and the Sources of Medieval History*, ed. Joel T. Rosenthal (Athens, GA: University of Georgia Press, 1990), 210–36; *Married Women and the Law in Premodern Northwest Europe*, eds. Cordelia Beattie and Matthew Frank Stephens (Woodbridge, Suffolk: Boydell Press, 2013). For Ermengarde of Narbonne, see Frederic L. Cheyette, *Ermengarde of Narbonne and the World of the Troubadours* (Ithaca, NY: Cornell University Press, 1999).

For wives in sermon literature, in addition to Katharina M. Wilson and Elizabeth M. Makowski, *Wykked Wyves and the Woes of Marriage: Misogamous Literature from Juvenal to Chaucer* (Albany: State University of New York Press, 1990), see Ruth Mazo Karras, "Misogyny and the Medieval Exemplum: Gendered Sin in John of Bromyard's 'Summa Praedicantium'," *Traditio* 47 (1992), 233–57. There is a huge literature on Chaucer's Wife of Bath, some of it excerpted in *The Wife of Bath*, ed. Peter G. Beidler (Boston: Bedford Books, 1996); see Ruth Mazo Karras, "The Wife of Bath," in *Historians on Chaucer: The General Prologue to the Canterbury Tales*, ed. Stephen Rigby (Oxford University Press, 2014), 319–33.

On the role of reproduction in marriage, see Peter Biller, *The Measure of Multitude: Population in Medieval Thought* (Oxford: Oxford University Press, 2000); on reproduction as a good of marriage see Ruth Mazo Karras, "The Reproduction of Medieval Christianity," in *The Oxford Handbook of Gender and Christian Theology*, ed. by Adrian Thatcher (Oxford University Press, 2014), 271–86.

The material on medical thought is once again taken largely from Joan Cadden, *The Meanings of Sex Difference in the Middle Ages: Medicine, Science, and Culture* (Cambridge: Cambridge University Press, 1993), as well as from Danielle Jacquart and Claude Thomasset, *Sexuality and Medicine in the Middle Ages*, trans. Matthew Adamson (Princeton: Princeton University Press, 1988); Monica Green, "Bodies, Gender, Health, Disease: Recent Work on Medieval Women's Medicine," *Studies in Medieval and Renaissance History* 3rd Series 2 (2005), 1–49; Monica Green, *Making Women's Medicine Masculine: The Rise of Male Authority in Pre-Modern Gynaecology* (Oxford: Oxford University Press, 2008); Katharine Park, "Medicine and Natural Philosophy: Naturalistic Traditions," in Bennett and Karras, *Oxford Handbook of Women and Gender in Medieval Europe*, 84–100.

On the revaluation of marriage in the twelfth century, see Duby, *The Knight, the Lady, and the Priest*; Jo Ann McNamara, "The 'Herrenfrage': The Restructuring of the Gender System, 1050–1150," in *Medieval Masculinities: Regarding Men in the Middle Ages*, eds. Clare A. Lees with Thelma Fenster and Jo Ann McNamara (Minneapolis: University of Minnesota Press, 1994), 3–29; and R.I. Moore, *The First European Revolution, c. 971–1215* (Oxford: Blackwell, 2000). On married

231

people coming to be venerated as saints in the later Middle Ages, see Donald Weinstein and Rudolph M. Bell, *Saints and Society: The Two Worlds of Western Christianity, 1000–1700* (Chicago: University of Chicago Press, 1982). On chastity within marriage in the eastern Church, see Eve Levin, *Sex and Society in the World of the Orthodox Slavs, 900–1700* (Ithaca, NY: Cornell University Press, 1989). On priests' wives see Dyan Elliott, *Fallen Bodies: Pollution, Sexuality, and Demonology in the Middle Ages* (Philadelphia: University of Pennsylvania Press, 1999). On the Cathars the standard general work in English is Malcolm Lambert, *The Cathars* (Oxford: Blackwell, 1998).

On the canon law of marriage see Brundage, *Law, Sex, and Christian Society*. The dating and attribution of the *Decretum* are discussed by Anders Winroth, *The Making of Gratian's Decretum* (Cambridge: Cambridge University Press, 2000). The *Decretum* itself is not available in English translation; the original Latin may be found in vol. 1 of *Corpus iuris canonici*, ed. Emil Friedberg (Graz: Akademische Druck- u. Verlagsanstalt, 1959). On Peter Lombard's *Sentences*, the key work is Marcia Colish, *Peter Lombard* (Leiden: E. J. Brill, 1994).

On the nature of marriage vows and the role of present consent, see Helmholz, *Marriage Litigation in Medieval England*. On the jury of matrons, see Jacqueline Murray, "On the Origins and Role of 'Wise Women' in Causes for Annulment on the Grounds of Male Impotence," *Journal of Medieval History* 16 (1990), 235–49. The fact that the "jury of matrons" actually consisted of prostitutes was pointed out by P.J.P. Goldberg, "Women in Fifteenth-Century Town Life," in *Towns and Townspeople in the Fifteenth Century*, ed. John A.F. Thompson (Gloucester: Alan Sutton, 1988), 107–28.

On the use of contraception and the sinfulness of non-reproductive sex, besides Biller, *Measure of Multitude*, see John T. Noonan, Jr., *Contraception: A History of Its Treatment by the Catholic Theologians and Canonists*, 2nd edition (Cambridge, MA: Harvard University Press, 1986). On contraceptive practices themselves, see John M. Riddle, *Contraception and Abortion from the Ancient World to the Renaissance* (Cambridge, MA: Harvard University Press, 1992), and *Eve's Herbs: A History of Contraception and Abortion in the West* (Cambridge, MA: Harvard University Press, 1997). For Islam see Musallam, *Sex and Society*. Brożyna, *Gender and Sexuality* includes excerpts from some medical texts that discuss contraception. Catherine Rider, *Magic and Impotence in the Middle Ages* (Oxford: Oxford University Press, 2006) provides a detailed account of the idea of magically caused impotence in canon law, theology, and medicine.

The forbidden days for sex are discussed in Brundage, *Law, Sex, and Christian Society*. See also Jean-Louis Flandrin, *Un temps pour embrasser: aux origines de la morale sexuelle occidentale (VIe–XIe siècle)* (Paris: Editions du Seuil, 1983). The couple punished for having sex in a church by being stuck together like dogs is discussed in Elliott, *Fallen Bodies*.

On the churching of women, see Gail Gibson, "Blessing from Sun and Moon: Churching as Women's Theater," in *Bodies and Disciplines: Intersections of Literature and History in Fifteenth-Century England*, eds. Barbara A. Hanawalt and David Wallace (Minneapolis: University of Minnesota Press, 1996), 139–54; Paula M. Rieder, *On the Purification of Women: Churching in Northern France, 1100–1500* (New York: Palgrave Macmillan, 2006).

On Jewish women see David Biale, *Eros and the Jews: From Biblical Israel to Contemporary America* (New York: Basic Books, 1992); Ze'ev Falk, *Jewish Matrimonial Law in the Middle Ages* (Oxford: Oxford University Press, 1966); Judith R. Baskin, *Midrashic Women: Formations of the Feminine in Rabbinic Literature* (Hanover: Brandeis University Press, 2002); Judith R. Baskin, "Jewish Women in the Middle Ages," in *Jewish Women in Historical Perspective*, ed. Baskin (Detroit: Wayne State University Press, 1998), 101–27; Judith R. Baskin, "Male Piety, Female Bodies: Men, Women, and Ritual Immersion in Medieval Ashkenaz," in *Studies in Medieval Halakhah in Honor of Stephen M. Passamaneck*, eds. Alyssa Gray and Bernard Jackson, *Jewish Law Association Studies* 17 (2007), 11–30.

On the lustfulness of widows see Bernhard Jussen, *Der Name der Witwe: Erkundungen zur Semantik der mittelalterlichen Busskultur* (Göttingen: Vandenhoeck & Ruprecht, 2000); see also James A. Brundage, "Widows and Remarriage: Moral Conflicts and Their Resolution in Classical Canon Law," in *Wife and Widow in Medieval England*, ed. Sue Sheridan Walker (Ann Arbor: University of Michigan Press, 1993), 19–31.

For separate bedrooms see *A History of Private Life, vol. 2, Revelations of the Medieval World*, eds. Philippe Ariès and Georges Duby (Cambridge, MA: Harvard University Press, 1988); C.M. Woolgar, *The Great Household in Medieval England* (New Haven, CT: Yale University Press, 1999). For artistic representations of couples in bed, see Camille, *The Medieval Art of Love*, and Diane Wolfthal, *In and out of the Marital Bed: Seeing Sex in Renaissance Europe* (New Haven: Yale University Press, 2010). On candles see Christopher Dyer, *Standards of Living in the Later Middle Ages: Social Change in England, c. 1200–1520* (Cambridge: Cambridge University Press, 1989). On nakedness see Albrecht Classen, "Naked Men in Medieval German Literature and Art: Anthropological, Cultural-Historical, and Mental-Historical Investigations," in Classen, *Sexuality*, 143–69. On sexual positions see James A. Brundage, "'Let Me Count the Ways': Canonists and Theologians Contemplate Coital Positions," *Journal of Medieval History* 10 (1984), 81–93. On marital sodomy, see Robert Sturges, "Purgatory in the Marriage Bed: Conjugal Sodomy in 'The Gast of Gy'," in *Framing the Family: Narrative and Representation in the Medieval and Early Modern Periods*, eds. Rosalynn Voaden and Diane Wolfthal (Tempe: CMRS, 2005), 57–78.

On the relationship of marital sex to financial exchange, see Ruth Mazo Karras, *Common Women: Prostitution and Sexuality in Medieval England* (New York: Oxford University Press, 1996), and Sheila Delany, "Sexual Economics, Chaucer's Wife of Bath, and 'The Book of Margery Kempe'," in *Writing Woman: Women Writers and Women in Literature, Medieval to Modern* (New York: Schocken Books, 1983), 76–92.

4 Women outside of marriage

Most work on medieval women talks about them mainly in the context of marriage, work, or religion, and there are no scholarly works devoted to a discussion of women's sexual activity outside of marriage *per se*. A number of general histories of medieval women do exist, however, which provide important background on the subject: Margaret Wade LaBarge, *A Small Sound of the Trumpet: Women in Medieval Life* (Boston: Beacon, 1986); Shulamith Shahar, *The Fourth Estate: A History of Women in the Middle Ages*, trans. Chaya Galai (London: Methuen, 1983); Edith Ennen, *The Medieval Woman*, trans. Edmund Jephcott (Oxford: Blackwell, 1989); A *History of Women in the West, vol. 2, Silences of the Middle Ages*, ed. Christiane Klapisch-Zuber (Cambridge, MA: Harvard University Press, 1992). None of these books place much emphasis on the early Middle Ages (the last has a chapter on it), for which see Lisa M. Bitel, *Women in Early Medieval Europe 400–1100* (Cambridge: Cambridge University Press, 2002). Information on women in Jewish and Muslim societies can be found in Avraham Grossman, *Pious and Rebellious: Jewish Women in Medieval Europe*, trans. Jonathan Chipman (Waltham, MA: Brandeis University Press, 2004), and in Yossef Rapoport, *Marriage, Money and Divorce in Medieval Islamic Society* (Cambridge: Cambridge University Press, 2007).

On women bathing see Olivia Remie Constable, "From Hygiene to Heresy: Changing Perceptions of Women and Bathing in Medieval and Early Modern Iberia," in *La cohabitation religieuse dans les villes européennes, Xe-XVe siècles*, eds. Stéphane Boissellier and John Victor Tolan (Turnhout: Brepols, 2014), 185–206. On French queens and adultery, see Charles T. Wood, *Joan of Arc and Richard III: Sex, Saints, and Government in the Middle Ages* (Oxford: Oxford University Press, 1988). For lust (and other vices) as women in medieval art, see Adolf Katzenellenbogen, *Allegories of the Virtues and Vices in Medieval Art from Early Christian Times to the Thirteenth Century* (Toronto: University of Toronto Press, 1989), including the famous capital from Vézelay; also Anthony Weir and James Jarman, *Images of Lust: Sexual Carvings on Medieval Churches* (London: B. T. Batsford, 1986).

Sumptuary laws are discussed in Ruth Mazo Karras, *Common Women: Prostitution and Sexuality in Medieval England* (New York: Oxford University Press, 1996), and the dress of matrons in Dyan Elliott, "Dress as Mediator between Inner and Outer Self: The Pious Matron of the High and Later Middle Ages," *Mediaeval Studies* 53 (1991), 279–308. The material on the Byzantine and Slavic Orthodox churches comes from Eve Levin, *Sex and Society in the World of the Orthodox Slavs, 900–1700* (Ithaca: Cornell University Press, 1989). For the French fabliaux, see R. Howard Bloch, *The Scandal of the Fabliaux* (Chicago: University of Chicago Press, 1986); Marie-Thérèse Lorcin, *Façons de sentir et de penser: les fabliaux français* (Paris: Honoré Champion, 1979).

The term "courtly love" was coined by Gaston Paris in 1883; see David Hult, "Gaston Paris and the Invention of Courtly Love," in *Medievalism and the Modernist Temper*, eds. R. Howard Bloch and Stephen G. Nichols (Baltimore: Johns Hopkins University Press, 1996), 192–224. William D. Paden, "The Troubadour's Lady through Thick History," *Exemplaria* 11 (1999), 221–44, and further discussion at "An Exchange between Don A. Monson and William D. Paden: The Troubadour's Lady," <http://web.english.ufl.edu/exemplaria/exchanges/main.htm>, debate the extent to which the troubadour poetry represents adulterous desire. James Schultz, *Courtly Love, the Love of Courtliness, and the History of Sexuality* (Chicago: University of Chicago Press, 2006) is the best account of the genre in Middle High German.

The classic article doubting the reality of courtly love is John Benton, "Clio and Venus: An Historical View of Medieval Love," in *The Meaning of Courtly Love*, ed. Francis X. Newman (Albany: SUNY Press, 1969), 19–42. Maria Rosa Menocal, *The Arabic Role in Medieval Literary History: A Forgotten Heritage* (Philadelphia: University of Pennsylvania Press, 1987), discusses its origins in Arabic literature. Georges Duby, "Youth in Aristocratic Society: Northwestern France in the Twelfth Century," in *The Chivalrous Society*, trans. Cynthia Postan (London: Edward Arnold, 1977), 111–22, suggests that in northern France the courtly love literature displaced a real possibility of female adultery with an unmarried man onto a less threatening path. John T. Noonan, Jr., *Contraception: A History of Its Treatment by the Catholic Theologians and Canonists*, 2nd edition (Cambridge, MA: Harvard University Press, 1986), suggests that the phenomenon may be related to Cathar heretical beliefs. Frederic Cheyette, "Women, Poets and Politics in Occitania," in *Aristocratic Women in Medieval France*, ed. Theodore Evergates (Philadelphia: University of Pennsylvania Press, 1999), 138–77, uses Ermengarde of Narbonne as an example to show that the literature reflected the real power of women. Joan Kelly, "Did Women Have a Renaissance?," in *Women, History and Theory: The Essays of Joan Kelly* (Chicago: University of Chicago Press, 1984), 19–50, argued that this tradition buttressed women's social position. Tova Rosen, *Unveiling Eve: Reading Gender in Medieval Hebrew Literature* (Philadelphia: University of Pennsylvania Press, 2003), argues that a comparable tradition in Jewish literature was in fact misogynistic.

On simple fornication, see Ruth Mazo Karras, "Two Models, Two Standards: Moral Teaching and Sexual Mores," in *Bodies and Disciplines: Intersections of Literature and History in Fifteenth-Century England*, eds. Barbara A. Hanawalt and David Wallace (Minneapolis: University of Minnesota Press, 1996), 123–38; Shannon McSheffrey, "Men and Masculinity in Late Medieval London Civic Culture: Governance, Patriarchy, and Reputation," in *Conflicted Identities and Multiple Masculinities: Men in the Medieval West*, ed. Jacqueline Murray (New York: Garland, 1999), 234–78, argues that the double standard is not as absolute as some authors, including Karras, have made it sound.

On leyrwite, see Judith M. Bennett, "Writing Fornication: Medieval Leyrwite and Its Historians," *Transactions of the Royal Historical Society*, 6th Series 13 (2003), 131–62. On *droit de seigneur* see Alain Boureau, *The Lord's First Night: The Myth of the Droit de Cuissage*, trans. Lydia G. Cochrane (Chicago: University of Chicago Press, 1998). On fornication and church courts see Michael M. Sheehan, "Theory and Practice: Marriage of the Unfree and Poor in Medieval Society," *Mediaeval Studies* 50 (1988), 457–87, now reprinted along with other related studies in *Marriage, Family and Law in Medieval Europe: Collected Studies*, ed. James K. Farge (Toronto: University of Toronto Press, 1996), and L.R. Poos, "Sex, Lies, and the Church Courts of Pre-Reformation England," *Journal of Interdisciplinary History* 25 (1995), 585–607, along with R.H. Helmholz, *Marriage Litigation in Medieval England* (Cambridge: Cambridge University Press, 1974). The statistics for the early modern period come from Keith Wrightson, *English Society 1580–1680* (New Brunswick: Rutgers University Press, 1982). The Venetian case comes from Guido Ruggiero, *The Boundaries of Eros: Sex Crime and Sexuality in Renaissance Venice* (Oxford: Oxford University Press, 1985). Brożyna, *Gender and Sexuality*, includes some excerpts from church court records from England and Poland.

On peasant sex in the pastourelle, see Kathryn M. Gravdal, *Ravishing Maidens: Writing Rape in Medieval French Literature and Law* (Philadelphia: University of Pennsylvania Press, 1991). On "priests' concubines" see Dyan Elliott, *Fallen Bodies: Pollution, Sexuality, and Demonology in the Middle Ages* (Philadelphia: University of Pennsylvania Press, 1999). On the village of Montaillou, see Emmanuel Le Roy Ladurie, *Montaillou: The Promised Land of Error*, trans. Barbara Bray (New York: G. Braziller, 1978). For slave women see many articles by Sally McKee, including "Slavery," in *The Oxford Handbook of Women and Gender in Medieval Europe*, eds. Judith M. Bennett and Ruth Mazo Karras (Oxford: Oxford University Press, 2013), 281–94, and Deborah Blumenthal, *Enemies and Familiars: Slavery and Mastery in Fifteenth-Century Valencia* (Ithaca: Cornell University Press, 2009).

There is a great deal of literature on Abelard and Heloise. The authenticity of the letters of Heloise is defended in Barbara Newman, *From Virile Woman to Woman Christ: Studies in Medieval Religion and Literature* (Philadelphia: University of Pennsylvania Press, 1995). Marilynn Desmond, "'Dominus/ Ancilla': Rhetorical Subjectivity and Sexual Violence in the Letters of Heloise," in *The Tongue of the Fathers: Gender and Ideology in Twelfth-Century Latin*, eds. David Townsend and Andrew Taylor (Philadelphia: University of Pennsylvania Press, 1998), 35–54, discusses some of the sexual aspects; see also Juanita Feros Ruys, "Heloise, Monastic Temptation, and 'Memoria': Rethinking Autobiography, Sexual Experience, and Ethics," in Classen, *Sexuality*, 383–404. On the authenticity of the *Epistolae duorum amantium*, otherwise known as the "Lost Love Letters" of Abelard and Heloise, see Constant J. Mews, *The Lost Love Letters of Heloise and Abelard: Perceptions of Dialogue in Twelfth-Century France* (New York: Palgrave Macmillan, 1999); Jan M. Ziolkowski, "Lost and Not Yet Found: Heloise, Abelard, and the 'Epistolae duorum amantium'," *Journal of Medieval Latin* 14 (2004), 171–202; C. Stephen Jaeger, "'Epistolae duorum amantium' and the Ascription to Heloise and Abelard,"; Giles Constable, "The Authorship of the 'Epistolae duorum amantium': A Reconsideration," and C. Stephen Jaeger, "A Reply to Giles Constable," in *Voices in Dialogue: Reading Women in the Middle Ages*, eds. Linda Olson and Kathryn Kerby-Fulton (Notre Dame, IN: University of Notre Dame Press, 2005), 125–86. See also Karma Lochrie, *Heterosyncrasies: Female Sexuality When Normal Wasn't* (Minneapolis: University of Minnesota Press, 2005).

On prostitution see Karras, *Common Women*; Jacques Rossiaud, *Medieval Prostitution*, trans. Lydia G. Cochrane (Oxford: Basil Blackwell, 1988); Lydia Leah Otis, *Prostitution in Medieval Society: The History of an Urban Institution in Languedoc* (Chicago: University of Chicago Press, 1985); Richard Trexler, "La prostitution florentine au XVe siècle: patronages et clienteles," *Annales: Economies, societe's, civilizations* 36 (1981), 983–1015; Peter Schuster, *Das Frauenhaus: Städtische Bordelle in Deutschland (1350–1600)* (Paderborn: Ferdinand Schöningh, 1992); Ruggiero, *The Boundaries of Eros*; Guy Dupont, *Maagdenverleidsters, hoeren en speculanten: Prostitutie in Brugge tijdens de Bourgondische periode (1385–1515)* (Bruges: Marc Van de Wiele, 1996). Excerpts from English legislation on brothels may be found in Brożyna, *Gender and Sexuality*. The German woodcut is discussed in Gertrud Blaschitz, "Das Freudenhaus im Mittelalter: 'In der stat was gesessen/ain unrainer pulian' . . ." in Classen, *Sexuality*, 715–50. *Church*, eds. Vern

L. Bullough and James A. Brundage (Buffalo: Prometheus Books, 1982), 187–205. Information on "lesbian" relationships in Arabic texts comes from Sahar Amer, *Crossing Borders: Love between Women in Medieval French and Arabic Literatures* (Philadelphia: University of Pennsylvania Press, 2008). The story of Budur and Hayat al-Nufus may be found in *The Arabian Nights II: Sindbad and Other Popular Stories*, trans. Husain Haddawy (New York: Norton, 1995), although Amer points out that Haddawy's translation is not based on an edition using the earliest manuscript, and translates some of the terminology in a more overtly sexual manner.

On sexual irregularities among nuns (or the lack thereof) see Penelope Johnson, *Equal in Monastic Profession: Religious Women in Medieval France* (Chicago: University of Chicago Press, 1991); on the penitentials, see Payer, *Sex and the Penitentials: The Development of a Sexual Code 550–1150* (Toronto: University of Toronto Press, 1984). On the Lollards' critique of nuns, see Lochrie, *Heterosyncrasies*. See also Louis Crompton, "The Myth of Lesbian Impunity: Capital Laws from 1270 to 1791," *Journal of Homosexuality* 6 (1980), 11–26. For the cross-dressing university student, see Michael H. Shank, "A Female University Student in Late Medieval Krakow," *Signs: Journal of Women in Culture and Society* 12 (1987), 373–80.

On gynecological handbooks see Monica H. Green, *The Trotula: A Medieval Compendium of Women's Medicine* (Philadelphia: University of Pennsylvania Press, 2001), and her *Women's Healthcare in the Medieval West: Texts and Contexts* (Aldershot: Ashgate, 2000). On contraception see notably John M. Riddle, *Contraception and Abortion from the Ancient World to the Renaissance* (Cambridge, MA: Harvard University Press, 1992), and *Eve's Herbs: A History of Contraception and Abortion in the West* (Cambridge, MA: Harvard University Press, 1997), and Noonan, *Contraception*.

On incest the major work is Elizabeth Archibald, *Incest and the Medieval Imagination* (Oxford: Oxford University Press, 2001). On rape see Gravdal, *Ravishing Maidens*, and *Representing Rape in Medieval and Early Modern Literature*, eds. Elizabeth Robertson and Christine M. Rose (New York: Palgrave, 2001). Both of these works rely primarily on literary materials. John Marshall Carter, *Rape in Medieval England: An Historical and Sociological Study* (Lanham, MD: University Press of America, 1985) uses court records but should be read with caution.

On Mediterranean slavery see Susan M. Stuard, "Ancillary Evidence for the Decline of Medieval Slavery," *Past & Present* 149 (November 1995), 3–28; Sally McKee, "Domestic Slavery in Renaissance Italy," *Slavery and Abolition* 29 (2008), 305–26; McKee, "The Implications of Slave Women's Sexual Service in Late Medieval Italy," in *Unfreie Arbeit: Ökonomische und kulturgeschichtliche Perspektiven*, eds. M. Erdem Kabadayi and Tobias Reichardt (Hildesheim: Georg Olms Verlag, 2007), 101–14. Sexual exploitation of slave women is also discussed in Steven A. Epstein, *Speaking of Slavery: Color, Ethnicity, and Human Bondage in Italy* (Ithaca, NY: Cornell University Press, 2001). On slavery and sexual coercion in Old Norse society see Ruth Mazo Karras, "Servitude and Sexuality in Medieval Iceland," in *From Sagas to Society: Comparative Approaches to Early Iceland*, ed. Gísli Pálsson (Enfield Lock, Herts: Hisarlik Press, 1992), 289–304. On slavery in Islam, see R. Brunschvig, "'Abd," in *Encyclopedia of Islam, vol. 1*, eds. P. Bearman, T. Bianquis, C. E. Bosworth, E. van Donzel, and W. P. Heinrichs (Leiden:

The canon lawyers' views on the number of sex partners a woman had to have to be considered a prostitute come from James A. Brundage, *Law, Sex, and Christian Society in Medieval Europe* (Chicago: University of Chicago Press, 1987). On twelfth-century Parisian thought on prostitution (and other issues) see John W. Baldwin, *Masters, Princes, and Merchants: The Social Views of Peter the Chanter and His Circle, 2 vols.* (Princeton, NJ: Princeton University Press, 1970). On Mary Magdalene see Katherine Ludwig Jansen, *The Making of the Magdalen: Preaching and Popular Devotion in the Later Middle Ages* (Princeton: Princeton University Press, 2000), and Ruth Mazo Karras, "Holy Harlots: Prostitute Saints in Medieval Legend," *Journal of the History of Sexuality* 1 (1990), 3–32. On St. Nicholas see Charles W. Jones, *St. Nicholas of Myra, Bari, and Manhattan: Biography of a Legend* (Chicago: University of Chicago Press, 1978).

On prostitutes and Jews in Spain see David Nirenberg, "Religious and Sexual Boundaries in the Medieval Crown of Aragon," in *Christians, Muslims, and Jews in Medieval and Early Modern Spain: Interaction and Cultural Change*, eds. Mark D. Meyerson and Edward D. English (Notre Dame: Notre Dame University Press, 1999), 141–60, and "Conversion, Sex, and Segregation: Jews and Christians in Medieval Spain," *American Historical Review* 107 (2002), 1065–93; and Mark D. Meyerson, "Prostitution of Muslim Women in the Kingdom of Valencia: Religious and Sexual Discrimination in a Medieval Plural Society," in *The Medieval Mediterranean: Cross-Cultural Contacts*, eds. Marilyn J. Chiat and Kathryn L. Reyerson (St. Cloud, MN: North Star Press, 1988), 87–95. On the marriage with a rich widow, see Poos, "Sex, Lies, and the Church Courts." The article by P.J.P. Goldberg that identifies female witnesses in impotence cases as prostitutes is in "Women in Fifteenth-Century Town Life," in *Towns and Townspeople in the Fifteenth Century*, ed. John A. F. Thompson (Gloucester: Alan Sutton, 1988), 107–28.

On women who did not marry, see Judith M. Bennett and Amy M. Froide, *Singlewomen in the European Past 1250–1800* (Philadelphia: University of Pennsylvania Press, 1999).

Judith M. Bennett, " 'Lesbian-Like' and the Social History of Medieval Lesbianisms," *Journal of the History of Sexuality* 9 (2000), 1–24, and E. Ann Matter, "My Sister, My Spouse: Woman-Identified Women in Medieval Christianity," *Journal of Feminist Studies in Religion* 2 (1986), 81–93, along with Karma Lochrie, "Between Women," in *The Cambridge Companion to Medieval Women's Writing*, ed. Carolyn Dinshaw and David Wallace (Cambridge: Cambridge University Press, 2003), 70–88, and Jacqueline Murray, "Twice Marginal and Twice Invisible: Lesbians in the Middle Ages," in *Handbook of Medieval Sexuality*, eds. Vern L. Bullough and James A. Brundage (New York: Garland, 1996), 191–222, are some of the basic works on female same-sex relations in the Middle Ages; see also articles in *Same Sex Love and Desire among Women in the Middle Ages*, eds. Francesca Canadé Sautman and Pamela Sheingorn (New York: Palgrave, 2001), and *The Lesbian Premodern*, eds. Noreen Giffney, Michelle M. Sauer and Diane Watt (London: Palgrave Macmillan, 2011). The example of Elizabeth Etchingham and Agnes Oxenbridge is from Judith M. Bennett, "Remembering Elizabeth Etchingham and Agnes Oxenbridge," in Giffney, Sauer, and Watt, *The Lesbian Premodern*, 132–43.

For William of Saliceto, see Helen Rodnite Lemay, "Human Sexuality in Twelfth-through Fifteenth-Century Scientific Writings," in *Sexual Practices and the Medieval*

Brill, 1960), 24–40. Information on slavery in eastern Europe comes from Eve Levin, *Sex and Society in the World of the Orthodox Slavs, 900–1700* (Ithaca, NY: Cornell University Press, 1989).

The literature on witchcraft is huge, but much of it deals mainly with the early modern period, which was the age of the major witch hunts. Still a good introduction to the phenomenon in the Middle Ages is Richard Kieckhefer, *European Witch Trials: Their Foundations in Popular and Learned Culture* (London: Routledge, 1976). The *Malleus Maleficarum* is discussed most recently in Walter Stephens, *Demon Lovers: Witchcraft, Sex, and the Crisis of Belief* (Chicago: University of Chicago Press, 2002), which argues that the misogynistic aspects of works like the *Malleus Maleficarum* exist mainly to emphasize the reality and corporeality of demons. On enchantresses in literature see Corinne Saunders, "Erotic Magic: The Enchantress in Middle English Romance," in Hopkins and Rushton, 38–52; for the Jewish text see *The Book of Women's Love and Jewish Medieval Medical Literature on Women: Sefer Ahavat Nashim*, ed. and trans. Carmen Caballero-Navas (London: Kegan Paul, 2004).

5 Men outside of marriage

There is little published work on men's sexuality in particular; Jacqueline Murray, "Hiding behind the Universal Man: Male Sexuality in the Middle Ages," in *Medieval Sexuality: A Handbook*, eds. Vern L. Bullough and James A. Brundage (New York: Garland, 1996), 123–52, is a notable exception. On masculinity generally there are several essay collections: *Medieval Masculinities: Regarding Men in the Middle Ages*, eds. Clare A. Lees with Thelma Fenster and Jo Ann McNamara (Minneapolis: University of Minnesota Press, 1994); *Masculinity in Medieval Europe*, ed. D.M. Hadley (New York: Longman, 1999); *Conflicted Identities and Multiple Masculinities: Men in the Medieval West*, ed. Jacqueline Murray (New York: Garland, 1999); *Becoming Male in the Middle Ages*, eds. Jeffrey Jerome Cohen and Bonnie Wheeler (New York: Garland, 1997). For Paul the Deacon see Ross Balzaretti, "Sexuality in Late Lombard Italy, c. 700–800 AD," in *Medieval Sexuality: A Casebook*, eds. April Harper and Caroline Proctor (New York: Routledge, 2008), 7–31.

Evidence on age at marriage and other demographic issues are discussed by P. J. P. Goldberg, *Women, Work, and Life-Cycle in a Medieval Economy: Women in York and Yorkshire c. 1300–1520* (Oxford: Oxford University Press, 1992) for England, and David Herlihy and Christiane Klapisch-Zuber, *Tuscans and Their Families: A Study of the Florentine Catasto of 1427* (New Haven: Yale University Press, 1985).

For young men visiting brothels in relation to marital strategies see Guido Ruggiero, *The Boundaries of Eros: Sex Crime and Sexuality in Renaissance Venice* (New York: Oxford University Press, 1985); Richard Trexler, "La prostitution florentine au XVe siècle: patronages et clientèles," *Annales: Economies, sociétés, civilizations* 36 (1981), 983–1015. On apprentices and visits to brothels see Ruth Mazo Karras, *From Boys to Men: Formations of Masculinity in Later Medieval Europe* (Philadelphia: University of Pennsylvania Press, 2003).

On the penitentials see Pierre J. Payer, *Sex and the Penitentials: The Development of a Sexual Code 550–1150* (Toronto: University of Toronto Press, 1984). On masturbation and other aspects of the male body see Jacqueline Murray, " 'The Law of Sin That Is in My Members': The Problem of Male Embodiment," in *Gender and Holiness: Men, Women, and Saints in Late Medieval Europe*, eds. Samantha J. E. Riches and Sarah Salih (London: Routledge, 2002), 1–22. For sex crimes against God, see Ruggiero, *Boundaries of Eros*, and Dyan Elliott, *Fallen Bodies: Pollution, Sexuality, and Demonology in the Middle Ages* (Philadelphia: University of Pennsylvania Press, 1999). On the sexual connotations of names, see Dave Postles, *Talking Ballocs: Nicknames and English Medieval Sociolinguistics* (Leicester: University of Leicester, 2003).

On the Normans and marriage *more danico*, see Eleanor Searle, *Predatory Kinship and the Creation of Norman Power* (Berkeley: University of California Press, 1988). On Henry I see C. Warren Hollister, *Henry I*, ed. Amanda Clark Frost (New Haven: Yale University Press, 2001). On Lambert of Ardres see Georges Duby, *The Knight, the Lady and the Priest: The Making of Modern Marriage in Medieval France*, trans. Barbara Bray (Chicago: University of Chicago Press, 1993); Cameron Bradley and Ruth Mazo Karras, "Masculine Sexuality and a Double Standard in Early Thirteenth-Century Flanders?" *Leidschrift* 25 (2010), 63–77.

The discussion of rape in various genres of French literature draws heavily on Kathryn Gravdal, *Ravishing Maidens: Writing Rape in Medieval French Literature and Law* (Philadelphia: University of Pennsylvania Press, 1991). See also Barbara Hanawalt, *Of Good and Ill Repute: Gender and Social Control in Medieval England* (Oxford: Oxford University Press, 1998), for a London case. The data on rape in Venice are found in Ruggiero, *Boundaries of Eros*. The information on Bologna comes from Didier Lett, "Genre, enfance et violence sexuelle dans les archives judiciaires de Bologne au XVe siècle," in *Clio: Femmes, genre, histoire* 42 (2015), 202–15. On gang rape in Dijon see Jacques Rossiaud, *Medieval Prostitution*, trans. Lydia G. Cochrane (Oxford: Basil Blackwell, 1988). The story of Rodrigo is discussed in Thomas Deswarte, "Le viol comis par Rodrigue et la perte de l'Espagne dans la tradition mozarabe (VIIIe–XIIe siècles)," in *Mariage et sexualité au Moyen Age: Accord ou crise?* ed. Michel Rouche (Paris: Presses de l'Université de Paris-Sorbonne, 2000), 69–79. On inter-ethnic liaisons see Mark Meyerson, "Prostitution of Muslim Women in the Kingdom of Valencia: Religious and Sexual Discrimination in a Medieval Plural Society," in *The Medieval Mediterranean: Cross-Cultural Contacts*, eds. Marilyn J. Chiat and Kathryn L. Reyerson (St. Cloud, MN: North Star Press, 1988), 87–95. On the Fourth Lateran Council see Steven F. Kruger, "Conversion and Medieval Sexual, Religious, and Racial Categories," in *Constructing Medieval Sexuality*, eds. Karma Lochrie, Peggy McCracken and James A. Schultz (Minneapolis: University of Minnesota Press, 1997), 158–78.

On Arnold of Verniolles, see Michael Goodich, *The Unmentionable Vice: Homosexuality in the Later Medieval Period* (Santa Barbara, CA: ABC-Clio, 1979). David Halperin's four-part schema comes from his *How to Do the History of Homosexuality* (Chicago: University of Chicago Press, 2002). The discussion of effeminacy and eunuchs in Baghdad draws on Everett Rowson, "Gender Irregularity as Entertainment: Institutionalized Transvestism at the Caliphal Court in

Medieval Baghdad," in *Gender and Difference in the Middle Ages*, eds. Sharon Farmer and Carol Braun Pasternack (Minneapolis: University of Minnesota Press, 2003), 45–72, and Hugh Kennedy, "Al-Jāḥiẓ and the Construction of Sexuality at the Abbasid Court," in Harper and Proctor, *Sexuality*, 175–88.

For defamation cases in the London church courts, see Richard M. Wunderli, *London Church Courts and Society on the Eve of the Reformation* (Cambridge, MA: Medieval Academy of America, 1981). On sexual insults in Old Norse culture, see Preben Meulengracht Sørenson, *The Unmanly Man: Concepts of Sexual Defamation in Early Northern Society*, trans. Joan Turville-Petre (Odense: Odense University Press, 1983), and Kari Ellen Gade, "Homosexuality and Rape of Males in Old Norse Law and Literature," *Scandinavian Studies* 58 (1986), 124–41. David Clark, *Between Medieval Men: Male Friendship and Desire in Early Medieval English Literature* (Oxford: Oxford University Press, 2009) discusses the Anglo-Saxon cognates of the Norse *argr* and the overlapping connotations of cowardice, effeminacy, and moral baseness.

On the connection of sodomy with otherness in Jewish society see Ruth Mazo Karras, "The Aerial Battle in the 'Toledot Yeshu' and Sodomy in the Late Middle Ages," *Medieval Encounters* 19 (2013), 493–533. For the use of "heretic" for "sodomite" in Germany (as well as for most of the other information on homosexual relations in late medieval Germany) see Helmut Puff, *Sodomy in Reformation Germany and Switzerland, 1400–1600* (Chicago: University of Chicago Press, 2003). On Hrotsvitha's Pelagius, see Mark D. Jordan, *The Invention of Sodomy in Christian Theology* (Chicago: University of Chicago Press, 1997). On the image of Muslims as sodomites see Gregory S. Hutcheson, "The Sodomitic Moor: Queerness in the Narrative of 'Reconquista'," in Burger and Kruger, *Queering the Middle Ages*, 99–122. See also various articles in *Queer Iberia: Sexualities, Cultures, and Crossings from the Middle Ages to the Renaissance*, eds. Josiah Blackmore and Gregory S. Hutcheson (Durham, NC: Duke University Press, 1999). On Asia see Kim M. Phillips, " 'They Do Not Know the Use of Men': The Absence of Sodomy in Medieval Accounts of the Far East," in Harper and Proctor, *Sexuality*, 189–208.

On sex between Jewish men and Christian women, see Ariel Toaff, *Love, Work, and Death: Jewish Life in Medieval Umbria*, trans. Judith Landry (London: Litman Library of Jewish Civilization, 1998); the articles by David Nirenberg, "Religious and Sexual Boundaries in the Medieval Crown of Aragon," in *Christians, Muslims, and Jews in Medieval and Early Modern Spain: Interaction and Cultural Change*, eds. Mark D. Meyerson and Edward D. English (Notre Dame: Notre Dame University Press, 1999), 141–60, and "Conversion, Sex, and Segregation: Jews and Christians in Medieval Spain," *American Historical Review* 107 (2002), 1065–93.

A lucid history of the use and meanings of "sodomy" in the patristic and early medieval periods is provided in Clark, *Between Medieval Men*. A broad overview of all the evidence on male same-sex relations, focused on one country and period, is Tom Linkinen, *Same-Sex Sexuality in Later Medieval English Culture* (Amsterdam: Amsterdam University Press, 2015). On Peraldus and the sin against nature, see Karma Lochrie, *Covert Operations: The Medieval Uses of Secrecy* (Philadelphia: University of Pennsylvania Press, 1999). On the accusations against the Templars see Malcolm Barber, *The Trial of the Templars* (Cambridge: Cambridge University Press, 1978). On the Lollards and same-sex relations see Carolyn Dinshaw, *Getting Medieval: Sexualities and Communities, Pre- and Post-Modern* (Durham, NC: Duke University Press, 1999). Peter Damian is discussed in William E. Burgwinkle, *Sodomy, Masculinity, and Law in Medieval Literature: France and England, 1050–1230* (Cambridge: Cambridge University Press, 2004); Jordan, *Invention of Sodomy;* and Larry Scanlon, "Unmanned Men and Eunuchs of God: Peter Damian's 'Liber Gomorrhianus' and the Sexual Politics of Papal Reform," *New Medieval Literatures* 2 (1998), 38–64, and excerpts from his *Book of Gomorrah* are translated in Brożyna, *Gender and Sexuality.* Other aspects of monasticism in relation to sodomy, along with much else, are discussed in Robert Mills, *Seeing Sodomy in the Middle Ages* (Chicago: University of Chicago Press, 2015).

On the eastern church see once again Eve Levin, *Sex and Society in the World of the Orthodox Slavs, 900–1700* (Ithaca, NY: Cornell University Press, 1989). On *adelphopoiia* see Dion C. Smythe, "In Denial: Same-Sex Desire in Byzantium," in Liz James, *Desire*, 139–48; John Boswell, *Same-Sex Unions in Premodern Europe* (New York: Villard, 1994); and Claudia Rapp, "Ritual Brotherhood in Byzantium," *Traditio* 52 (1997), 285–326.

On Aquinas see once again Jordan, *Invention of Sodomy.* Peter of Abano is discussed in Joan Cadden, "Sciences/Silences: The Natures and Languages of 'Sodomy' in Peter of Abano's 'Problemata' Commentary," in *Constructing Medieval Sexuality*, 40–57, Joan Cadden, *Nothing Natural is Shameful: Sodomy and Science in Late Medieval Europe* (Philadelphia: University of Pennsylvania Press, 2013), and William Burgwinkle, " 'The Form of Our Desire': Arnaut Daniel and the Homoerotic Subject in Dante's 'Commedia'," *GLQ: A Journal of Lesbian and Gay Studies* 10 (2004), 565–97. The information about laws in various secular jurisdictions comes from John Boswell, *Christianity, Social Tolerance, and Homosexuality: Gay People in Western Europe from the Beginning of the Christian Era to the Fourteenth Century* (Chicago: University of Chicago Press, 1980), and James Brundage, *Law, Sex, and Christian Society in Medieval Europe* (Chicago: University of Chicago Press, 1987). For artistic representations of punishment for sodomy see Robert Mills, *Suspended Animation: Pain, Pleasure, and Punishment in Medieval Culture* (London: Reaktion Books, 2005).

On Dante see Michael Camille, "The Pose of the Queer: Dante's Gaze, Brunetto Latini's Body," in Burger and Kruger, *Queering the Middle Ages*, 57–86, with ample references to previous scholarship; Joseph Pequigney, "Sodomy in Dante's 'Inferno' and 'Purgatorio'," *Representations* 26 (Autumn 1991), 22–42; John E. Boswell, "Dante and the Sodomites," *Dante Studies* 112 (1994), 63–76; and Gary P. Cestaro, "Queering Nature, Queering Gender: Dante and Sodomy," in *Dante for the New Millenium*, eds. Teodolinda Barolini and Wayne Storey (New York: Fordham University Press, 2003), 90–103.

Pierre Chaplais makes his argument denying a sexual relationship between Edward II and Piers Gaveston in *Piers Gaveston: Edward II's Adoptive Brother* (Oxford: Clarendon Press, 1994). See also Claire Sponsler, "The King's Boyfriend: Froissart's Political Theater of 1326," in Burger and Kruger, *Queering Medieval Sexuality*, 143–67. On Arnold of Verniolles, see Goodich, *Unmentionable Vice*. On the English transvestite John/Eleanor Rykener see Ruth Mazo Karras and David L.

Boyd, "'Ut Cum Muliere': A Male Transvestite Prostitute in Fourteenth-Century London," in *Premodern Sexualities*, eds. Louise Fradenburg and Carla Freccero (London: Routledge, 1996), 101–16, and discussion in Dinshaw, *Getting Medieval*, and in Ruth Mazo Karras and Tom Linkinen, "John/Eleanor Rykener Revisited," in *Founding Feminisms in Medieval Studies: Essays in Honor of E. Jane Burns*, eds. Laine E. Doggett and Daniel E. O'Sullivan (Cambridge: DS Brewer, 2016), Gallica 39, 111–21, On "florentzen" as slang in Germany, see Bernd-Ulrich Hergemöller, *Sodom and Gomorrah: On the Everyday Reality and Persecution of Homosexuals in the Middle Ages*, trans. John Phillips (London: Free Association Books, 2001).

On Bernardino of Siena see Franco Mormando, *The Preacher's Demons: Bernardino of Siena and the Social Underworld of Early Renaissance Italy* (Chicago: University of Chicago Press, 1999). On the brothel in Florence and its relation to sodomy, see Richard Trexler, "La prostitution florentine au XVe siècle: patronages et clientèles," *Annales: Economies, sociétés, civilizations* 36 (1981), 983–1015. All the information on the Office of the Night and sodomy in Florence comes from the indispensable work of Michael Rocke, *Forbidden Friendships: Homosexuality and Male Culture in Renaissance Florence* (Oxford: Oxford University Press, 1996). On the age pattern see also Dyan Elliott, "Sexual Scandal and the Clergy: A Medieval Blueprint for Disaster," in *Why the Middle Ages Matter: Medieval Light on Modern Injustice*, eds. Celia Chazelle, Simon Doubleday, Felice Lifshitz and Amy G. Remensnyder (London: Routledge, 2012), 90–105.

For the Avignon case, see Bernhard Degenhart, "Das Marienwunder von Avignon," *Pantheon* 33 (1975), 191–203, from BN Ms Lat 5931, fol. 99r; Michael Camille, "The Pose of the Queer: Dante's Gaze, Brunetto Latini's Body," in Burger and Kruger, *Queering the Middle Ages*, 57–86.

For the argument that the standard age pattern in homosexual relations remained constant from the Greeks until the modern era, see Randolph Trumbach, *Sex and the Gender Revolution* (Chicago: University of Chicago Press, 1998). On age asymmetry in Florentine marriage, see Herlihy and Klapisch-Zuber, *Tuscans and Their Families*.

On taverns as locations for sexual encounters, see A. Lynn Martin, *Alcohol, Sex, and Gender in Late Medieval and Early Modern Europe* (Basingstoke: Palgrave, 2001). Martin criticizes a number of scholars who have written about sexuality (including me) for ignoring the role alcohol plays in sexual behavior, but he himself discusses only heterosexual behavior.

For cases involving homosexual behavior elsewhere in Europe: Hergemöller, *Sodom and Gomorrah* (including the example from the latrines in Regensburg); Ruggiero, *The Boundaries of Eros*, on Venice (including the case of Rolandino/a Ronchaia); Marc Boone, "State Power and Illicit Sexuality: The Persecution of Sodomy in Late Medieval Bruges," *Journal of Medieval History* 22 (1996), 135–53; Puff, *Sodomy*. A few fifteenth-century cases are also discussed in N.S. Davidson, "Sodomy in Early Modern Venice," in *Sodomy in Early Modern Europe*, ed. Tom Betteridge (Manchester: Manchester University Press, 2002), 65–81. The interplay between sodomitical acts and gender definitions or inversions is discussed in Burgwinkle, *Sodomy, Masculinity, and Law*. Chivalry and masculinity are discussed in Ruth Mazo Karras, *From Boys to Men: Formations of Masculinity in Late Medieval*

Europe (Philadelphia: University of Pennsylvania Press, 2003). The account of attraction in love literature draws heavily on James Schultz, *Courtly Love, the Love of Courtliness, and the History of Sexuality* (Chicago: University of Chicago Press, 2006); on Old English literature see Clark, *Between Medieval Men.*

For loving relations among men, see Boswell, *Christianity, Social Tolerance, and Homosexuality*, including discussion of Aelred of Rievaulx. Boswell's use of the term "gay" is considered problematic by many historians. See also Linkinen, *Same-Sex Sexuality*. For love language in Byzantine letters see Margaret Mullett, "From Byzantium, with Love," in *Desire and Denial in Byzantium*, ed. James, 3–22. On the friendship between Richard I and Philip Augustus, see C. Stephen Jaeger, *Ennobling Love: In Search of a Lost Sensibility* (Philadelphia: University of Pennsylvania Press, 1999), and Burgwinkle, *Sodomy, Masculinity, and Law*. The relationship between two knights at Constantinople is discussed in Siegrid Düll, Anthony Luttrell and Maurice Keen, "Faithful unto Death: The Tomb Slab of Sir William Neville and Sir John Clanvowe, Constantinople 1391," *Antiquaries Journal* 71 (1991), 174–90. On Ganymede see Ilene Forsyth, "The Ganymede Capital at Vézelay," *Gesta* 15 (1976), 241–6. On whether medieval people made the connection between male friendship and sodomy, see Matthew S. Kuefler, "Male Friendship and the Suspicion of Sodomy in Twelfth-Century France," in *Gender and Difference*, eds. Farmer and Pasternack, 145–81. On love poetry from Muslim Spain, see Norman Roth, "A Note on Research into Jewish Sexuality in the Medieval Period," and "A Research Note on Sexuality and Muslim Civilization," in *Medieval Sexuality: A Handbook*, eds. Bullough and Brundage, 309–28.

For artistic representations involving fertility, see Michael Camille, *The Medieval Art of Love: Objects and Subjects of Desire* (New York: Abrams, 1998), especially the example at p. 100 pl. 85. On nocturnal emissions see Dyan Elliott, *Fallen Bodies: Pollution, Sexuality, and Demonology in the Middle Ages* (Philadelphia: University of Pennsylvania Press, 1999), and Marie Theres Fögen, "Unto the Pure All Things Are Pure: The Byzantine Canonist Zonaras on Nocturnal Pollution," in *Obscenity: Social Control and Artistic Creation in the European Middle Ages*, ed. Jan Ziolkowski (Leiden: Brill, 1998), 260–78.

Afterword

Although I have referred to carping and reactionary criticism of the recent scholarship on sexuality, the articles I cite here are not part of that trend, but rather offer thoughtful critiques of the scholarship in the context of the overall historiography of the Middle Ages and of a broader view of the medieval body, respectively: Paul Freedman and Gabrielle M. Spiegel, "Medievalisms Old and New: the Rediscovery of Alterity in North American Medieval Studies," *American Historical Review* 103 (1998), 677–704; Caroline Bynum, "Why All the Fuss about the Body? A Medievalist's Perspective," *Critical Inquiry* 22 (1995), 1–33. Bynum's now classic work on food is *Holy Feast and Holy Fast: The Religious Significance of Food to Medieval Women* (Berkeley: University of California Press, 1987).

Leo Steinberg, *The Sexuality of Christ in Renaissance Art and in Modern Oblivion*, 2nd ed. (Chicago: University of Chicago Press, 1996), makes the case for the importance of the demonstration of Christ's penis to his humanity. Caroline Bynum replies in "The Body of Christ in the Later Middle Ages: a Reply to Leo

Steinberg," *Renaissance Quarterly* 39 (1986), 399–439, reprinted in her *Fragmentation and Redemption: Essays on Gender and the Human Body in Medieval Religion* (New York: Zone Books, 1991), 79–117. She points out that Christ is also presented and described as feminine and no texts relate Christ's penis to masculinity or sexuality. The 1996 edition of Steinberg's book contains a reply to her article, making the case that breasts and penises in general, if not those of the Virgin Mary and Christ, did have significant sexual meanings in the Middle Ages.

On the omnipresence of death, including its representations in medieval art, see Paul Binski, *Medieval Death: Ritual and Representation* (Ithaca, NY: Cornell University Press, 1996); Colin Platt, *King Death: The Black Death and Its Aftermath in Late-Medieval England* (Toronto: University of Toronto Press, 1996).

On the place of the Middle Ages within the longer history of sexuality in Europe, see Anna Clark, *Desire: A History of European Sexuality* (New York and London: Routledge, 2008); Katherine Crawford, *European Sexualities, 1400–1800* (Cambridge: Cambridge University Press, 2007). Neither of these works draws a boundary between the late medieval and the early modern, as can be seen from Crawford's title and Clark's chapter covering the period from the thirteenth to the sixteenth century. On the importance of the Middle Ages to contemporary ideas about law and sexuality, see James A. Brundage, *Law, Sex, and Christian Society in Medieval Europe* (Chicago: University of Chicago Press, 1987). Thomas Laqueur's book on the construction of the body is *Making Sex: Body and Gender from the Greeks to Freud* (Cambridge, MA: Harvard University Press, 1990).

INDEX

Meir b. Baruch of Rothenburg, Rabbi 105
Memoriale Credencium 34n6
men 1–6, 9, 17–18, 28–32, 36, 38–46, 47–9; adultery 56, 120, 138, 142, 146, 150, 169, 185; bonding 201; desires 1, 48–9, 52–3, 67, 98, 107, 118, 123, 140, 169–71, 182, 184, 187, 203–4; extramarital sex 32, 91, 173; love between 197–207; male prostitution 184; and masculinity 7, 11, 24, 41, 46, 52–3, 95, 177, 204; passivity 5, 24, 29, 34, 178–82, 186, 191–4, 197, 200–1, 203; privilege 32, 91, 173; same-sex relationships 8–9, 27–9, 66–7, 149, 154, 178, 182–3, 186, 188, 190–5, 197–9, 205–6; and sexual opportunity 173–8; sexual prowess 43, 146, 169; transgression of gender roles 177–81, 193, 219
menstruation 99, 102; *menarche* 2
"Merchant's Tale" (Chaucer) 130, 165n13; *see also* Canterbury Tales; Chaucer
meretrix 141, 166n27
Merovingian era 50–1, 81
metaphor 13, 49, 53, 69, 79–80, 145, 148, 173, 215; *see also* allegory; symbolism
midwives' handbook(s) 63, 154
mikveh 101–2, *103*
"Miller's Tale" (Chaucer) 24, 130, 134–5, 165n14; *see also* Canterbury Tales; Chaucer
Mills, Robert 72, 78n56
miscegenation law(s) 32
misogynism 18, 43, 53, 72, 86–7, 89, 113, 123, 128, 162, 164
mitzvah 99
moderation 46–8, 62, 171, 187
modern attitude(s) 4, 7–8, 11, 17, 27–31, 38, 67, 72, 80, 149, 154, 187, 190, 201, 205–6, 210, 212, 214, 217–18
money and sex 22, 63, 111, 113–14, 141–3, 169, 179–80
monks/monasticism 1, 6, 12, 15, 26, 46–50, 54, 72, 182, 186, 197–8, 212, 216–17; chastity 46–7, 52–3, 57–8, 79, 200; and marriage 46; as men outside marriage 46, 52–3, 57; and modern attitudes 72, 212, 217; and nuns 2, 5
Montpellier medical school 89

"Moralized Bible" 149–50
moral status/standards 5, 53, 55, 61, 89–90, 99, 118
more danico marriages 173
moredet 87–8, 105
mortality 99, 157
mortality rates 157
mūkannathūn 179
Muslim invasion of Spain 177
Muslims/Islamic tradition 98, 119, 159, 168, 191, 216; extramarital 32, 135–6, 146, 173, 176, 183–4, 205; marital 39, 79, 84, 96, 170
mutuality 5, 29

Nag Hammadi texts 41, 75n3
nakedness 18, 69, 72, 94, 108–10, 125–6, 144, 156, 163, 210, 214
naming practices 172
natural philosophy/philosophers 22, 186
nature/the natural 4–5, 22–3, 28, 61, 96, 186, 213; sodomy as sin against 5, 22, 111, 147, 185–8, 190–1
negotiations: marriage 81, 169
Newman, Barbara 140
Nicholas, St. 142
niddah 101
Njal's Saga 95, 116n9, 208n16
nocturnal emissions 36, 48, 62–4, 171
non-reproductive sex 9, 11, 22, 28, 97–8, 182, 191
Noonan, John T. 116n12
Norman tradition 20, 173, 182
norms/normality discourse 8–9, 11, 60, 85, 164, 169, 192, 215
nuns 2, 5–6, 18, 26, 46–7, 50, 53, 57–9, 61, 68, 70–1, 79, 148–51

obedience 47
Odo of Cheriton 123, 165n5
Office of Honesty, Florence 91, 191
Office of the Night, Florence 192
one-seed theory 218
One Thousand and One Nights 24, 153, 128, 153, 170
Opera Arnaldi de Villanova 166n40
oral sex 113, 147, 193
orgasm 30, 63–4, 76n36, 104, 154, 163
Origen of Alexandria 39
original sin 37, 102, 118
Origo, Iris 167n47
Orthodox Church 57, 91, 100, 216
Oswald von Wolkenstein 147–8